THE
INFLUENCE
OF SOROS

Politics, Power,
AND THE Struggle
FOR AN Open
Society

THE
INFLUENCE
OF SOROS

Emily Tamkin

HARPER

An Imprint of HarperCollins*Publishers*

HarperCollins books may be purchased for educational, business, or sales promotional use. For information, please email the Special Markets Department at SPsales @harpercollins.com.

FIRST EDITION

Library of Congress Cataloging-in-Publication Data has been applied for.

ISBN 978-0-06-297263-7

20 21 22 23 24   LSC   10 9 8 7 6 5 4 3 2 1

For my parents, and for Neil

Thinking can never quite catch up with reality; reality is always richer than our comprehension. Reality has the power to surprise thinking, and thinking has the power to create reality. But we must remember the unintended consequences—the outcome always differs from expectations.

—GEORGE SOROS

And it seemed to them that they were within an inch of arriving at a decision, and that then a new, beautiful life would begin. And they both realized that the end was still far, far away, and that the hardest, the most complicated part was only just beginning.

—ANTON CHEKHOV

Even when we're empowered, it doesn't mean we're in control.

—LORENE SCAFARIA

CONTENTS

THE
INFLUENCE
OF SOROS

INTRODUCTION

If one believes conspiracy theorists, world leaders, and conspiracy theorists who are world leaders, George Soros's influence is everywhere and all-encompassing.

In the past few years alone, Turkish President Recep Tayyip Erdoğan has accused Soros of trying to divide and destroy nations;[1] Israeli Prime Minister Benjamin Netanyahu posted on Facebook that the Hungarian-born Jewish billionaire was coordinating with the Iranian regime by communicating with its foreign minister;[2] Romanian political kingmaker Liviu Dragnea suggested first that nongovernmental organizations linked to Soros had "financed evil" in the country around the time of anticorruption protests in the capital of Bucharest,[3] and then that Soros was behind an assassination attempt on his life;[4] former Slovak Prime Minister Robert Fico blamed Soros for the series of protests that ultimately forced him to resign;[5] and U.S. President Donald Trump alleged that Soros was the force behind those protesting against then–Supreme Court nominee Brett Kavanaugh, who was accused of having attempted to sexually assault Dr. Christine Blasey Ford while in high school (and was nevertheless confirmed to a lifetime appointment).[6]

Trump also suggested that Soros was responsible for a caravan of Central American migrants heading toward the U.S. border, echoing Soros's most committed foe: Hungarian Prime Minister Viktor Orbán. Orbán, who was once given a scholarship to Oxford by Soros's organization, successfully ran his reelection campaign by maligning Soros and his foundations, accusing him of trying to flood the country with migrants.[7] That was not enough for Orbán; he also worked to banish Central European University, which Soros founded in Budapest in the early 1990s in order to ensure advanced research, teaching, and intellectual inquiry would exist in Central and Eastern Europe.[8]

It is not only heads of government and state who look to blame Soros for the ills of the world. According to many in the right-wing media, he is remaking America in his own nefarious image. In a broadcast on criminal justice reform, Fox News host Tucker Carlson said Soros is "hijacking our democracy."[9] Conservative outlet the *Daily Signal* warned its readers to "Beware Soros-Funded Hijacking of US Census."[10] When Facebook, which is not technically a media company but is nevertheless where many of its users get their news, was looking to do damage control after it let misinformation run rampant on its site during the 2016 U.S. presidential election, it hired a Republican-linked public relations firm that attempted to discredit the company's critics by linking them to Soros.[11]

To those on the political left, although Soros is not the stuff of outright conspiracy theory, he is still sometimes blamed for global ills. In 2015, leftist outlet *Jacobin* ran an article titled "Counting on Billionaires," which argued that "Philanthrocapitalists like George Soros want us to believe they can remedy the economic misery that they themselves create."

Introduction

In this telling, Soros is responsible for the ills of the global financial system and papers over his misdeeds with self-serving charity. While the right obsesses over the idea of Soros as a sort of godfather of the left, some on the actual left call for soaking the rich and argue that every billionaire is a policy failure. On the right, Soros has enemies; on the political far left, he has few friends.[12]

THIS BOOK IS NOT A biography of George Soros.

A biography of George Soros would include interviews with wives and children, and try to get at the man's most personal and private moments, and attempt to share with the reader a version of the man never seen before.

This book does not do any of that.

This is not a biography of George Soros; rather, this is the story of George Soros's influence.

And what is that influence? The rumors, lies, outright conspiracy theories, and sweeping statements about eighty-nine-year-old George Soros are so omnipresent and overwhelming that they threaten to obfuscate the truth, which is that George Soros has wielded and continues to have tremendous influence—just not in the ways that his most famous detractors would have us believe.

It may be an understatement to say that George Soros is influential in finance. Soros, who survived the Nazi occupation of Hungary as a teenager by pretending to be a Christian, went on to study at the London School of Economics and then to work in finance in London and later in New York. He became one of the fathers of the modern-day hedge fund, establishing his own fund, Quantum (advised through the firm retaining his name, Soros Fund Management). He is perhaps the most famous currency speculator in history, credited with (or blamed for, depending on your perspective) "breaking the Bank of England" by shorting the pound and forcing the United Kingdom out of the European Exchange Rate Mechanism in 1992.

It is also an understatement to say that George Soros is influential in philanthropy. In the late 1970s, concerned that he would die only worrying about money, he began a foundation called "Open Society," named after a book by his tutor at the London School of Economics, Karl Popper.

That book, *The Open Society and Its Enemies*, inspired the idea at the core of Soros's philanthropic work. It is a repudiation of Plato, Hegel, Marx, and, most of all, totalitarianism. An open society, according to Popper, is one that promotes freedom, knowledge, progress, and cooperation. It may, in its promotion of individualism and freedom, leave some feeling isolated and anxious, but that, Popper writes, "is the price we have to pay for being human."[13]

In addition to paying the price for being human, Soros has spent billions toward the cause—$32 billion since 1984.[14] That's somewhere between the GDPs of Latvia and Lithuania, according to the Organisation for Economic Co-operation and Development. Since the establishment of Open Society, Soros has been philanthropically engaged, primarily across Central and Eastern Europe and Russia in the 1980s and 1990s, and then throughout the world. Through his Open Society Foundations, "the world's largest private funder of independent groups working for justice, democratic governance, and human rights," Soros has, for decades, committed himself and his money to the project of making ours a world in which more people have a better chance at full civic participation.[15]

It is also an understatement to say that George Soros is influential in politics. In 2004, he threw his financial weight behind then-Senator John Kerry in the hope of defeating the incumbent, President George W. Bush, by backing voter mobilization efforts across the country. He saw Bush, with his war in Iraq and response to 9/11, as the greatest threat to open society: Bush, in Soros's view, was using military might to impose the idea of American supremacy in a way that was completely counter to the ideals Soros held dear. Despite his best efforts on behalf of the Democratic candidate, Bush was reelected. But Soros is still, to this day, a political backer, primarily for politicians and political causes on the left. In July 2019, he created a PAC for the 2020 election called Democracy PAC and promptly put $5.1 million into it.[16]

Soros may not wield his influence to destroy nations and smuggle in caravans, but he has still done quite a lot.

THIS BOOK IS DIVIDED INTO nine chapters that explore episodes from Soros's life in which he was particularly influential. Soros has done so much that there was a seemingly endless selection of events from which to choose and on which to focus. I selected the nine that I thought were the most influential and provided the best material with which to attempt the following three tasks. That judgment was shaped by my previous reporting on Soros, about whom I had written extensively before I ever started this book, by my journalistic work on related subjects like nationalism, populism, and foreign affairs, and by my research background in Russia and Central and Eastern Europe. Still, I will allow that another person could easily look at his life and choose to focus on a completely different set of experiences.

The three tasks are: First, to try to assess what Soros's influence in the space of finance, philanthropy, and politics has been.

Second, to disentangle that influence from the conspiracy theories that today threaten to undermine it while examining where these ideas come from and what about Soros in particular is so attractive to illiberal leaders looking for a bogeyman on whom to blame their every problem.

And third, to ask whether the notion of a fairer, freer, more equitable society is not inherently at odds with the existence of a billionaire trying to use his power and influence to make it so. To ask, in other words, whether the idea of open societies can be reconciled with the idea of a man who has given millions upon millions away to make them.

ORIGINALLY, I HAD HOPED THAT this book would include a sit-down interview with its subject. But after months of back-and-forth with his (very patient and helpful) communications team and updates of "we'll see what we can do" and "we're trying to see what's possible," I was told that Soros was not doing any interviews. He was willing, however, to answer my questions via email.

My first question was whether he thinks about what his influence has been and, if so, how he would describe or define it.

He responded, "Through my philanthropy, I have tried to make the world a better place. But outcomes don't always correspond to expectations. This is a core idea of my philosophical framework. Given our inherent imperfect understanding, our actions often have unintended consequences. But I maintain my commitment and my passion because I care about the values and principles of the open society. I have been extremely privileged to translate some of my dreams into reality. Though I have not sought recognition or gratitude, I realize that I have in fact been able to help a large number of people."

That is his answer. The following is mine.

CHAPTER 1

Birth of a Myth

George Soros was never born.

György Schwartz,[1] however, was born in 1930 in Budapest, the younger of two sons of upper-middle-class, secular Jews. It was not until 1936 that György Schwartz became a Soros; his father had the entire family—György, and his older brother, Paul (born Pál)—change their names to protect themselves against increasing antisemitism in Hungary.[2] In the 1940s, the Soros family hid out under a false Christian identity after the Nazis took over Hungary. György's father procured documentation and alternate housing not only for his own family but for several other Hungarian Jews. After World War II, György enrolled in the London School of Economics. Decades later he became George Soros the Financial Genius, and then George Soros the Ambitious Philanthropist, and then George Soros the World's Bogeyman.

BUT FIRST HE WAS GYÖRGY Schwartz, born into a Hungary that had learned to hate people like György Schwartz and his family—that had recently learned, in other words, to hate and blame the Jewish people. To understand the Soros family and the accusations of Nazi collaboration that surround them, one must first understand how Jews in Hungary were Hungarians, until non-Jewish Hungarians decided that they weren't.

For generations, Hungary was an example of successful Jewish assimilation. "There is no other example in all of the eastern part of Central Europe of such complete, rapid, and, to all appearances, successful assimilation and equality as that of Hungarian Jews," Robert A. Kann, the Austrian historian, wrote in 1945. Karl Lueger, who served as mayor of Vienna in the late nineteenth and early twentieth centuries and had a penchant for antisemitic rhetoric, helpfully dubbed Budapest "Judapest."[3]

Unlike some other places in Europe, in the Austro-Hungarian Empire, Hungarian Jews thought of themselves, by and large, as Hungarians first. They assimilated more quickly than Jews did elsewhere in Central and Eastern Europe. Successful Jews were in a sort of alliance with the Hungarian political elite: Jews spoke Hungarian, and identified with Magyarization, the cause of Hungarian nationalism within the Austro-Hungarian Empire.[4] And while Magyar aristocrats may not have wanted to live and work full-time in the city, contented as they were with their manors and estates and traditions, Jews, who made up just 5 percent of the country's population but a full fifth of Budapest's residents by 1900, did. "We have Jews to do the work for us," Count Mihály Károlyi is said to have told a visiting German diplomat. Jews made up half the doctors and lawyers in Budapest by 1910, and they converted the city into something of a financial and cultural powerhouse.[5] Hungarian Jews also proved their loyalty on the battlefield during World War I; 10,000 of them died for the emperor.[6]

George Soros's father, Tivadar Soros (born Tivadar Schwartz), was a lawyer. George's mother, Erzebet, was a gentle, nervous woman to whom his father was not faithful. The pair had one son before George: Paul, who was four years older and passed away in 2013.

Tivadar Soros is a major character in Soros's narrative telling of his own life, and his father's life was its own story, too, full of twists and turns: When Tivadar was still a university student, he, like tens of thousands of other Hungarian Jews, went off to fight in World War I. Tivadar later wrote that he joined not because he was a patriot, but because he thought it would be an adventure, and helpful to his future legal career. He was young; he had ambitions.[7]

Those ambitions were quashed by reality. He was taken as a prisoner of war and transported to a dismal camp in Siberia, where he became editor of a prisoners' newspaper, *The Plank*, so called because it was, after being written by hand, nailed to a plank. Tivadar Schwartz eventually escaped the camp, but got lost, and found himself in the midst of the Russian Revolution. "He returned to Hungary a changed man. He had lost his ambition. He didn't want to be prominent anymore," his younger son later recalled. "My father wanted to enjoy life and maintain his independence, but he did not want to become wealthy or influential."[8]

Tivadar Schwartz had been changed by his wanton odyssey, and he came back to a Hungary that had changed, too.

THE GREAT, GLITTERING BUDAPEST OF the early 1900s, the one in which Hungarian nobility happily let Jews count themselves as Hungarians so long as they contributed to Hungary's national cause and financial prosperity, was not the Budapest in which Paul and George Soros were to grow up. Growing antisemitism would have Tivadar Schwartz change the family name. The name Schwartz signified that they were Jewish. It meant that they weren't Hungarian, not really, and, increasingly, that was a dangerous thing.

When World War I ended, Hungary was on the losing side. Then, in 1918, a revolution led by Count Mihály Károlyi brought about the First Hungarian Republic. The republic was short-lived. Károlyi struggled with land reform (the proletariat thought his reforms too slow, the landowners, too radical) and a rising and discontented political left. In March 1919, French Colonel Vyx passed on the Allies' ultimatum that old Magyar lands would be cut off from Hungary. Defeated, Károlyi decided to pass power to the Social Democrats so that they could form a new government.[9]

The Social Democrats, unbeknownst to Károlyi, had made a pact with the Communists, which meant that the First Hungarian Republic was succeeded by a Hungarian Soviet Republic under the leadership of revolutionary Communist Béla Kun, who kept Károlyi under house arrest until he fled the country that July. Some of the leadership of the Hungarian Soviet Republic was of Jewish origin, but Communism was an explicitly antireligious project, and the Communists, in Hungary and elsewhere, who happened to be of Jewish descent were hardly there to promote their own Jewish identity. What's more, many Jews were also hurt by the Hungarian "Red Terror," political oppression against real and imagined opponents of Communism.[10]

The Hungarian Soviet Republic lasted just 133 days. The Hungarian Red Army unsuccessfully fought its Romanian counterpart (Romania was aligned with France, Britain, and Russia and so stood to gain territorially from the Treaty of Versailles, whereas Hungary did not so much as get the invitation it was promised to the conference). The Hungarians lost, and the Hungarian Soviet Republic was sent packing into history.[11] Admiral Miklós Horthy's government came to power in late 1919—France and Britain, happy to see the Communists out of power, as well as Romania helped bring in his right-wing government.

So, too, was the Hungarian Soviet Republic followed by the Treaty of Trianon, the Austro-Hungarian equivalent to the Treaty of Versailles. The Treaty of Trianon was presented to Hungary by the victors of World War I in June 1920. The treaty formally and finally ended the First World War between the Allies and Hungary. Romania, Czechoslovakia, and the new kingdom of Serbs, Croats, and Slovenes carved up the independent Kingdom of Hungary that resulted from the treaty—and that was left with roughly 93,000 of the 282,000 square miles it had had before the war. A 1920 census showed that post-Trianon Hungary had 7.6 million people, compared to 18.3 million before. Almost every family was impacted, finding itself with members who were suddenly minorities in a different country.[12]

In looking for an internal enemy to blame for their trauma, the new right-wing rulers of interwar Hungary settled on the Jews.

Why were the Jews of Hungary blamed when the Jews had not ruled the country when World War I began and were not in charge when it ended?

They were blamed because Count Károlyi, who had argued for ties with the British and French, had Jewish advisors. They were blamed because there were the Jewish Bolsheviks of the Soviet Republic and its Red Terror. They were blamed because the Jewish intellectuals who had previously been in league with the nobility could now be painted as turning the country from its core Christian values, and because Jewish millionaires were seen as making money off of Hungary, even while it was nearing bankruptcy. They were blamed because somebody had to be.

"In short, the Jews and they alone were responsible for Trianon and the Hungarian tragedy," the Hungarian-Austrian historian and journalist Paul Lendvai wrote dryly. The historic pact between the Hungarian ruling class and Hungarian Jews was no more.[13]

In 1920, the first anti-Jewish law was passed by Horthy (who was actually in charge when the Treaty of Trianon was signed) and his prime minister, Pál Teleki, who was also decidedly antisemitic. The law decreed only 6 percent of university students could be Jewish.

"This was the beginning of an unmistakable official Christian-nationalist, right-wing conservative counterrevolution, giving expression to an anti-Semitism of a kind which had been alien to the liberal elite of a multinational Hungary," Lendvai wrote.[14] Jews had been permitted to be Hungarians; now they were only Jewish.

"The antisemitic agitation between 1919 and 1945 . . . sought to belittle the degree of the Jews' assimilation and their profound emotional loyalty to the Hungarian fatherland by vague and manipulative concepts such as 'the deep Magyar race,' 'the Magyar soul,' 'the Magyar nation,' and the 'Magyar genius,' and to discredit the loyalty of outstanding figures of cultural and scientific life as 'mimicry.'"[15]

Jewish Hungarians had contributed to the Magyar nation, to Magyar genius, but after World War I and the Soviet Republic's government, "Magyar" did not include Jewish people.

In 1934, Jewish people in Hungary watched from afar as the Nazis engineered the murder of the chancellor of Austria, Engelbert Dollfuss, and, in 1936, as the swastika flew over the Olympics in Berlin.[16]

As Tivadar saw the signs of increasing antisemitism and with his sons both in school, he decided that the family name had to change. If Jewish names were increasingly not Hungarian, then Tivadar would not have his family use an obviously Jewish name. In 1936, Schwartz became Soros. In Hungarian, the name means "the one who is next in line," but there was another meaning, too.

Tivadar Soros was involved in the Esperanto movement, Esperanto being an international language developed in the nineteenth century by Ludwik Lejzer Zamenhof, a Polish Jew who had hoped his constructed language could be used to forge greater understanding between people and overcome petty nationalism. In Esperanto, Soros is the future tense of the verb "to soar."[17]

IN 1939, WHEN GEORGE SOROS was nine years old, Hungary passed a new law. There were quotas enacted for Jews in professions; Jews could not fully own businesses. Only those Jews whose families came to Hungary before 1914 could claim Hungarian citizenship. Jews who had acquired citizenship through naturalization after 1914 lost their citizenship.[18]

The slow erosion of Jewish rights and dignity was about to pick up, and quickly.

In 1941, the prime minister—Pál Teleki, back in office—shot himself, not because he was ashamed of his own antisemitic legal history, but because he was so conflicted about how Hungary was behaving toward Germany. This was a turning point, or, at least, a signal; the partnership with Germany was now out of Hungary's control.

Hungary, as Germany's neighbor and as a fellow nationalistic traveler, was an obvious choice for an ally. Hungary stood to benefit geographically by its alliance with Germany, and Hungary joined the Axis Powers in 1940. In December of that same year, Teleki signed a Pact of Eternal Friendship with Yugoslavia; a few months later, Hitler's troops used Hungary, marching across the country to crush its new "eternal friend."

"We broke our word, out of cowardice," Teleki's suicide note read. "The nation feels it, and we have thrown away its honor. We have allied ourselves to scoundrels . . . We will become body-snatchers! A nation of trash. I did not hold you back. I am guilty."[19]

"Teleki acted, one might say, as the noble aristocrat he was: in his family there were plenty of examples of resolving personal conflict through suicide," Tivadar Soros observed in his memoir, a line that demonstrates some of the scorn felt for the ruling class that had cast Jews aside.[20]

The Soros family continued to live their life in Budapest, with Tivadar Soros working the quiet lawyer's life he'd wanted for himself. Then, three years later, in 1944, with Hitler worrying that Hungary was trying to negotiate an armistice with the United States and the United Kingdom, Nazi Germans took over Hungary. George Soros was thirteen years old. His father had earlier made plans to get his wife and children over to America, but Erzebet, perhaps suspecting that her husband was trying to get her out of the country in order to carry on a passionate love affair in wartime, insisted that the family was to stay together in Budapest.[21] And so they were in Budapest when the Nazis came.

"For years the threat of occupation had been hanging over our heads—in fact for so long that we had forgotten all about it. The news took me completely by surprise," Tivadar Soros wrote.[22]

When the Nazis took over a country during World War II, they would, early on, establish what was known as a Jewish Council. The Jewish Council was comprised of leaders of the Jewish community who carried out German orders. In exchange, their families were exempt from those orders, at least at first. "If they did not comply they would be the first to be punished; if they did, they would be safe—or so they thought," Tivadar Soros wrote.

Jewish students and teachers, no longer permitted to go to school, were sent to Council headquarters. The students were "enlisted" as couriers. In Tivadar Soros's telling, after George Soros's second day at the Jewish Council, he came home and said that he went to specific addresses to deliver notices telling people to report to the rabbinical center with a blanket and enough food for two days.

"Do you know what this means?" his father asked.

"I guess . . . they'll be interned," his son said.

Tivadar Soros said that the Jewish Council had no right to tell people to round themselves up. George Soros said that he'd tried to tell them not to go. Nevertheless, Tivadar Soros wrote, he forbade him from ever going back to the Jewish Council.[23]

George Soros remembered it somewhat differently, and said that his father told him to deliver the set of notices but warn the recipients that they would be deported if they obeyed.[24]

Tivadar Soros had no qualms about telling his son to go against orders. "The citizen should not accept arbitrariness from the state to which he belongs. If his life is endangered by an unjust action of the state, he is justified in fighting back," he wrote. "So I felt no compunction about breaking the law. For me the law ceased to have moral sanction the day the Germans occupied the country."[25]

"We have nothing to protect us against Hitler's threats; there is nobody we can turn to; we are on our own. We must fight for ourselves," Tivadar Soros said, and recalled in his memoir, *Masquerade*. "And since we can't stand up to Hitler's fury, we must hide from it."[26]

If the family worked within the system, they would be powerless before Hitler. And so they worked outside of it.

Tivadar Soros set about finding documents under which his family—and their friends, and, eventually, friends of friends of friends—could hide. He found new apartments, too, splitting up his family for safety.

Less than two weeks after the Germans arrived, Jews were ordered to put stars on their clothing; the Soros family did, but only to see what it felt like to walk around marked as Jews. Tivadar Soros approached occupation with a sense of intellectual curiosity.

(Granted, he also had the privilege, even as a Jew and even in such times, because he was of a certain socioeconomic class and had the means to save himself and others; countless others were not so lucky.)

But he also understood the importance of action and continued his search for Christian identities.

His original plan was to obtain documents from Christians whose identity roughly fit their own. But time passed, and he hadn't found enough real documents for all of the people he wanted to help—though he did for some, including his younger son, who hid out as Sándor Kiss. And so he set about finding fake documents. Eventually, he found a forger who could produce counterfeit documents in large numbers.[27]

George Soros as Sándor Kiss hid out with a man by the name of Baumbach, a Ministry of Agriculture employee (who was in turn hiding his Jewish wife in the countryside). Tivadar Soros paid the man to take young George in and pretend he was his godson. When Baumbach was ordered to go to a Jewish aristocrat's estate to take inventory, he brought his "godson" with him. Shortly thereafter, George was spotted by an old schoolmate on Baumbach's balcony and had to move to a new hiding place.

Decades later, the fact that teenage Soros hid out as a Christian would turn into a rumor that Soros was a Nazi collaborator. In 1998, Steve Kroft, interviewing George Soros on *60 Minutes*, noted that Tivadar Soros had "bribed a government official to swear that you were his godson," adding, "as hundreds of thousands of Jews were being shipped off to the Nazi death camps, a thirteen-year-old George Soros accompanied his phony godfather on his rounds, confiscating property from the Jews."[28] Soros, taken by surprise, only managed to say that he was but a spectator. The idea of Soros's culpability stuck: In 2010, right-wing personality Glenn Beck said of Soros, "Here's a Jewish boy helping send the Jews to the death camps." In 2017, Dinesh D'Souza, a conservative commentator with a propensity for conspiracy theories, tweeted, "YES, REALLY: George Soros, who now funds violent 'anti-fascist' groups in America, confiscated the property of Jews for Hitler during WWII."[29] In 2018, reactionary comedian Roseanne Barr tweeted at Chelsea Clinton, the daughter of former U.S. President Bill Clinton and former Secretary of State and failed presidential candidate Hillary Clinton, "George Soros is a Nazi who turned in his fellow Jews to be murdered in German concentration camps and stole their wealth."[30]

In 1944, however, the Soros family wasn't worried about being accused of Nazi collaboration. They were concerned with surviving the Nazis.

From May 15 to July 9 that year, 440,000 Jews were deported from Hungary by Hungarian officials under the guidance of German SS officers. They were mostly sent to Auschwitz-Birkenau, where, after inspection and selection, the majority were killed in gas chambers. Others were sent to the Austrian border, where they were made to dig fortification trenches.[31]

"I was not yet 14," Soros said years later. "That was my father's finest hour, because he knew how to act. He understood the situation; he realized that the normal rules did not apply. Obeying the law became a dangerous addiction; flaunting it was a way to survive."

This was a lesson Soros learned at a young age: Rules are meant to be fairly obeyed, unless the rules themselves are inherently unfair and unjust, in which case they must be broken.

"Having experienced the Russian revolution, he knew what to do," George later wrote of Tivadar. "He made arrangements for the family to get false identity papers, and he found places for us to live or hide. He helped not only his immediate family, but a fairly large number of other people around him. I can truthfully say he saved dozens of lives."[32]

For some people, whom he believed could afford it—the friend,

Lajos Ozma, with whom he hid out in cramped quarters, for example—Tivadar Soros charged quite a lot to obtain fake documents. For others, he charged nothing.[33]

The family was able to move about more freely than they would have if they had not had false identities, to put it mildly, although they did have a few close calls. At one point, officers confronted Tivadar's wife—George Soros's mother—about her identity. She successfully convinced them that she was not Erzebet, but a woman named Julia.[34] At another, the attendant at the pool where Tivadar Soros would meet his sons inexplicably thanked George Soros in the name of the religious community—the Jewish religious community. The family concluded that it must have been a joke; all the same, they decided not to go back to the pool. "At the time, to give up swimming was to give up one of the few pleasures of life," Tivadar wrote.[35]

The war, and the way in which they survived it, was a formative experience for father and son alike.

"The state of war I had lived through since the Germans invaded had changed my emotional world. Living as a victim of persecution had changed my sense of empathy: the condition of all such victims of persecution became my affair, a part of my condition," Tivadar Soros wrote in *Masquerade*. "The atrocities of the Japanese government made *me* ashamed; the measures taken against South African blacks were offenses against *me*. It was as though I felt responsibility for the whole world." He tried, he said, to pass that sense on to his sons.[36]

His younger son learned that lesson. But he learned another one, too: survival.

"The important and paradoxical point is that 1944 was the happiest year of my life. This is a strange, almost offensive thing to say because 1944 was the year of the Holocaust, but it is true," Soros recalled in the 1990s. "I was 14 years old. I had a father whom

I adored, who was in command of the situation, who knew what to do and who helped others. We were in mortal danger, but I was convinced that I was exempt. When you are 14 years old, you believe that you can't really be hurt."

He added, "It had a formative effect on my life because I learned the art of survival from a grandmaster."[37] In the following years, he would scrape his way through London, start a new life in New York, stand toe-to-toe with the Hungarian Communist Party, lose and win and lose and win tremendous amounts of money, and be vilified by seemingly everyone.

But he would survive. His father had taught him how.

There is another story about another lesson learned that one person who has known Soros for years says he likes to tell: On one of the days that father and son met up from their respective hiding places, they went together to buy cigarettes. Jews were banned from buying tobacco, but they lived under Christian identities, and so went forth and made the purchase.

Outside the tobacco shop, some young Jews stopped and asked if they could buy the cigarettes from Tivadar Soros, who gave them all away. His young son asked him why he did that. It wasn't only that they had just purchased the cigarettes; it was dangerous for them to give them to Jews.

"I didn't want them to think all Christians are bad," his father said.[38]

I asked Soros about this story. He noted first that the Jews in the story were shopkeepers, not boys. Did he agree, I asked, that this explains a lot about his mentality?

"This story of the cigarettes is just one of many examples that illustrate what type of man my father was. It was not that he wanted the Jewish shopkeepers to think Christians were good, it was that he did not want them to think that all Christians were bad. He recognized the dangers of hatred and extremism," he wrote.

And then I understood: I had thought that the story meant that his father wanted to give other Jewish people hope in their fellow man. Actually, his father was trying to keep Jewish Hungarians from hating Christians. He didn't want one group to hate another. He needed the different pieces of this society to coexist. Years later, his younger son would spend billions toward the same aim.

"My father had a genuine interest in other people's fate. He taught me how to deal with the world. If it were not for my father, who recognized the dangers early enough to take action, I might have perished during the Holocaust," his emailed response continued. "And so would the dozens of others that my father helped to survive the Nazi occupation of Hungary by providing advice to them and helping to arrange false identities. In the end, despite the odds, we prevailed against what was truly an evil force. This was the formative experience of my life."

HUNGARY WENT FROM BEING GOVERNED by Nazis (and then the Arrow Cross, the far-right Hungarian party) to being "liberated" by the Soviet Union—and so being put under one-party socialist control. George Soros found life in socialist Hungary constricting. He may not have been in hiding anymore, but at school he had gotten into trouble for a newspaper he was producing—an emulation of his father's publication *The Plank*. An article in the paper ended with the word "amen." The youngest Soros had meant it to mean "so be it," but his fellow students claimed he had offended their religious feelings.[39]

By 1947, Soros had had enough. He had been listening to the BBC and so had some frame of reference for the United Kingdom. He decided to go to England.

Soros got out of Hungary by traveling to Switzerland. His papers hadn't arrived in time for the Esperanto conference at which he was meeting his father, so he got on the train without his permit. When Tivadar went back to Hungary, his son waited in Switzerland. When his visa came through roughly two weeks later, George Soros went to England.[40]

At first, he worked menial jobs, failed his English exam, and generally felt himself on the outside of a part of London—the intellectual, cultural, stylish part—to which he badly wanted to belong. "I had never wanted to be friends with Nazis or Hungarians or anti-Semites," he later recalled. "Being excluded [in London], and trying to break into a closed society as an outsider, that was new and painful."[41]

But in the spring of 1949, he managed to achieve a sufficient score on his exams, meaning he could, finally, enroll at the London School of Economics, with all of its sophistication, intellectual rigor, and influence on political thinking.[42] There he was introduced to the writings of Karl Popper. Popper was not Soros's regular teacher at LSE, but Soros finished his regular studies a year early, and so, in his third and final (and required) year, he selected Popper as his tutor.

"I had lived through Nazi persecution and Soviet occupation," Soros later said. "Popper's book, *Open Society and Its Enemies*, struck me with the force of revelation—it showed that fascism and communism have a lot in common, and they both stand in opposition to a different principle of social organization, the principle of open society."[43]

Popper's theory was basically this: nothing can be known with absolute certainty, and so people should have an open society, with lots of different ideas, where individuals can, together, move toward a better understanding. Popper's approach, Soros once said, is "based on a hidden assumption, namely that the main purpose of thinking is to gain a better understanding of reality."[44]

Popper and Soros were not particularly close, but Popper's

philosophy—that there is no perfect truth, that we can each be wrong, that our expectations will never quite match with reality, and that all people, with all their flaws, should be allowed to participate in a society to try to strive toward understanding—became the core of Soros's life. When he eventually turned to his own charitable work, Popper's writings would be a sort of North Star.

But in his early London days, Soros was receiving, not giving, charity, and his early interaction with charity showed him how easily it can be manipulated by its recipients. The Jewish Board of Guardians, a charity established by the upper-class Jewish community in the nineteenth century, turned him down as a recipient for stipends—evidently, they didn't think he was a sufficiently worthy cause. Soros was then working and broke his leg. He went back to the Jewish Board of Guardians and told them he had been working illegally and so was ineligible for National Assistance. This was untrue, but the Jewish Board of Guardians didn't know or bother to find out, and so agreed to give him money, provided he came to their office, climbing stairs with a broken leg, to get it. Soros then wrote the chairman of the board and said that he was hurt to find that this is how one Jew treats another. They sent him money, and he kept collecting money from the Jewish Board of Guardians long after his broken leg had healed.[45]

"I learned that it is the task of the applicant to get money out of the foundation and it is the task of the foundation to protect itself . . . I also discovered that charity . . . can have unintended consequences. The paradox of charity is that it turns the recipients . . . into objects of charity," he later said.[46] When he set up his own philanthropic foundation, he tried to ensure that its recipients did not become objects of charity—and could not try to take advantage of his generosity.

At this point he was still years away from becoming a

philanthropist. After graduating from the LSE, Soros first worked at a fancy goods manufacturer in England, and then went to work for a customer who was a wholesaler.

"I became a traveling salesman selling to retailers in Welsh seaside resorts, and that was a low point in my career. It took me very far away from my concept of myself," Soros said.[47] He wanted to be somebody. He wanted to do what his surname suggested: soar.

So he wrote to all the merchant banks in London. At one, he was told that he wasn't from the right college or circles, or even the right country, and he was told to give up. But at Singer & Friedlander, he was from the right country: one of the managing directors was Hungarian.

He got a job there in 1953 and worked in arbitrage and the stock exchange. But the job wasn't what he'd thought it would be.

Before too much time had elapsed at Singer & Friedlander, Soros missed a day of work—he had flown to Paris to spend an extra weekend with his brother and sister-in-law, Daisy, and his return was delayed by fog—and was asked to explain himself. He took the opportunity to ask what his prospects were. Soros was meant to be working in arbitrage—buying something in one market and selling it in another—but the firm wasn't particularly pleased with how he was doing and felt he was a fifth wheel. When he was told they wouldn't find a niche for him, he asked to look for work elsewhere. Permission was granted.

In 1948, his brother, Paul Soros, a skier, learned a leg injury would keep him from participating in the Olympics. Traveling with the ski team to Switzerland, Paul Soros defected, and moved to the United States. Several months after asking to seek gainful employment outside of Singer & Friedlander, George followed his brother and moved to America to work at a small brokerage firm on Wall Street owned by the father of one of his coworkers at Singer & Friedlander.

George Soros moved to New York City to work in international arbitrage.[48] He had arrived in London thinking that it would be the sort of place where the sky was the limit; as a working man, he found that that London no longer existed, if it ever had.[49] He hoped New York City would be the kind of city he had in mind. He lived first with his brother in Queens and then in a two-bedroom apartment on Riverside Drive where his parents briefly stayed on their arrival to America—they were among the thousands who fled their native country following the Hungarian Revolution of 1956.[50]

Soros stayed at the brokerage firm, F. M. Mayer, for three years, but then, in 1959, moved to Wertheim & Co., an investment firm. He felt his business decisions were being questioned at Mayer and believed that he had earned trust, and so resented having to answer to someone. The next year, in 1960, he married his first wife—Annaliese Witschak,[51] an ethnic German immigrant, with whom he moved to an apartment on Sheridan Square and built a house in Southampton.

All was not well for long at Wertheim. In 1962, Soros had taken on a large position in a Japanese insurance company. When word got out that President John F. Kennedy was planning to put a tax on foreign securities, there was some concern as to whether potential buyers would, in fact, buy—or if Wertheim would be left with Soros's Japanese acquisitions, meaning the company would lose money and Soros would be blamed for the loss.

Worse than that was that his boss denied knowing of or approving the venture. "Of course he knew about it and authorized it," Soros later protested. But evidently there was no paper trail, and, in any event, it was his word against that of a superior. He realized he would never rise to the highest level of the firm, "and though by then I did not want to be a partner I knew it was time to leave. Toward the end of 1962 I left Wertheim."[52]

It wasn't long until another firm, Arnhold & S. Bleichroeder, came calling. Soros began there in 1963, taking time in between jobs to focus on his philosophy.

He pulled together a manuscript for a work called "The Burden of Consciousness," which was, by his own admission, "very much a regurgitation" of Popper's ideas. (He showed it to Popper, who was excited that someone had understood him until learning Soros wasn't American, a reality that somehow wasn't evident to Popper while he was Soros's tutor. If Soros had been American, "That meant I had managed to communicate my ideas. But you lived through it all, so you don't count and that's why I'm disappointed," Popper said, at least in Soros's telling.)[53] In 1966, Soros invited a group of philosophers to spend a weekend at his estate in Bedford, New York, for a discussion of his ideas (or his take on Popper's ideas). Jonathan Wolff from University College London later noted that Soros "had apparently read no philosophy since the fifties and had made clear that he did not think that much of significance has occurred in the field since then" but also said, "These were interesting ideas and arguments and very much worth discussing. I had assumed that it was to be an exercise in vanity, but in fact the discussions were of good quality and he was a full participant. Also a very good host."[54]

His treatise discussed but at an intellectual dead end, Soros turned back to finance. In 1966, at Arnhold & S. Bleichroeder, he set up a model account with $100,000 of the firm's money.[55] The model performed well. Based on that, the firm set up a small investment fund for him to manage: First Eagle Fund. In 1969, he used $4 million to set up a hedge fund, a long/short stock-picking mechanism, named Double Eagle Fund.[56]

Soros was guided by the wisdom of Wall Street, and also by what he learned from his old tutor, Karl Popper. Popper's theory was that nothing can be known. Soros broke that into two propositions: fallibility, or the idea that the world is full of people, and people get things wrong, and reflexivity, or the idea that false views lead to the wrong course of action. "Popper's philosophy made me more sensitive to the role of misconceptions in financial markets," Soros said decades later. People believe that markets don't lie and should be trusted; but that isn't true, Soros knew. Markets react to humans, and humans are fallible. Instead of looking at the money being made, or, as Sebastian Mallaby put it in *More Money Than God*, his book on the history of hedge funds, "the psychology that drove investors' appetites," Soros looked at how the one impacted the other, "predicting that each would drive the other forward until the trusts were so completely overvalued that a crash was inevitable."

The Double Eagle Fund was successful—and successfully presented a conflict. Soros was recommending stocks to clients that he was also potentially buying for his own account, and so could have been accused of recommending stocks to make his own stocks perform better.

And so Soros gave up his model, left, and went to set up his own hedge fund in 1973. His fund was called the Soros Fund. He brought along Jim Rogers, a former coworker (Rogers had been an analyst at Bleichroeder), and they opened an office on Columbus Circle, not far from Soros's home at the time at 25 Central Park West.[57] In 1978, the fund changed its name to Quantum Fund.[58] (This was also around the time that Rogers left the fund.)[59]

By 1981, the fund had gained assets worth $381 million. Soros had a personal fortune of $100 million. That June, a magazine called *Institutional Investor* declared him "the world's greatest money manager." George Soros the Financial Genius was born.

THE CONCEPT OF A HEDGE fund was still relatively new in the late 1970s and early 1980s. The idea of a hedge fund dates back to 1949, when journalist turned moneymaker A. W. Jones founded one. The notion was to take different positions on companies' shares in a particular industry so as to hedge against macroeconomic factors and benefit from specific companies that were nevertheless doing well.[60]

If the idea of hedge funds was still relatively new, George Soros's idea of how to run a hedge fund was even newer.

Soros said that his financial strategy was informed by his philosophy, but it was executed by instinct; he believed he could tell there was trouble ahead for his portfolio when he felt a pain in his back, something definitely not covered in Popper's writings.[61] And when he believed there was opportunity ahead, he went in for the kill. In 1973, for example, the Arab-Israeli War had shifted tectonic plates in the defense industry. Egypt had used Soviet weaponry, and it had worked, meaning that the United States had a legitimate challenger. Soros guessed that the Pentagon would go to Congress for authorization of further spending; he bought defense stocks and made money.[62]

If his strategy was different, so, too, was his style, and not just because there were only so many financiers with Hungarian accents who admitted "I fancied myself some kind of god" working in hedge funds. In the course of reporting this book, a former colleague of mine from graduate school got in touch; her father had a story about Soros that he wanted to share with me.

"I joined the British merchant bank Kleinwort Benson back in late '78 or early '79," her father, Andrew Morrison, now the Viscount Dunrossil, told me in his posh British accent.

"One day my manager said that there was someone who had walked in—nobody ever walked into the bank—would I go with him to meet with this person. We went into a little conference room, the three of us. The person was George Soros." Soros, Morrison remembers, said that he had gone to the London School of

Economics, was living in New York, and "ran something called the Quantum Fund."

"He said he wanted a loan for 50 million pounds, which was a large loan for our bank. We were also used to loans . . . being made to corporations that said, five years of profit history that you could spread, look at the history of profits, look at the interest/coverage ratios," he added. "And this was not like that. He didn't have a balance sheet. He just said, I want to use this money to buy British Government Securities and you can keep the gilts [bonds issued by the British government] as collateral."

Morrison described it as "unusual in so many ways. We were used to soliciting and going out to talk to people. And here's a guy who walks into our bank and says, I've got a deal, I've got an idea for you, will you listen." Soros didn't have spreadsheets, and it wasn't business as usual, but he had a big idea he wanted to go for.

"This was so different. It was what working in a merchant bank really should be all about. George Soros made things fun in my brief experience with him," Morrison said.[63] "It was the very first credit proposal I got to present to the bank's committee and to defend. They went for it. We now know what he did with the money—he was shorting sterling."[64]

We now know what he did with the money because shorting currencies proved, for Soros, profitable. So profitable that he became famous doing it.

IN THE LATE 1970S AND early 1980s, Soros wanted to live a larger life or, as his son Robert put it, he wanted to be a "grander persona." He didn't yet want to be famous, exactly, but he wanted to be a known person. As Soros put it, "I changed my attitude. I accepted the fact that I was successful."[65] This, according to Robert Soros, is what led to the demise of Soros's first marriage to the private Annaliese Witschak, who evidently did not want to be married to a known person, or a society man. The two separated. Soros met Susan Weber, twenty-five years his junior. He had met the recent Barnard College graduate previously, but they reconnected at a chance meeting at the tennis courts on Columbus Avenue in 1978, the same year he left Witschak; the two married in 1983, five years after his separation[66] and the same year of his first divorce.[67]

The desire for more public engagement was reflected in his public and professional life, too.

In 1985, Soros believed the dollar, which had been rising, was due for a reversal. He started keeping a diary that August, believing the time was almost ripe: President Ronald Reagan was making changes to his team, apparently to bring down the U.S. dollar to reduce the country's trade deficit, and interest rates were falling.

As of August 16, Mallaby writes, Quantum owned $720 million worth of the primary currencies against which the dollar was expected to fall. "The only competitive edge I have," Soros wrote, "is the theory of reflexivity."

At first, it looked like Soros had made a mistake. On September 9, Quantum had lost $20 million. But Soros saw that the Reagan administration was bent on getting the deficit down and stuck to his bet.

And then, on September 22, James Baker, the U.S. treasury secretary, met his counterparts from Britain, France, Japan, and West Germany at the Plaza Hotel in New York, where the five agreed to coordinate intervention in currency markets to drive down the dollar. Soros made $30 million. Soros called brokers in Hong Kong and instructed them to buy more yen for his portfolio. He bought up more yen, more German marks—$500 million worth of the two, plus nearly $300 million to his short position of the dollar.

In four months, the fund had increased by 35 percent. The profit was $230 million. Soros published his diary two years later, in 1987, under the title *The Alchemy of Finance*.[68]

A *Fortune* magazine cover story published that September said he was possibly ahead of Warren Buffett in being "the most prescient investor of his generation."

It was a title that was about to be challenged.

As Mallaby notes in his *More Money Than God*, that same *Fortune* magazine cover had a line asking, "Are stocks too high?"[69]

Soros thought the answer was no. "Just because the market is overvalued does not mean it is not sustainable," he said.[70]

As it turned out, he was wrong. Soros was short on Japan and long on the U.S. market. In fact, on October 14, Soros published a *Financial Times* article predicting a crash would hit Tokyo before Wall Street. But Japan would be relatively spared the crash, in part because the Japanese government intervened to urge large brokers not to sell.[71]

The Wednesday of the week his *FT* article was published, the Dow Jones Industrial Average dropped 3.8 percent. Stocks kept falling Thursday and Friday. Stanley Druckenmiller, already a Soros confidant (and soon to be brought in by Soros to run Quantum Fund on a day-to-day basis), whom Soros met that Friday, thought that the prices had fallen to a point from which they would bounce back. The next day, Druckenmiller concluded that things were worse than he'd realized; the stocks were in free fall. On Monday, he sold as much as he could as quickly as he could.[72] But Quantum Fund was too big to do so quickly.

Stocks had been too high. The market was overvalued, and now it had come crashing down. On October 19, 1987—now known as Black Monday—stock markets around the world crashed. The Dow Jones index lost 22.6 percent of its value.[73]

That Thursday, Soros saw the London market fall, and thought it meant another sell-off in New York was coming. He decided to move to cash. But here, again, Quantum was too big. In selling a $1 billion position quickly, Soros moved the market; other investors saw they could let the market fall and then take profit on short positions. Soros's Thursday decision lost his fund $200 million, and $840 million over the week—the fund had gone from being up 60 percent for the year to being down 10 percent.[74]

Then, around two weeks after Black Monday, Soros saw an opportunity to short the dollar. He did what he always did when he saw an opening and went in for the kill. Quantum ended the year that was supposed to kill George Soros up 13 percent. At the end of the year, *Financial World* listed him as the second-highest earner on Wall Street.[75] George Soros became famous in 1985 for making money; in 1987, he became famous for losing it and then, undaunted, making more.

BUT ALL OF THIS—MAKING A name, making money, losing money, and making more—was only part of what George Soros was doing in the late 1970s and throughout the 1980s.

From the outside, Soros was, at the time, an innovator, pushing boundaries and making it look, if not easy, then at least thrilling.

But in 1979, Soros himself decided he was not thrilled; in fact, he was exhausted. The stress of running a hedge fund was taking a strain on his body, so much so that he was finally pushed to ask himself what the physical and emotional toll of the stress was for.

"The strain of risk-taking on a leveraged basis was enormous," he later wrote. "On one occasion, I subscribed to a very large amount of a new issue of British government bonds on short notice without previously arranging the necessary financing. I was rushing around London trying to find a credit line, and walking down Leadenhall Street I thought I was having a heart attack. 'I took this risk to make a killing,' I told myself, 'but if I die now I end up as the loser. It doesn't make sense to risk my life to make money.'"[76]

He could also afford to risk his life on something else: His fund had reached $100 million, about $40 million of which was his. "That was more than enough for me and my family, I felt."

Soros's father had taught him that money was a means to an end, and Soros himself later said that he didn't particularly like making money; he was just good at it. But what was the end?[77] What was it all for?

If George Soros was going to feel like he was about to die of a heart attack, then he was going to have the stress and strain be for a good cause.

"That is when I decided to do something worthwhile with my money and set up a foundation. I thought long and hard about what I really cared about. I relied on my rather abstract conceptual framework for guidance and I honed [sic] in on the concept of open society, which is one of the cornerstones of that framework."[78]

In 1979 he decided to embark on opening society, with foundations intended to open closed societies, make open societies more viable, and promote critical thinking.

Almost fifty years after György Schwartz's birth, George Soros the Ambitious Philanthropist came into the world.

CHAPTER 2

1984

An open society is one in which it is understood that none of us can know for certain what is right and what is wrong. That is not to say that everything is morally equivalent; it is to say that none of us can ever really know for certain what is morally superior, or even what is true. For that reason, an open society is one in which every individual from every background has the right to contribute to the civic discussion and debate. To increase each individual's chance at equitable participation in the discourse is to increase the collective's chance of arriving at true understanding. An open society is one that eschews tribalism and totalitarianism in thought; it is one in which the individual's dignity and freedom to participate in that discussion is protected. This was what Soros took from Popper, and this was the cause to which Soros wanted to give his money.

Soros's determination to open society led to two important questions: Where does one go to open society? And, having found societies that need opening, how, exactly, does one open them?

The answer to the first question was relatively easy: Soros had a friend from apartheid-era South Africa, and so set out there, and when he decided that his efforts there were not working, he went back to his native Hungary. The answer to the question of how to open a society was, and is, more complicated.

IN 1979, SOROS ESTABLISHED THE Open Society Fund as a charitable lead trust. His motives were not entirely altruistic. "A charitable lead trust is a very interesting tax gimmick. The idea is that you commit your assets to a trust and you put a certain amount of money into charity every year," he explained in the early 2000s. "And then after you have given the money for however many years, the principal that remains can be left [to one's heirs] without estate or gift tax. So this was the way I set up the trust for my children." He expected to contribute up to $3 million a year for up to twenty years.[1]

Philanthropy, in addition to being a way to ostensibly make the world a better place, is effectively a legal form of tax evasion, and Soros is one of many wealthy people who have set up charitable trusts or philanthropic organizations at least in part toward these ends. Those with enough money can use it to make a name for themselves as something other than good at making money, but they can also use it to hold on to their money for themselves and their heirs. This isn't to say that Soros wasn't genuine in caring about the principle of an open society; it is to acknowledge that, by his own admission, he first set up a charitable lead trust to keep more money in the family and hand less of it over to the state for redistribution.

In deciding where to make the contributions, Soros first looked not to the country of his birth, nor around the United States. Nor, despite his Jewish heritage and World War II experience, did he try to give his money expressly to Israel or Jewish organizations.

Soros's Jewish identity is, to this day, a subject of discussion and debate, as is the extent to which criticism of him is antisemitic. When world leaders accused Soros's money of being behind attempts to undermine society—when Viktor Orbán, for example, said that he, Orbán, was fighting an enemy that is different from them, that "does not have its own homeland but feels it owns the whole world"—and were accused of spewing antisemitism, those same world leaders pointed to their support of and close relationship to Israel and Prime Minister Benjamin Netanyahu, who is himself critical of Soros, a supporter of Palestinian rights. This argument presumes not only that supporters of Israel cannot be antisemitic, but also that one can only have a Jewish identity if one identifies with the state of Israel. Neither of these things is true.

Soros's sense of Jewishness is not tied to Israel. In the early 1990s, Soros wrote, "My Jewishness did not express itself in a sense of tribal loyalty that would have led me to support Israel. On the contrary, I took pride in being in the minority, an outsider who was capable of seeing the other point of view. Only the ability to think critically and to rise above a particular point of view could make up for the dangers and indignities that being a Hungarian Jew had inflicted on me."[2]

That his identity and self perception was shaped both by an experience of being persecuted for his Jewishness and also by an experience dealing with an ostensibly pro-Jewish organization that frustrated him in his time of need is perhaps not surprising. In any event, Soros's sense of Jewishness did not make him feel connected to other Jews, but rather made him want to help further freedom of expression—and those who found themselves under the wheel, as he, being Jewish, had once found himself.

"I realized that I cared passionately about the concept of an open society in which people like me could enjoy freedom without being hounded to death. Accordingly, I called my foundation the

Open Society Fund, with the objective of making open societies viable and helping to open up closed societies."[3]

And the first closed society he sought to open was South Africa.

"I had a Zulu friend in New York, Herbert Vilakazi, who was a university lecturer in Connecticut," Soros recalled in 2011. "He returned to South Africa to take up a post at the University of Transkal [*sic*]—one of the homelands under the apartheid system. I visited him . . . and gained insight into South Africa from an unusual angle. Here was a closed society with all the institutions of a first world country, but they were off limits to the majority of the population on racial grounds. Where could I find a better opportunity for opening up a closed society?"[4]

Soros decided to try to open South African society by offering scholarships to black South African students, giving them, through access to academia and knowledge, a fairer chance at a platform through which to reform their country and community.

That Soros started in South Africa at a university in particular is significant, not only because he would go on to provide scholarships to people all over the world and found a university, and not only because it is an early example of his use of philanthropy to try to reform a system from within. It is significant because of the reason he started there; he happened to know an interesting person who led him to approach philanthropy through scholarship. This pattern—that Soros would happen to meet someone, find that person interesting, and follow that person to a new philanthropic endeavor—would be a pattern in his philanthropic career. In this way, Soros would cultivate and empower local, talented individuals; in this way, he would also come to be blamed for promoting certain groups of people, leaving those who were in the know a world apart from those who were not. If one relies on people one knows and the people they know, one risks creating in-groups and out-groups, something of a paradox for a philanthropist whose fundamental idea is that conditions must be created so that society can have and hold different opinions and views of the world.

None of that became clear in South Africa, but something else did. Soros soon discovered a lesson one might have imagined he'd already learned: power works to protect power, and systems set up by power work to protect power, too. Perhaps Soros should have known or expected this, but he believed that the people with whom he was dealing were dealing in good faith, as he was. They were not.

"The system was so insidious that whatever I did made me an accomplice of the system," Soros later said.[5] On a visit the following year, he learned that the University of Cape Town, the institution that was supposed to give out his scholarships, was not quite as committed to the idea of openness as it had made itself seem to Soros when he set out to give his money away. Black student enrollment had not increased as much as the number of scholarships he was providing would suggest. The money was not being used to supplement the state's contribution, but as a replacement for it. The black students with whom he met felt discriminated against, and felt angry—not necessarily with Soros, but certainly with the system.[6]

Frustrated, Soros discontinued his work in South Africa, though he did see the original group of students through their education. But he stuck with the idea of giving out scholarships: In 1980, he turned to a place where he was more familiar, awarding scholarships to dissidents in Eastern Europe who were advocating for human rights. Soros knew firsthand the impact that education could have on broadening a person's perspective and horizons; his foundation carried the name it did because of his own education at the London School of Economics. In giving students an opportunity to achieve an education, he was trying to give them footing for participating in society.

He also began directly financially supporting dissident movements like Solidarity in Poland (a labor union outside of the

Communist Party that pushed for workers' rights and social change), Charter 77 in Czechoslovakia (a group led by intellectuals pushing for human rights in the country), and physicist Andrei Sakharov's prodemocratization movement in Soviet Russia. The idea that Soros has, in his time, funded groups that worked against the ruling government or party is not, technically, untrue.[7]

Soros would go back to philanthropy in South Africa in 1987, providing financial support to business and political leaders taking part in an early dialogue for the dismantlement of the apartheid system.[8] But it would only be later, after apartheid ended in South Africa in 1994, that Soros would look back at his student scholarship plan and wish that he had not felt so quickly defeated by the system, and that instead he had stuck with his intention to try to change it, and society, for the better.[9]

INITIALLY, SOROS GOT INVOLVED IN Hungary by giving scholarships to dissidents. But the dissidents themselves suggested to him that being personally selected for foreign-funded scholarships was discrediting them, setting them aside and apart from the country and community they were trying to change and improve.

The opinion and work of the dissidents meant a lot to Soros—who, it should be noted, was still running a highly successful hedge fund during this time—and so he took their warning to heart and decided it would be more effective to change the way in which he was giving his money away in Hungary.[10]

In 1984, he approached Hungary's ambassador to the United States, Vencel Hazi, to ask if he could give out cultural and education scholarships in Hungary. This way, the scholarships would be given out with government cooperation and not to a select segment of society. To his surprise, the ambassador said yes. That Soros started in Hungary—as opposed to, say, in Poland, where the dissident movement was more established and politically potent—was, he said, down to the fact that he spoke the language.[11]

The Hungarian branch of Open Society was, at this point, being run out of Soros's home by his second wife, Susan Weber (she said it caused marital tension—working for one's highly demanding spouse can have that effect—and therefore gave up running the foundation in the early 1990s).[12] In Hungary, Open Society had to be called the Soros Foundation because the name Open Society was evidently too political for the Hungarian powers that were. It was established in cooperation with the Hungarian Academy of Sciences under the regime, and had executive directors from both the government and the Soros side (Party man Janos Quittner and sociologist László Kardos, respectively), but was really run by a third Soros pick: Miklós Vásárhelyi, who was the last surviving defendant in the trial of Imre Nagy.[13] Nagy was the leader of the thwarted Hungarian Revolution of 1956.[14] While Vásárhelyi had survived, Nagy was hanged for treason; the Party did not admit that this was a "fabricated political trial" and concede that the execution had been illegal until 1989—five years after Soros began working in Hungary.[15]

Choosing Vásárhelyi (who had spent years in prison and could have been sentenced to death,[16] and who had a record of opposing the government) to work at the foundation was a clear sign of the independence that Soros intended for the institution. Annual grants of $3 million were given from the foundation for language courses, support for journals and literature, and scholarships for students and researchers traveling abroad.

The dissidents had warned that special selection for scholarships might hurt the scholarship recipients. That was part of the reason for making work in Hungary more formal in the first place. Still, the Soros Foundation in Hungary, once established, continued to operate on a somewhat selective and secretive basis.

Soros was not trying to ignore the dissidents' warning; in having established a more formal process of giving out scholarships, he probably thought he was heeding it. He was trying to avoid his foundation's being exploited.

From his experience scamming the Jewish Board of Guardians in his London days, Soros learned that foundations try to protect themselves while recipients try to get money out of them; years later, he remembered that charities can turn their recipients into objects of charity. Soros saw two routes through which he could avoid this paradox. "One is to become very bureaucratic like the Ford Foundation, and the other is not to become visible at all—to make grants without inviting applications and to remain anonymous. I chose the latter alternative."[17]

Today, Open Society is a large organization that could very well be described as bureaucratic. But at its beginning, it was nimble and meant to adapt quickly to what were perceived as the needs of the society—and Soros was trying to keep it that way.

"We made a policy of supporting practically any initiative that was spontaneous and nongovernmental," Soros said. "The name of the Soros Foundation kept on cropping up in the most unexpected places. The foundation attained a mythical quality exactly because it received so little publicity. For those who were politically conscious, it became an instrument of civil society; for the public at large, it was manna from heaven."[18]

From its earliest days, there was—by design—something secretive about how George Soros gave the money away. Today, that air of mystery has contributed to conspiracy theories, but back in 1984, it was part of what made the project electrifying—the money and the work were like an unexpected jolt to the society Soros was trying to help open.

The shocking nature of the work held even when Soros made attempts at transparency. The organization's bylaws stipulated that a press release had to be sent to newspapers to announce which scholars had been selected as recipients. But the third time that they sent out the list of recipients, it wasn't published by the Hungarian papers. The decision not to publish, Soros learned from editors at the economic weekly publication *HGV*, came directly from General Secretary János Kádár; one approved grant was for a biography of Mátyás Rákosi, postwar Hungary's Communist leader, and Kádár felt only the Party could determine who could write what about such figures.

Soros decided that he would go on a weekly radio show, *168 Hours*, the following weekend to announce that either the government had to allow outlets to publicize which grants the foundation had awarded or he would withdraw from Hungary. Three days later, an editor at *HGV* called to say the paper had been informed it could publish the names.

At that moment, Soros became more than a very rich man; he was a very rich man who successfully delivered an ultimatum to the Hungarian leadership. Until the first free and fair elections in 1990 (or, rather, the first free and fair elections since the 1940s), that party had a hold on political power in the country. That Soros wrested some of it away and bent the party to his will was not just a neat trick; it meant that he had real power.

That was the myth of Soros at the time; he was a benefactor who was somehow of two continents and had given money to scholars in need, of all people, and who was politically powerful.[19]

He was also known as being very rich: Géza Jeszenszky, who was minister of foreign affairs for József Antall, leader of the Hungarian Democratic Forum in 1989 and then the first democratically elected prime minister of Hungary, told me over email that Soros offered to settle Hungary's national debt in exchange for stock in Hungary's state-owned companies. Jeszenszky remembers the meeting as being in the fall of 1989 "at what was then called Hotel

Novotel near the Southern Railway Terminal. It was convened by General Béla Király, the commander of the Hungarian National Guard during the 1956 Revolution, who then lived in the U.S." Antall consulted experts and then turned down the offer, wanting instead, Jeszenszky wrote, to give the stocks to the highest bidder. Soros's spokesperson disputed this account. The spokesperson said that Soros did have an idea for Central and Eastern European national debts to be canceled in exchange for some Western stock in state-owned companies, but that Soros did not mean he personally wanted to own the stock or make money off of Hungary. In any case, the very fact that the anecdote persists (Jeszenszky has told it to Hungarian journalists, too) suggests that Soros and his wealth made an impression on the political elites of the day.

Those who remember Soros from the 1980s often begin their stories by saying that they'd heard about this American who was originally from Hungary and was giving money away. This is how András Bozóki, who went on to be Hungary's minister of culture in the early 2000s, first came across Soros's foundation. In 1987, Bozóki was in the United States. He'd been in Indianapolis and then came to New York courtesy of the New School, he told me in his tidy, comfortable apartment in Buda over coffee and seltzer one warm June day in 2019. He had very little money, and had heard about this rich Hungarian American, and so sought out the Open Society offices. He was told to come back another time. In an unlucky turn of events, Bozóki's visit coincided with Black Monday.

"Probably they lost millions on that day," he said. "Still, they could have given me a hundred dollars," he added with a glint in his eye.

Bozóki ultimately did get money from Soros. From the fall of 1988 to the spring of 1989, Bozóki went on a Soros research fellowship at the University of California, Los Angeles.

"That was a life-changing experience for me," he said. And while Bozóki was involved in a nascent political movement called Fidesz in Hungary, he didn't want to run to be in Hungary's first freely elected parliament when the time came. Having seen in California how serious research was done, he wanted to pursue a career in academia. He is still today, he told me earnestly, thankful to Soros for his career.[20]

When I walked away from our interview, this anecdote stayed with me for two reasons. First, because of what the money meant to Bozóki; a Soros scholarship could change the course of a person's entire life. And second, because the story reminded me of another Soros scholarship recipient, one who did not go into academia. As I sat there with the professor who had largely turned down a political career—though in the end he became a minister of culture—I thought of the Soros scholarship recipient who took on a prominent role in Fidesz and ended up running the whole country: Viktor Orbán.

IN ADDITION TO GIVING OUT scholarships, one of the Hungarian Soros Foundation's first projects was to offer photocopiers to institutions. Previously, the distribution of photocopiers had been controlled by institutions run by the state so that the state, in turn, could control the information that the photocopiers were used to distribute. Soros provided so many photocopiers that the information they were used to distribute couldn't be controlled or regulated. It was subversive—Soros was, in effect, funding underground or unregulated information—but the party badly needed these institutions to have photocopiers, so how could it refuse?

"That was the most fantastic, marvelous time we ever had. The foundation enabled people who were not dissidents to act, in effect, like dissidents," Soros said a decade later. "Nothing that we have done since quite compares with it."[21] It was their first real, successful foray into philanthropy as subversion.

There were also more day-to-day projects funded with Soros's money. A friend of mine, the Hungarian journalist Szabolcs Panyi, told me that the first time he remembered hearing Soros's name was as a child in Budapest; he heard that the milk he drank at lunch was paid for by George Soros, he recalled matter-of-factly.[22] Soros was giving money not only for sustenance of the mind, but also for literal sustenance.

So, too, were there some projects that Soros supported that didn't immediately seem to have a cultural component. Bálint Magyar, a tall, gregarious man, who, in the mid-1990s and early 2000s, had been Hungary's minister of education, told me over an iced coffee on the sidewalk of a spacious and popular Budapest café in the summer of 2019 that, while he only got to know Soros in the 1990s, he received funding from Soros for a project in 1985. Stuck without a passport in a rural town, Magyar found himself charged with organizing the second rural farmers association. I asked Magyar why he, the son of a theater director, was organizing the second rural farmers association. "I was a sociologist there," he answered without pause, as though sociologists who find themselves working in villages naturally assume farm association responsibilities.

The farm association was relevant, even if I still didn't fully understand why Magyar was involved: the Soros Foundation paid for the building out of which the association operated.[23] Soros was everywhere—or seemed to be.

In the beginning, Soros's influence wasn't resented; it was celebrated. In the 1980s, "Even the actual government looked at him as the benefactor of Hungary," Gábor Horn, who, in the late 1980s and early 1990s, received support from Soros as a representative of an independent labor union, told me through a translator in an email. "There wasn't any progressive cultural and scientific activity that wasn't connected to Soros and his foundation." He described the politics of the foundation as "multicolored."

The Party begrudgingly worked with him. And everyone else worked at least in part because of him. "There wasn't any [opposition] movement or group that didn't get support from him."[24]

ONE-PARTY SOCIALIST RULE CAME TO an end in Hungary in 1989. That year, inspired by events in Poland, Hungary saw "Round Table Talks"—discussions between the party and various opposition groups—lead to free elections. The Hungarian People's Republic became the Republic of Hungary.

After 1989, there was more than one philanthropic game in town. But, as Soros put it in 1995, "from 1984 to 1989, the foundation was really the center of intellectual life in Hungary."[25] And that included funding movements and groups that were in opposition to one-party control.

The Soros Foundation was not the only institution to support democratic opposition movements, as Timothy Garton Ash, a journalist in Central and Eastern Europe at the time and now a professor of European studies at Oxford, told me over the phone from the United Kingdom.

Garton Ash is now based at Oxford's St. Antony's College, where I got my master's degree; I remember him primarily for wearing scarves indoors and asking hard-hitting questions of visiting lecturers. He got to know Soros "fairly quickly" because he was traveling around Central and Eastern Europe in the 1980s writing for the *New York Review of Books*. He described Soros as a "very important supporter of democratic opposition movements" but "not a predominant one." There were others involved, like the Ford Foundation and the Rockefeller Foundation. It was not just Soros.[26]

But Soros was indeed there supporting these opposition groups, including that group of young activists Bozóki had mentioned: Fidesz.

Bibo István Special College for law students in Hungary was, according to the historian Paul Lendvai, an "island of autonomy and self-determination" in Eastern Bloc Hungary. It was so in part because of George Soros, "who from 1986 onwards promoted the college and generously subsidized its politically active students, as well as their journal *Szazadvég*, through language courses, bursaries, foreign trips, printing costs, and so on." The college was also where a young man named Viktor Orbán forged his politically active group of friends.[27]

In 1988, those young students founded Fidesz, a politically minded youth group. That same year, Orbán, who in 1988 was only in his twenties, attracted some fame for a staunchly anti-Soviet speech he delivered in Budapest. In 1989, Fidesz transitioned from a youth organization to a political party so that it could participate in the first free elections. Orbán had been working part-time for Open Society since 1988, and, in 1989, went to Oxford University's Pembroke College on a Soros fellowship. He returned to Budapest in 1990, determined to throw himself into politics.[28]

"We supported a number of self-governing student colleges (faculty dormitories where students instituted their own educational programs)," Soros proudly recalled in his early 1990s book, *Underwriting Democracy*. "They became the incubators of Fidesz (Association of Young Democrats), which later spearheaded the transition to democracy and is currently one of the two major opposition parties in Parliament. Several members of our first group of scholars at Oxford later became leaders of Fidesz."[29]

Almost everyone, back then, thought of Orbán and Fidesz as young defenders of democracy.

Magyar (the sociologist and onetime rural farm organizer) told me he had thought otherwise. Orbán had always been Orbán. Back when he first got into politics, he thought that what the people wanted to hear was the language of inclusive democracy. "This liberal, secular, rational language was the language of regime change," he told me between sips of his coffee and puffs of his cigar. Later, when Orbán learned that they'd rather hear something else—something conservative, and religious, and exclusive—he changed what he was saying.

But the "utility of language for power," Magyar told me—that is what Viktor Orbán, a young man fresh off of a Soros scholarship, learned all the way back in 1988.[30] Orbán has always been Orbán. He has always wanted power. It is the substance of his speeches that has changed, not him.

SOROS MAY HAVE LOOKED BACK most fondly on his work in Hungary in the 1980s, but it was far from the only country in which he was seriously involved during that time.

Soros tried to re-create the success he'd had in Hungary in China. As in Hungary, his foundation would be run by and for local actors, and would partner with a local organization—later on, Soros would set up his own foundations, but at the start, this was a way to ensure on-the-ground knowledge and at least some measure of local buy-in. In China's case, the partner was to be the Research Institute for the Reform of the Economic Structure. RIRES was directed by Chen Yizi, who was economic advisor to Zhao Ziyang. Zhao ranked behind Deng Xiaoping, leader of the People's Republic of China at the time, and was a powerful force. Notably, he had an angle: Zhao was in favor of economic liberalization within Chinese Party politics. With his blessing, in 1986, Soros had an agreement with RIRES for his Chinese foundation.[31]

At first, it looked like Soros's success in Budapest might be matched in Beijing. By 1988, there were over 2,000 annual applications for scholarships and other similar grants; 209 were approved, including some projects that were critical of the government.[32]

But many of them were awarded to individuals associated with RIRES, much to Soros's consternation. Soros's fund was a victim of political factions. The fund existed because of Zhao's support, and was seen as an extension of the proreform group. Soros wanted to offer an open society to everyone; in reality, the foundation gave grants to people associated with the proreform political faction and institution.[33]

As a part of Chinese political infighting, the fund attracted Chinese political concern, and, in 1987, Chinese hard-liners passed around a dossier accusing Soros of being a CIA agent and of attempting to use the foundation to undermine Communism (nothing came of this particular dossier, but it wouldn't be the last time Soros would be accused of being in league with U.S. intelligence agencies; in 2019, Donald Trump's lawyer, Rudy Giuliani, accused Soros of having hired a former FBI agent to bring down the U.S. president). At one point, a high Party council ruled the fund should be closed. It remained open only because Zhao personally intervened.[34]

Eventually, it was Soros himself who brought down the curtain on the Chinese operation. In 1989, he learned from Dai Qing, a Chinese journalist who was a Soros fund recipient, that state security operatives were involved in the fund. Soros decided to end the Chinese fund, which closed that year.[35] There wasn't enough support or space for an independent institution in China, so Soros didn't want to be involved at all. And unlike in South Africa, he did not go back.

"It became clear to me in retrospect that I had made a mistake in setting up a foundation in China," Soros wrote in *Underwriting Democracy*. "China was not ready for it because there were no independent or dissident intelligentsia. The people on whom I based the foundation were members of a party faction. They could not be totally open and honest with me because they were beholden to their faction."[36]

Today, there are five foundation offices in the Asia-Pacific: in Afghanistan, Indonesia, Mongolia, Myanmar, and Pakistan. But there still isn't one in China. Soros, however, has recently turned his attention back to the country, giving speeches about how Chinese leader Xi Jinping is the most powerful threat to open societies. The Chinese government is presumably still not comprised of supporters of Soros's work.

BACK IN CENTRAL AND EASTERN Europe, Soros was also having some difficulty.

On the face of it, Poland was an ideal place for a foundation. As a part of the Communist-controlled Eastern Bloc, it was a relatively closed society: the party was not to be questioned, and free thought was by and large still a dangerous thing. However, Poland had Lech Walesa and the Solidarity movement, which was arguably the most robust dissident movement anywhere behind the Iron Curtain: in Solidarity, the workers and the intellectuals joined together to create a political force.

Soros founded the Stefan Batory Foundation—Poland's Open Society, named for the sixteenth-century Hungarian who became a Polish monarch—in 1988. For day-to-day operations, he relied on Okno, the cultural wing of the Solidarity movement.

But the leadership of Okno did not know how to run an organization.

"They couldn't even manage to get a telephone line installed," Soros told an interviewer in the 1990s.[37]

Soros then tried letting Zbigniew Bujak, one of the heroes of the Solidarity movement, run the foundation. "But that didn't work too well either," he later admitted, though, in that interview, Soros did not specify why.[38]

While the foundation was floundering, Poland was transforming. In 1989, the Polish government and the opposition movement held talks that led to the peaceful transition out of Communism. For this, Soros can possibly take some credit; he worked to convince Poland's last Polish United Workers' Party leader, General Wojciech Jaruzelski, to enter negotiations with representatives of Solidarity, and the general did agree to the roundtable talks. (Soros also consulted with Polish economists who drew up the post-Communist finance minister Leszek Balcerowicz's economic transformation plan, which did eventually achieve growth and make Poland's a market economy, though not without pain, particularly for Poland's poorest people.)[39]

But the Stefan Batory Foundation was less impactful. Until, finally, Soros found Aleksander Smolar. Or, rather, Smolar found him.

"Let's say I was acquainted with activities—Soros activities—before coming back to Poland," Smolar told me over the phone from France in the spring of 2019.

At the time, Smolar had been in France for twenty years and was working in Paris. He first heard of Soros when the rector of the institution he was at asked him for help distributing fellowships from "a rich man," who was American but of Hungarian descent, for Central and Eastern European students.

Although that was the first time Smolar had heard of Soros, he went on to meet him several times at various conferences before he returned to Poland in 1989 to advise the first post–one-party-rule prime minister, Tadeusz Mazowiecki.

A year later, when Smolar's government position was wrapping up, he was looking for something that would allow him to keep one foot in academia and in France and another in Poland (to this day, he shuttles back and forth between the two).

Then friends told him about the Stefan Batory Foundation. "I was advised to, let's say, to postulate the chairman of the foundation."

Soros was living in London at the time, having moved his family over in the 1980s to be closer to his philanthropic work (they moved back to New York in the early 1990s).

"I asked him for a rendezvous, to have an occasion to meet him. I visited him in London and we started to talk, we were walking around—he has a house in London, and a sort of small garden . . . this is a big square, actually, big with a lot of trees, his private garden, let's say—I told him, 'George, I would like to take care of your money in Poland.'"

"He was a little bit surprised," he added, half laughing. "He asked about my situation. He understood very well why I wanted to do this job, and he asked what I would have out of it, what would be [the] advantage—I presented him sort of a program of what I think the foundation can and should do to play a much bigger social, cultural, educational role in Poland."[40]

Smolar was elected to the board (Soros's support was "decisive" in determining his election), and took over the operation of the Stefan Batory Foundation, which he still runs to this day. He turned it into, in Soros's estimation, "one of the best foundations in the network."

Smolar is emblematic of one of Soros's skills, Garton Ash told me. Everywhere in the region that one went, particularly after 1989, Soros would find "the very major local figures," these forces of intellectual life, and "in all these societies," Garton Ash said, "there are significant figures grouped around the work of the OSF."[41]

Garton Ash presented this as a positive attribute of Soros's work, but it has also been characterized negatively. Soros can be criticized for promoting people of a certain class and worldview within a society, perhaps planting them on a pedestal apart from those they were trying to help. The figures to whom Soros gravitated and with whom he entrusted his foundations tended to be intellectuals living in the major cities, which means, too, that they tended to come from a certain level of privilege. How could a society be opened, and how could opportunity to participate in it be made more equitable, if the people who were charged with opening it all came from a similar social stratum?

To this, Garton Ash replied that this "is a generic problem related to all NGOs," and that "actually I think George personally and the foundations more broadly were very good at identifying the local actors . . . People who would have played a significant role in their societies anyway."[42]

If Soros thought highly of Smolar, so, too, did Smolar hold Soros in high esteem. "It was quite fascinating how much he was involved in the first years of the foundation in Central Europe, how much he was involved in the activities," he told me. "He knew almost everything."

"We were very influential and quite popular," Smolar told me. "Prestigious." Nobody was trying to smear them or accuse them of being something other than what they said they were, he said. Except for, "of course," those who were ideologically motivated, he added—attacks by people who, for whatever reason, were fundamentally opposed to the idea of having theirs be an open society.[43]

SOROS'S MOST AMBITIOUS UNDERTAKING IN the 1980s was arguably in Soviet Russia.

In 1987, Soros went to set up a foundation in Soviet Russia. Originally, he approached Andrei Sakharov, a physicist and one of the most renowned dissidents in Soviet Russia. Sakharov had been made to live in internal exile in the Urals, but in 1986 was told by Mikhail Gorbachev, the last leader of the Soviet Union, who was trying to reform and hold together his country, that he could return to Moscow. Soros took this as a sign that a major shift was coming, and that the society would be open enough for an Open Society Foundation.[44]

Soros clearly had high hopes for Gorbachev, even presenting him with what he called the Shatalin plan, an economic reform package designed by Soviet economists under Soros's direction. Gorbachev ultimately rejected the plan, which would have involved some decentralization of power, a thing that the central government was reluctant to let happen.[45]

Sakharov was not as optimistic about his country. The foundation, he warned, would inevitably end up enriching the state security services. Nevertheless, Soros, undaunted, assembled a board: the sociologist Tatyana Zaslavskaya; the historian Yuri Afanasiev; and the writer Valentin Rasputin, who, not a decade later, became a nationalist.[46]

The foundation was called the Cultural Initiative Foundation, and management of it very quickly fell into the hands of officials from the Communist Youth League. As Sakharov had warned him, the foundation would ultimately get pulled into the thrall of the state. Soros tried to get them to shake their "Soviet mentality," with its allegiance to the Soviet Union and to the Party and to profound distrust of expressing independent thought in public. When he saw they would not, he pulled off what he described as a putsch, which preceded the actual putsch of August 1991 in which Communist hard-liners tried to overthrow Gorbachev. The hard-liners were opposed by Boris Yeltsin, who, after the Soviet Union disintegrated in the weeks and months following the attempted coup, became the first president of the Russian Federation after Gorbachev resigned in December of that year. Soros later said that his lawyer in Moscow organized the foundation's minicoup—but turned the organization into his personal playground, which resulted in a second putsch to get rid of him.[47]

The Cultural Initiative finally hit its stride with the Transformation Project, which was meant to replace Marxist-Leninist teachings in schools by, for example, commissioning textbooks and training school principals, all with full cooperation of the Russian authorities. Soros said that it was so successful in such a short period of time that he decided to throw more money at it—and that doing so turned out to be a mistake. In the 1990s, Russia turned into a financial wild west, and robber capitalists ran roughshod over the country. In the first half of 1994, shares of Russian enterprises were given away in a mass-privatization voucher program. People who did not yet fully understand capitalism sold their vouchers for much less than they were worth, making some who sensed which way the wind was blowing very rich. "Everybody with money was making money hand-over-fist," Soros, who had been opposed to the voucher scheme, lamented in 1995.

This had something of a trickle-down effect on the broader population, and on some of the foundation's administrators. Soros and his people discovered that $12 million of the foundation's money had been deposited "in a less-than-first-class bank." The money was recovered, but there had to be an audit, and personnel obviously had to be let go. The foundation, Soros said, was five years behind where it should have been.[48]

In addition to the roller coaster that was the Cultural Initiative, Soros set up the arguably more successful International Science Foundation in partnership with the International Soros Science Education Program. The International Science Foundation was meant to save the best of natural science teaching from the former Soviet Union by giving grants to scientists and making the internet universally available. Soros gave the International Science Foundation $100 million in 1992. It was all spent in less than two years. The Science Education Program had a separate annual budget of over $20 million.

"I wanted to prove that Western aid can be effective," he said in 1995, "and natural science was the best field in which to prove it . . . Soviet science represented an outstanding achievement of the human intellect, a somewhat different strain from Western science, that deserved to be preserved."

There was another reason, too.

"Scientists had been, and remain, in the forefront of the struggle for an open society."[49]

"THE TRANSFORMATION OF A CLOSED society into an open one is a systematic transformation . . . What the foundations have done is to change the way the transformation is brought about," Soros later wrote. "In each country, we found a group of people who shared belief in open society and entrusted them with establishing priorities." Those priorities, he stressed, were not imposed from the outside.[50]

There was one priority, or at least idea, that Soros did hope to impress upon people, however, one notion that held from Budapest to Warsaw to Moscow, and one he wanted to enshrine in an institution that he thought would outlast any of the foundations.

"He understood perhaps better than many people that there was a danger that Communism would be followed by nationalism," the British sociologist Paul Stubbs, who has researched Soros and his role throughout Eastern Europe, told me over the phone in 2017. Perhaps this was because of his experience in interwar Hungary; perhaps it was because he had read Popper. Perhaps he was just the person willing to act on the suspicion that nationalism was right around the corner; whether many other people did in fact understand this, the reality was that the competition to help former Eastern Bloc countries was perhaps not as stiff as some might have thought.[51]

"I thought that I would blaze the trail, I would lead and others would follow. But now that I look back, I find that there was practically nobody behind me. I ask myself what went wrong," Soros admitted in 1995.[52]

It would not be the only time Soros noted publicly that there was no great rush to help him help Eastern Europe. "The East was in the midst of a systemic collapse; in the West it was business as usual. When I proposed a new Marshall Plan for the Soviet empire at an East-West conference in the spring of 1989 in Potsdam, which was then still in East Germany, I was literally laughed at," Soros recalled.[53]

There was no appetite in the West for such a thing. The cavalry wasn't coming; there wouldn't be a second Marshall Plan.

Still, even without as much support from the West as Soros had envisioned, change did come. It was an exciting, but also precarious, time. The revolutions of 1989 were about, among other things, the right to hold and express different ideas in a free and open society. "I recognized the need for an institution that would preserve and develop the spirit of that revolution," Soros recalled in 1995. That institution was Central European University, which was originally meant to have three campuses in Central and Eastern Europe.

The impetus for the university was twofold. The first was an international university summit in Dubrovnik, Croatia, attended by Soros in the summer of 1989. People throughout the region came to discuss and debate ideas. What was then Yugoslavia had been, throughout the post–World War II era, the most liberal part of the former Eastern Bloc, and so it is perhaps unsurprising that it was not Central Europe but Yugoslavia that served as the germ of the idea for the university.

The second was that one system was collapsing, and Soros saw that people needed new skills. They needed to know business law, and economics, and political science—subjects that were viewed with suspicion by the socialist workers' parties across the region or were seen as incompatible with their version of socialism and so hadn't been taught.

At first, Soros wanted to establish a high-level vocational school. He approached a man by the name of István Rév, who was working in the economic history department at Budapest's Karl Marx University of Economics.

When I met Rév in June 2019, he spoke solemnly and purposefully, sitting back in his chair in his office in Budapest. He had a pouf of curly hair atop his head and wore glasses with chic red frames, which rested on the table between us, but which he occasionally picked up to make a point. Rév, in our interview, told me Soros "saw [nationalism] could become a serious danger." Rév began speaking to me of the University of Bologna, where the elite studied in early medieval times. When war broke out, there was nevertheless an elite that had studied together and had a language with which to talk to each other.

Rév, however, was reluctant. He thought that there was a need not for a vocational school, but for a robust university. He turned Soros down.

Half a year later, Soros asked him again. This time, Rév agreed, but only for six months and only for free. He took a sabbatical from his actual job. It was only when Soros agreed that there could be a medieval studies department—shorthand for an acknowledgment that Rév was right, and that it should be a true university—that Rév quit his job and became the director of CEU's Budapest college. He is now the director of the Vera and Donald Blinken Open Society Archives, housed in a Budapest CEU building.[54]

Just as the early foundations found their key staff members in intellectual circles, with people who happened to know people finding themselves before Soros, so, too, was CEU, at first, staffed somewhat spontaneously.

Bozóki, whose fellowship at UCLA was Soros-sponsored, for example, gave a talk in Poland about why the rule of law had to take precedence over a sense of justice during decommunization, asserting that some might be left feeling that others had gotten away with something, but the important thing was that all were treated equally before the law, whatever role they had played in the decades prior.

As it happened, János Kis, the leader of the Alliance of Free Democrats, the liberal opposition group, had been at the talk and was on Bozóki's flight back to Budapest. Kis told Bozóki about a new university and invited him to join the political science department. Bozóki at first turned down the job, believing he was "quite alright" in the state university. He called back a week later to change his answer.

There was no job interview, Bozóki told me, his house slippers dangling from his feet. It wasn't a competitive job process. "I was lucky," he told me. "But I also deserved it."[55]

FROM ALMOST THE VERY BEGINNING, Soros and those running CEU found themselves in conflict with the authorities of the countries in which campuses were set up—the Czech Republic and Hungary. (There was a third campus in Poland, but it offered only sociology and closed down in 2003.)[56]

In 1991, the president of Czechoslovakia who agreed to the foundation of CEU in Prague was the dissident and intellectual Václav Havel. But the leader of the Czech portion of Czechoslovakia, Václav Klaus, was in many ways Havel's opposite—and did not want Soros or CEU there. Klaus "has a personal animosity toward me . . . He believes in the pursuit of self-interest and, accordingly, finds my concept of open society—which requires people to make sacrifices for the common good—objectionable," Soros said in 1995.[57]

Rév had another idea as to why Klaus objected to CEU.

The university's Prague branch, he told me at our meeting, was always going to be fighting an uphill battle. After Prague Spring—the calls for openness and reform in 1968 that were followed by a Soviet invasion and societal crackdown—very few intellectuals were in university jobs, Rév explained. The people who had scholarly jobs lost them. They worked in the zoo, he said, or they went west. They didn't stay around to be able to staff the Prague campus of a university that hadn't been invented yet. Some were still in the country, and one—Ernest Gellner, the British and Czech philosopher—agreed to come back to Prague to lead CEU's Prague college.

Klaus had other ideas. In 1992, Klaus and Vladimír Mečiar, his Slovak counterpart, decided that Czechoslovakia should peacefully split between the Czech Republic and Slovakia. Mečiar had wanted more federalization; Klaus, more centralization. Rather than compromise, the two divided the country.

Klaus, who then became prime minister not of Czechoslovakia, but of the Czech Republic (and who went on to become the Czech president in 2003), has since become "a Euroskeptic jerk," Rév told me. "He was a jerk at that time," but one who believed in the idea of Europe and of the Czech Republic's place in it. After the secession of Slovakia, Klaus believed he could clearly argue that the Czech Republic was a western nation. The very name of the university, then, emphasizing its place in Central Europe, "reminded them of the existence of this region," Rév said. Klaus immediately kicked the university out.[58] In a way, he was kicking the path that Soros was trying to offer away from nationalism and toward liberalism out with it.

There was still the Budapest campus, although that ran into

issues, too. The conservative Hungarian Democratic Forum won the elections of 1990; the previous socialist government had been eager to work with Soros to gain some liberal legitimacy, but they were out, and the Free Democrats, which was the party most people mentally associated with Soros and Open Society, was in the opposition.

The Democratic Forum had a "rabid antisemitic wing," in Soros's telling, and so the CEU in Budapest, as well as the foundation, shortly after being established, found themselves on the receiving end of public pressure.[59] István Csurka, the party's deputy chairman, said that his criticism of Jews was just meant to keep Communists from coming to power again. He claimed that "'as a result of history' people with Jewish background are more likely to be in higher positions but can never 'really be Hungarian.'" Csurka said Soros was trying to overthrow the Democratic Forum. Csurka, in hindsight, was ahead of his time; a politician who knew how to rail against someone who was not running for office in an attempt to score political points, and to use a people's latent antisemitism for his own professional gain.[60]

This "conservative, provincial" government, as Rév described it, resented CEU. It was so obvious that Yoko Ono, who had a Hungarian partner at the time, wrote to Soros asking if there was anything she could do.[61]

There was a sense in which the conservative government, in criticizing CEU, could claim that it was articulating the will of the people. Nationalism had been actively repressed after the failed Hungarian revolution of 1956, and so nationalist sentiment was on the rise in this newly liberated Hungary. During this time, one anonymous scholar told me, there was some resentment at being told that they, the Hungarian people, still couldn't express pride in their Hungarian nation.[62]

However, the government, in making the attacks antisemitic,

tied together Hungarian nationalism and antisemitism, arguably proving Soros's point: that education and cultural offerings needed to be made to the people such that they would, intellectually and ideologically, have more than nationalism to sustain them.

SOROS LATER SAID THAT BEING attacked by the government was good, in a way; the previous government had wanted to cooperate with the university for a sense of prestige and legitimacy. The cooperation made things easier for the university, but the attacks renewed their sense of purpose.

Prague and Budapest were the only CEU campuses, but CEU was not only attacked in the Czech Republic and Hungary. Originally, Rév said, there was supposed to also be a campus in the Slovak capital of Bratislava. But the fact that Soros is Hungarian made the issue a nonstarter; Hungarians make up the largest minority in Slovakia, and there was, and is, some prejudice against them.

That was the problem in Bratislava. In Prague, the problem was that it was Central European. In Budapest, the problem was that he is Jewish.

"There is no place for us here in this part of the world," Rév said. But that was why it was so important that the university be there. The issue of the university in Budapest was, from the very beginning, "existential." Students at the university were not in an ivory tower, he argued; they were well aware of what was happening outside of the classroom walls, of what was at stake beyond them. "You could not remain neutral to the outside world," he told me solemnly.[63]

The university was meant to exist with such a spirit; it was part of the reason Soros hoped that the university would be the institution to remain and continue on after the foundations, and he, were gone.[64]

The Influence of Soros

BY THE 1990S, THERE WERE enough foundations established that Soros's work evolved into a network.[65] The staff in
New York was growing, too (and were sometimes derided by Soros and Weber, who found them frustratingly bureaucratic compared to those they dealt with in the Eastern Bloc and deemed
them "philanthropoids"),[66] and Soros ended up opening an office
space on Seventh Avenue. The space was chosen over an office in
then–real estate mogul Donald Trump's newest building. "How
could I expect people from my foundations to feel comfortable
when they visited me in a building like that," Soros reportedly said
of Trump's tower.[67]

In less than a decade, Soros's project had become bigger—and
certainly more expensive—than he'd anticipated at the outset.

"To achieve a systematic transformation requires a helping
hand from the outside. Everything needed to be done at once. So
when I received a proposal that seemed to be backed by an ability
to deliver, I usually approved it," Soros wrote years later. "That is
how expenditures of my Open Society Foundations jumped from
$3 million to more than $300 million in the space of a few years.
It could not have been done according to a plan."[68]

But contributing to systematic transformation in such a way
was not sustainable. Two things changed in the early 1990s that
would in turn change the nature of Soros's philanthropy.

In 1993, Soros brought Aryeh Neier over from Human Rights
Watch to run Open Society. Neier founded Human Rights
Watch—or, as it was originally known, Helsinki Watch—in 1978,
and Soros's attendance at its Wednesday meetings in the offices of
Random House, which were the closest thing the group had to a
board meeting in the beginning, was, in some ways, his introduction to the human rights movement.[69]

That Neier was brought in was a reflection of the reality that
the organization was no longer brand-new and nebulous, and was

in fact large and impactful enough that it needed to exist as just that—an organization. It was Neier's job to make sure that it was run like one.

That was the first thing. The second thing that happened that would irreversibly change how Soros and his philanthropy operated was this: Soros became infinitely higher-profile and more prominent in the early 1990s. "Soros became Soros in the nineties," Garton Ash told me. It was a sentiment similar to what the journalist Michael Lewis wrote in his profile of Soros for the *New Republic*: before 1992, "Soros was not much better known in the region than any Wall Street drone." Back in the 1980s, he was a man deeply committed to a cause and very good at making money, but he wasn't a one-name celebrity yet.[70] By 1994, when Lewis traveled with Soros through Eastern Europe, Soros was dining with multiple presidents in one day and told his interlocutor, "Just write that the former Soviet Empire is now called the Soros Empire."[71]

What changed? Soros's philanthropy had existed for a few years and received more attention following the fall of the Berlin Wall. But in larger part, Soros himself happened, not in Eastern Europe, but in England. That was where he broke the bank.

CHAPTER 3

Breaking the Banks

In 2009, believing that his personal success at averting catastrophe during the 2008 financial crisis meant that his philosophy should be taken seriously by the public, Soros delivered a series of lectures at his Central European University in Budapest. During these lectures, he said, "There is a deep-seated conflict between capitalism and open society, market values and social values. The distinguishing feature of the market mechanism is that it is *amoral*: one person's dollar is exactly the same as another person's, irrespective of how she came to possess it."

Soros said that the political process would be improved in an open society if people separated their role as market participants from their role as political participants. When they are acting as the former, people should act according to self-interest; when they are acting as the latter, they should consider first and foremost the public interest. "I have practiced what I preach," he said. "As a hedge fund manager I have played by the rules and tried to maximize my profits. As a citizen I try to improve the rules, even if the reforms go against my personal interests. For example, I support the regulation of hedge funds along with other financial institutions. I firmly believe that if more people followed this precept, our political system would function much better." This is partly what makes the attacks on Soros that call him a socialist so ludicrous; not only did he leave a socialist country by choice, but he then went into speculating. He was a professional capitalist.[1]

He tried, though, to be both a professional capitalist and a professional citizen. But the two cannot always coexist so peacefully. What happens when one's role as a market participant is large enough to force changes in or destabilize societies? What happens when one can, say, speculate on a currency so forcefully and successfully that one can be accused of breaking a national bank, or triggering a continent-wide financial crisis? What happens when maximizing profits makes countries rewrite rules in a way that they would not otherwise have rewritten them? What happens when one's fund is so great that it cannot pursue financial gain without someone, or some country, losing?

This tension—between Soros's financial abilities and his philanthropic ambitions—is at the core of his work. On multiple occasions in the 1990s, that tension was on particular display.

STANLEY DRUCKENMILLER—THE FINANCIER WITH WHOM Soros regularly discussed financial matters in the run-up to the stock market crash of 1987—finally came to join him at Soros Fund Management, the Quantum Fund's advisory firm, in 1988. Soros decided that, since he was increasingly consumed with his philanthropic work, he would step back a bit and hand day-to-day operations over to Druckenmiller.

"He had told me that he was ready to retire from active money management. He said that he didn't want to do this anymore, he was not even sure he could do this anymore, he really wanted to focus on his philanthropy," Druckenmiller told me in a September 2019 phone call.

"I had about four or five advisors, all of whom told me not to go there. I figured worst case I could continue running Duquesne [Druckenmiller's own capital management firm] if it didn't work out, and probably learn something valuable before that happened," he recalled in his surprisingly soothing voice. "Obviously, things worked out very well for both of us."[2]

Two years later, in October 1990, the United Kingdom joined something called the European Exchange Rate Mechanism. The ERM originated over a decade earlier, in 1979. It was launched as part of the European Monetary System, which was meant to move Europe toward greater integration and was set up with the support of French President Valéry Giscard d'Estaing and German Chancellor Helmut Schmidt, and had eight original member states (Belgium, Denmark, France, Germany, Ireland, Italy, Luxembourg, and the Netherlands).[3] The ERM linked the value of currencies across the European community. The idea was to avoid large, damaging fluctuations in currency value and consequently trade balances among the participant nations. Immediately, the United Kingdom saw an impact from the Conservative government's decision to join: interest rates came down for the first time in a year from 15 to 14 percent, and share prices on the London Stock Exchange and the value of the British pound, also known as sterling, rose. These were seen as positive developments.[4]

The pound came into the ERM at a value of 2.95 Deutschmarks and could appreciate or depreciate in a narrow band of 6 percent—but no more. The British chancellor of the exchequer at the time, John Major, said that it had become clear that the government's policies were successfully decreasing inflationary pressures.

Only two years after this perceived financial improvement in Britain, the reality of financial chaos in Europe came to a head.

JOHN MAJOR, WHO HAD BECOME prime minister shortly after Britain joined the ERM, said that the pound would function as the European reserve currency. "That's like putting a red flag in front of a bull," Rob Johnson, who joined Soros and Druckenmiller in the fall of 1992, told me. The Germans were very proud of their Deutschmark.

In October 1990, the same month that the United Kingdom joined the ERM, East and West Germany reunified. German reunification created what Sebastian Mallaby, in *More Money Than God*, deemed "inflationary pressure within Germany," which meant that Germany's central bank, known as the Bundesbank, raised interest rates to support this investment environment. However, at the same time, other European countries were entering recessions, meaning they would have been served by going into their monetary toolkit to apply lower interest rates. High interest rates in Germany and low interest rates elsewhere meant that currencies like the Italian lira and the pound were at the bottom of the exchange range allowed by the ERM.[5]

"Germany had a history of absolute obsessive fear of inflation because of what they'd went through in the Weimar Republic," Druckenmiller told me. And so even though many suspected that reunification would be good for growth but bad for the Deutschmark, "I thought the Bundesbank would do whatever they could to make sure inflation wouldn't pick up."[6]

At Soros Fund Management, a portfolio manager by the name of Scott Bessent noted to Druckenmiller that interest rates on British mortgages weren't normally fixed, which meant that, when the Bank of England raised rates, mortgage payers felt the pain.

If the Bank of England raised rates to defend the sterling against the other currencies within the ERM, mortgage payers, who were already living in a recession, would feel it even more.

Druckenmiller started investing in Deutschmarks and against sterling, buying up the former and selling the latter. By August, he had invested $1.5 billion in that position.[7]

Meanwhile, as Mallaby recounts in his book, British Chancellor of the Exchequer Norman Lamont (John Major's successor) was begging Helmut Schlesinger, head of the German Central Bank, to lower German interest rates. Schlesinger said he saw no reason to cut or raise rates. Lamont took Schlesinger's pseudo-promise not to raise rates to the British media as a concession won, even though Germany hadn't really been expected to raise them; presumably he wanted to look as though he'd gotten something out of Schlesinger.

Schlesinger, who had not intended to concede a thing, pushed back at a surely lively congregation of central bankers in Basel. He said publicly that he would not guarantee anything about the future of interest rates.

Soros happened to be in the audience to hear this. He approached Schlesinger after the speech was done and asked him what he thought of the ECU—the European Currency Unit, a predecessor to the euro. Schlesinger said that he liked it but wished it had been called the mark. Soros understood maybe more than Schlesinger had said: the Germans were going to first protect the value and stability of their precious Deutschmark.

Back in New York, Soros, Druckenmiller, and Rob Johnson, who was moving over to Soros Fund Management from Bankers Trust, convened.[8]

Soros and Johnson had met in the late 1980s, when Johnson was the chief economist of the Senate Banking Committee. While the committee was going over and holding hearings on what went wrong in the stock market crash of 1987, Soros would often telephone and give Johnson his input on what had happened—he didn't want to testify, but he did want to give his input and offer insight, which Johnson found useful. Later, when Soros was working on his (ultimately rejected) Shatalin plan for the Soviet Union, he would call on Johnson to discuss the ideas in that, too—specifically, the relationship between central banks and other institutions and forms of governance.

In 1988, Johnson's boss in the Senate, William Proxmire, announced he was retiring. Johnson left the Senate to go to work for Bankers Trust Company. At this point Johnson wasn't working with Soros and Druckenmiller, but the trio of traders did often discuss matters of mutual interest.

At Bankers Trust, Johnson was increasingly focused as a portfolio manager working on European issues. This, he told me in an enthusiastic phone interview in September 2019, was before email. You had to go to these places, he explained, "you kind of had to see the whites of their eyes." Johnson was traveling throughout Europe, studying Greece, Portugal, Germany, and France, evaluating conditions both within and outside the ERM. He was also managing several billion dollars for Bankers Trust. And all the while, he was talking to Soros (who had a penchant for finding knowledgeable people and soaking up information from them) and Druckenmiller.

When, in 1992, Soros finally invited Johnson to come work with him, Johnson originally hesitated. Soros and Druckenmiller worked together, he told me, like Miles Davis and John Coltrane. What could he, Johnson, bring to the partnership?

To this, Soros told him, "If you want to stay in the womb and never be born, that's your problem."

Johnson decided to be born and joined Soros and Druckenmiller in what would become one of the most consequential financial decisions in history.

"George looks at me and said, what kind of leverage would you use" in betting against sterling, Johnson told me in his booming voice. "I said something in the neighborhood of three-to-one to five-to-one."[9]

In late summer 1992, the British government had only 22 billion pounds in reserves. Soros and Druckenmiller decided to supercharge Druckenmiller's $1.5 billion short position to $15 billion: ten times the bet Druckenmiller already had made against sterling. They were going to short the pound.[10]

When investors take a long position on an investment or asset class, they are holding on to that investment with the idea that it will increase in value. To take a short position, on the other hand, means to sell something—like a stock, or, in this case, a currency—that one does not actually own with the intention of buying it at a later date for a lower price. If the cost of what's being sold goes down, the seller makes a lot of money; if it goes the wrong way, it can be financially ruinous. The act of actually selling assets tends to put downward pressure on the market value of that asset—selling short, in other words, can be a self-fulfilling prophecy. However, the risk remains that other players in the market can take a contrary position on trades, resulting in disaster. If there turns out to be sufficient long interest in a particular asset, there can potentially be no real limit to how wrong a short trade can go. (To take a more recent example, in 2012, Bill Ackman took a tremendous short position on Herbalife and publicly trashed the stock. He expected to make a massive profit but was thwarted when Carl Icahn took an enormous long position on the stock. Icahn revealed that he made $1 billion off Herbalife; it took Ackman, on the other hand, a full six years to get out of his bearish bet.)[11]

But the beauty, insofar as there can be beauty in the world of finance and global capitalism, was that, due to the U.K.'s participation in the ERM, there was a limit to how wrong this could go for Soros and company. There was only so much they could possibly lose. Inasmuch as the pound resided within the convenient (for Soros et al.) safety net of the ERM, the pound was within a band. If they were wrong, and the value of sterling were to appreciate, it could only rise so high. But if it crashed out of the ERM, there was no limit to how far it could fall. It was a one-sided bet. There was always a chance, of course, that sufficient support from other countries within the ERM would arrive and the value of sterling would appreciate, but based on everything Soros, Druckenmiller, and Johnson had heard, that wasn't likely to happen.

Even so, Johnson is, to this day, impressed with Soros's conviction.

"That was maybe four times our capital," Johnson said, "and George was gonna go for it."

The British government's reserves to defend the pound were going to get wiped out, and Quantum could only sell sterling if someone could buy it. "We had to be kind of gentle and sneaky for a while," Johnson told me, "until we got big enough and exhausted their reserves and [they] were stressed out and raising rates."

The men proceeded with a caution bordering on paranoia. "I didn't talk to Stanley from my home," Johnson told me. "I went out to my car." His wife at the time worked for the New York Fed and had no idea what he was doing.

He'd only just arrived at Soros Fund Management. "These people were so courageous, and so knowledgeable," he told me, enthusiastically recalling this time in his professional life, surrounded by people who were so talented at what they did. "They would have done this if I was never alive. I think I added to our confidence and maybe our vigor, aggression, and size of leverage," he said, "but they were already there."[12]

THE FINNISH MARKKA HAD BEEN pegged to the ECU. But after Schlesinger's pronouncement about interest rates, the markka fell by nearly 15 points. This was profitable for traders, but the impact within the ERM was limited, because Finland wasn't part of the ERM. However, the Italian lira was.

The lira, like the pound, had already been at the bottom of the ERM band. On September 11, 1992, a formal devaluation had to be negotiated. Italy had indeed gotten begrudging support from the German central bank, which bought 24 billion Deutschmarks' worth of lira. But the Germans weren't happy about this and didn't want to have to do it again. They had done it for the stability of the ERM, but that stability would not matter as much to the annoyed Germans in the future.

The Bank of England, looking to fend off a similar attack, announced it was borrowing the equivalent of 7.25 billion pounds. The pound rose, as nobody knew that Soros and Druckenmiller were plotting to sell that and more.[13]

Then, on September 14, Schlesinger—the German central bank leader who liked the name "mark" better than "ECU"—gave an interview in which he said that it would be better to have a broad realignment of European currencies than a narrow adjustment of the lira. Effectively, this meant he was calling for sterling to devalue. Schlesinger clearly wasn't going to cut interest rates further; if not doing so meant that Britain was bounced from the ERM, that was clearly fine with the Bundesbank.

In Mallaby's meticulous retelling of the breaking of the bank, Schlesinger protested that he had thought that he would have been able to clear the quotes before the interview was published. But that mattered little to Soros, Druckenmiller, and Johnson.[14]

Druckenmiller told Soros that the time had come to move.

"I told him I was going to short another 5 billion pounds in the fund, taking the position to 100 percent of the fund," Druckenmiller told me.

"I told him my thesis. He looked puzzled, which really surprised me. But then he proceeded to tell me that my analysis didn't make any sense. He agreed with the theory, but that my actual execution didn't make any sense. Since it was a one-way bet . . . we should put two times the fund in it. Not one hundred percent of the fund."

In other words, the time had come to sell the full $15 billion. Soros told Druckenmiller: "Go for the jugular."

"Most of our conversations over the years were him pushing me to increase size on a position I liked," Druckenmiller said. "He was particularly adamant in this case. I thought about it. It made total sense."[15]

Johnson told me what Druckenmiller later told him: "The difference between George and everyone else is he knows when to go big."[16]

And Druckenmiller did. They borrowed sterling to sell it and then buy it back at a cheaper price, over and over, again and again, every few minutes. Before 8:30 A.M., the Bank of England had made two purchases of 300 million pounds. But Soros and Druckenmiller were selling in the billions, not millions, and they weren't stopping.[17]

"By mid-morning," *The Guardian* recalled two decades later, "the selling was so intense that Bank of England officials were buying £2bn of sterling an hour."[18]

IT WASN'T ENOUGH.

By the time John Major finally authorized a rate hike, it was too late. The pound didn't respond; its value had already been driven down too far to rise back up. And there was no time to negotiate a realignment within the ERM. Major tried another rate hike—and Soros and Druckenmiller went in for one final kill.

With the value of sterling lying on the proverbial floor and no support from other countries within the band, there was no way to keep the sterling within the ERM. On the evening of September 16, 1992, Lamont announced that Britain was leaving the mechanism. Black Wednesday had come to a close.[19]

AT FIRST, SOROS'S ROLE IN the short wasn't entirely clear.

It was only the next month, in October, that Soros's involvement came to light: that was when Gianni Agnelli, captain of Italian industry, shared that his investment in Quantum had earned him more money that year than his ownership of Fiat, his car company. (It was at this point, Johnson told me, that his then-wife asked if he had anything he wanted to share with her.) The very next day, the *Daily Mail* ran a photo of Soros with the headline, "I Made a Billion Crashing the Pound."[20] Soros himself didn't exactly downplay his role: in an interview with London *Times* journalist Anatole Kaletsky, who would go on to join the global board of Open Society, Soros said that Quantum and its offshoots had bet about ten billion dollars against sterling, and that that speculation had gotten roughly two billion dollars in profits.[21]

To some extent, Soros's role is still debated today by economists, journalists, and even those involved.

"Invisible investors like Soros, owing no allegiance as citizens, could place bets big enough to change economic outcomes for entire nations," Martin Vander Weyer, business editor of *The Spectator*, wrote for *The Telegraph* in 2012. "That was how the future was going to be, and 20 years on it should still frighten us all."[22]

In an interview, I asked Mallaby, who had so carefully chronicled the events of the summer and fall of 1992, what he thought. Was Soros responsible? Did he, as they say, break the bank? The central banks obviously had responsibility, and Soros was, of course, not the only foreign trader. But his was the face on the cover of the *Daily Mail*. Was that fair?

"I think the way to think about it is that countries can have unsustainable policies, which are going to end up—the unsustainable cannot be sustained," Mallaby told me over the phone in August 2019.

"If you want to zoom out . . . the speculator is not responsible for its bad policy," he said. "But clearly, the speculator is the trigger."

The defense of Soros in this case isn't that he wasn't responsible for the breaking of the bank, "which I think he was," Mallaby said. But Soros was hastening the inevitable, which was actually, Mallaby said, better for Britain.[23] Some argue that Black Wednesday forced the United Kingdom to change course and resulted in lower unemployment and higher economic growth. "Eventually, it turned and it became White Wednesday instead of Black Wednesday," Druckenmiller told me.[24]

But that it was going to happen eventually doesn't necessarily mean that it would have happened in the way that it did, as dramatically as it did. A country was thrown into economic chaos. Some—ironically, including Helmut Schlesinger—have argued that Black Wednesday was the beginning of what has culminated in Brexit, exposing divisions between Britain and powerhouses in Europe even as European countries were allegedly deepening integration. These were divisions that, one could argue, finally resulted in the referendum to leave the European Union. And this happened at least in part because Soros saw an opportunity to make a lot of money.

Soros himself later said that he overstated his own role in breaking the bank to help his philanthropy—curating his own legend and profile in order to attract support for his more noble endeavors.

"When the currency of the United Kingdom, the pound sterling, was forced out of the European Exchange Rate Mechanism, I became known as 'the man who broke the Bank of England.' This happened because I did not deny that my hedge fund had played a role in the event; the media then exaggerated my role," Soros wrote in 2011, almost two decades after the event. "I deliberately allowed it to happen in order to establish a platform from which I could speak on other issues. And it worked. Suddenly I had a voice that could be heard."[25]

Still, when challenged, he shied away from defending currency speculation. "I fight for many causes in my life, but I don't particularly feel like defending currency speculation. I consider it a necessary evil. I think it is better than currency restrictions, but a unified currency would be even better," he said in 1995.[26]

But that didn't mean that, two years later, he had qualms about breaking another national bank.

SHORTING THE POUND IS PERHAPS Soros's most famous move as a speculator. But arguably more controversial was shorting the Thai baht.

In 1994, two other men joined Team Soros and Druckenmiller: Rodney Jones and David Kowitz. Both men were Asian financial specialists. Johnson had originally brought Jones to Bankers Trust with him, and then, in early 1994, Jones followed him to Soros Fund Management. Jones, an economist, was based in Hong Kong. Kowitz, an Asian equities specialist, returned from Hong Kong in 1994. "There weren't so many specialists out there," he told me over the phone from the United Kingdom in September 2019, "and I had a pretty good reputation, I guess." He found his way over to Soros Fund Management, too.[27]

"We [the team] had discussed stresses of credit in Asia as early as 1995," Jones told me over the phone from New Zealand in September 2019. "One of the things that was unique about George Soros was he . . . recognized the dangers of the credit system we were building globally as early as the eighties. That was a unique insight at the time," he said, and "as early as 1995 Soros and Drucken-miller focused on the credit boom in Asia."[28]

Meanwhile, Soros and Druckenmiller restructured the fund—Druckenmiller had felt that the fund would have been better had it been slightly smaller while they were shorting sterling. Because they were the size that they were, they'd gone out to get $15 billion in sterling but had only been able to sell $10 billion of the $15 billion. Druckenmiller felt that if the fund had only tried to sell $10 billion, their percentage gain would have been higher. But Soros didn't want to be smaller; he wanted his empire to be grand and global.

Their compromise was that Soros Fund Management's assets wouldn't be allocated to just Quantum. By 1996, just under half of their $10 billion was at Quantum, while just over half was divided between three other funds: Quantum Emerging Growth, Quasar (to invest with outside managers), and Quota (managed by macro trader Nick Roditi). Soros brought in Arminio Fraga, an econo-mist, to run the startup funds.[29] (Incidentally, this was also around the time Soros got involved philanthropically in Myanmar, referred to by the Soros foundations at the time as Burma; in 1993, the Open Society Foundations' Burma Project was established to document the military junta's human rights abuses, and also to award schol-arships to students in Burma and refugee students in Thailand.)[30]

"Fraga was an economist, and a pretty respected, impressive economist," Kowitz told me. Fraga was more of a Latin America specialist, whereas Kowitz was an Asia expert. The two of them together, he said, ran the Quantum Emerging Market Fund, tak-ing meetings in their respective continents of expertise. Eventually, one of those meetings took place in Thailand.[31]

BY THE TIME FRAGA, JONES, and Kowitz came for their Bank of Thailand meeting, they'd already been watching stresses in Asian credit for years. As Mallaby describes, there was, if not a perfect storm of unfortunate conditions, then something fairly close: Thai exports were losing the competition to low-cost exports from China; the Thai currency was linked to a currency basket dominated by the dollar, meaning it was difficult for the baht to compete in world markets; and Thailand was running a trade deficit, but rather than letting go of its peg to the dollar to try to make the baht competitive, Thailand was consuming more than it was producing. The difference was being made up in foreign lending, with the threat of a withdrawal of this vital foreign investment hanging like a financial sword over Thailand's exposed neck.

In their meeting with the Bank of Thailand, the official with whom they were meeting conceded that, while Thailand had previously accepted the interest rates needed to "maintain the exchange rate within its designated band," banks were having trouble, and getting interest rates down might take priority over defending the currency level. The Thai peg, in other words, was unsustainable.[32]

"Central banks don't normally say things like what they told us," Kowitz recalled.[33]

Back in New York, the team shorted roughly $2 billion worth of Thai baht.

"In the months and years to come," Mallaby writes in *More Money Than God*, "a spirited argument would break out as to whether hedge funds precipitated Asia's financial crisis . . . but for now the opposite one stands out: why didn't Druckenmiller and Fraga do *more* to force a Thai devaluation?" Two billion dollars was hardly a small bet, but it was, after all, a relatively small amount of what they could have pursued.[34]

"It was a debate we had," Jones told me. "We'd gone to work in Asia and here you were taking large-scale short positions in countries with institutional fragility." Going for the jugular in the

United Kingdom was one thing; doing the same in Thailand was another.[35] The Bank of England would surely recover; Thailand was a developing economy, and it was unclear what impact outside investors could have.

Soros has justified speculation with the idea that it could serve as a kind of warning to governments. *Look, Thai government— the baht needs to devalue. Change your policy now before a currency collapse is devastating for your people.*

The trouble was that the Thai government didn't do this. Instead, it spent months using Bank of Thailand reserves to buy Thai baht. When it finally ran out in early summer 1997, the value of the baht plunged 32 percent against the dollar, and millions of Thai people lost their livelihoods. The Soros funds made $750 million.

The Thai financial crisis spread, becoming the Asia financial crisis, and Soros was blamed (a former college suitemate who is of Asian descent, on learning that I was writing this book, joked that Soros, in ridding her grandmother of her money, had at least cured her of her gambling problem). At the 1997 World Bank and International Monetary Fund (IMF) meetings, Malaysian Prime Minister Mahathir Mohamad called Soros a "criminal" and a "moron," and claimed that he single-handedly caused the crash of the Malaysian ringgit.[36]

The next month, in front of Malaysian villagers, Mahathir Mohamad offered that their woes were caused by the Jewish agenda. "Malaysian Premier Sees Jews Behind Nation's Money Crisis," the *New York Times* headline read.[37] (In 2019, the prime minister would go back to playing the antisemitic hits, telling a chortling audience at the Cambridge Union, "I have some Jewish friends, very good friends. They are not like the other Jews, that's why they are my friends."[38])

"I was surprised and angry," Kowitz told me of his response

to the Malaysian prime minister blaming them, "because it was absurd." The idea that they were trying to collapse Malaysia was just untrue.[39]

Soros, at the same World Bank and IMF meetings, told the crowd, "The main enemy of the open society, I believe, is no longer the communist but the capitalist threat."[40] The notion that markets should be left to do what they will—"The laissez-faire idea"—had, he said, become influential. But it was, in Soros's opinion, "a dangerous idea." Markets, he knew, were impacted by human behavior, including human folly. And the market was only one thing that should be taken into account, but surely there were others. This was the case Soros was making—even as he himself was blamed for the Asian financial crisis.

And here, too, Soros's dual roles came into conflict. Soros had his team take a long position on the Indonesian rupiah, and held on to it even as the currency went into freefall. In the end, they lost about $800 million, canceling out what they'd made in Thailand. In some cases, pecuniary profit appeared to matter above all; in other cases, the stability of the country seemed to take precedence.

"It was like we were participating in an IMF program" in Indonesia, Jones told me.

Also frustrating for Jones was the case of South Korea. On a visit to that country, Jones realized how badly the crisis had hit South Korea, and that its central bank was misleading the markets. The IMF thought that the country was immune from the crisis; Jones discovered otherwise. Jones sent over a memo to headquarters saying as much. But, Jones told me, they "had no position in Korea." I asked about the conflict of Soros the financial genius and Soros the philanthropist. "Absolutely. There was a real conflict. And in the case of Korea, there was a conflict, absolutely" between what he wanted to do and what his boss actually did.

"Rodney was quite frustrated," Johnson told me. "George

wanted to hold back in Korea when Rodney saw an opportunity because George knew the leaders there."[41]

"Rodney was like myself, a younger guy . . . he didn't really have a philanthropic state of mind at the time," Johnson said.

"I see people who try to demonize George. They act as though his philanthropic work is a Trojan horse for moneymaking," Johnson went on. "I experienced it the opposite way, which is that he curtailed his raw insight into moneymaking out of his philanthropic conscience."

This was particularly frustrating to some Soros employees because each of them was expected to have money in all four funds so that they'd all be literally invested in watching over one another. You had "all these smart people keeping an eye on everything," Johnson said. It was all of their money; younger players particularly were motivated to keep an eye out for any decisions that might cost them.

"The dilemma of that is George, for philanthropic reasons, wants to take a position in Russia—if we go in, the capital goes in. There's a problem with that. I'm not, age thirty-three, interested in philanthropy." He wanted to make money, and not lose money in Russia because Soros wanted to see the country turned around.[42]

Incidentally, this scenario did play out in Russia.

In the early 1990s, Soros made the decision to let the fund invest in Russia. In an interview in the 1990s, he said that his foundations were strong enough to resist blackmail, and that Soros Fund Management investments could not be "held hostage in order to influence the behavior of my foundations." He justified making investments in countries where he was philanthropically involved by saying, "My experience shows that people take me much more seriously as an investor than as a philanthropist. So if I really want to have an influence in these countries, I can do better as a potential investor."

Soros's 1995 book *Soros on Soros* was actually a series of long interviews, in which one of his interviewers observed to Soros that, had Soros refrained from making investments, he would have "reduced the grounds on which [Soros] can be attacked."

"To be a selfless benefactor was just a little too good to be true," Soros replied. "It fed my self-image as a godlike creature, above the fray, doing good and fighting evil . . . I became an awesome figure, and I could see, particularly in Russia, that people simply could not understand what I was all about."

Soros's argument was that acting as a selfless benefactor fed into his own messiah complex, and also made him distrusted in Russia; surely, a person wouldn't come into a foreign country and just give his money away for the good of that country. His argument was that being a philanthropist was therefore less beneficial both to him and to Russia than being a financier and philanthropist.

People in Russia were so caught up fighting for the day-to-day that "pursuit of an abstract good like open society hardly seems credible." He said he made the decision to start investing "at the height of the robber capitalist episode. It seemed to me that to appear as a robber capitalist who is concerned with cultural and political values was more credible than to be a disembodied intellect arguing for the merits of an open society. I could serve as a role model for the budding robber capitalists of Russia. And by entering the fray as an investor, I descended from Mount Olympus and became a flesh and blood human being."

The countries of Eastern Europe, he went on, need financial markets. Investors contribute to their development.

"Of course, we don't do that as a public service," he said. "We do it to make money. It may not be in the interest of these countries that we take away the profits we make there, but that's the nature of financial markets."[43]

Soros's argument was that it was better for Russia if he was more human—that Russians would then find his philanthropic work more credible. But, one could ask, in the era of Russian robber capitalists, did Russia really need one more person looking to make money off of Russia? More to the point, if Russians couldn't believe that somebody would be purely selfless, didn't acting selfishly in one's professional life just prove them right? Soros seemed to be arguing that, by potentially taking profit from a society, he was a better philanthropist for it, an argument that sounds an awful lot like justification for behavior that might run directly counter to the aims of his philanthropy.

But two years later, in 1997, the argument took on an even stranger light when Soros invested almost $1 billion in Svyazinvest, Russia's state-owned telephone company, even though he knew the state of the Russian economy and governance, having just given President Boris Yeltsin a loan behind the back of the IMF. Soros hoped both that foreign direct investment would help Russia and that the privatization of Svyazinvest would mark a turning point for the country. A year after that, in 1998, Soros was personally trying to act as an intermediary between Russia and the U.S. Treasury and Congress. He knew that the ruble was going to need to be devalued, but he did not short it, or even try to get his money out. When Russia finally did devalue the ruble, between Svyazinvest and other Russian bonds and equities, Quantum and the other funds lost somewhere between $1 billion and $2 billion.[44]

"In my view, he could be, theoretically, entitled to have one view as a speculator on how he wanted to make money and a second view as an analyst in the way the world works," Mallaby told me in our interview. "Lots of people, after all, can have that dissonance in their life." Political spin doctors, he offered as an example, can acknowledge that they made their money in that field while saying that it's bad for society. "To be hypocritical in that sense is fairly human."

But what's interesting about Soros, he said, is that Soros is "overly apologetic for his speculation, and that this can kind of lead him into this kind of comic zigzagging when he was quite willing to speculate against Thailand but squeamish about doing so in South Korea."

"It's one thing to have two views," Mallaby said. "It's another thing that within your moneymaking, you do it one day and refuse to do it the next. That's what's very jarring about him."[45]

Druckenmiller remembered it somewhat differently, though his understanding of Soros as making money to make philanthropic gifts was the same.

"I didn't sense a conflict," he told me. "My impression was he compartmentalized the two. The more money he made, the more money he could then target to his philanthropic work."[46]

I BELIEVE THAT THE PHILANTHROPIC work was an end in itself—that is, that Soros was deeply committed to the ideas of the foundation for their own sake, not as a way to launder his reputation or as a way to make more money. He very publicly gave to causes that he believed would open society for decades. If it was a charade, it was an impressively sustained and consistent one. And I believe Johnson and Jones when they talk about situations in which Soros pursued philanthropy over opportunity for financial gain.

But the reality remains that Soros's day job and his passion were in conflict. He was vitally interested in the civic health of Europe, yet he shorted the British pound. He wanted a world in which everyone had a fairer chance at civic participation, but he and his employees helped trigger the Asian financial crisis. Perhaps, if the government had taken it as a sign to correct course, their speculation could have been an opportunity to prevent a Thai economic downturn.

"The industry in which he made his money is an industry whose norms and rules have generally served to disenfranchise regular people over the last thirty, forty years," said Anand Giridharadas, author of *Winners Take All: The Elite Charade of Changing the World*, a look at the way in which the very wealthy use philanthropy to protect the status quo and paper over problems they themselves have created, in a September 2019 phone interview with me. "If you are the beneficiary of a system that has fundamentally been harmful to average people, it calls into question how strenuously you push back against the system that was benefiting you and harming others."

Soros did say, very publicly, that his philanthropy was possible because of a system that should be changed. But ultimately he was still participating in a system that actively disenfranchises people.

This is what Giridharadas describes in his book as "the only schmuck problem." Who wants to be the person to opt out when there's money to be made, especially when you're so good at making it?[47]

I ASKED SOROS WHAT HIS response was to the idea that the way in which he made his money and the concept of an open society are in tension.

"Nonsense. I have always operated with good intentions and within the rules," he responded. "If there is a breakdown in the rules, the blame lies with the authorities who set them. I only broke the rules in extraordinary times like during the Nazi occupation when they endangered the lives of those who obeyed them. I put the public interest ahead of my own personal interests, such as calling for higher taxes on the wealthy, which I continue to support today."

And it's true—he was working within the system and the law. He made money legally. Many people believe that making money in finance is not, in and of itself, at odds with a society in which everyone can participate. In other words, that Soros worked in the field of finance does not necessarily make him hypocritical, any more than it would have been hypocritical if he had worked in energy, or real estate, or technology, or any other field that can potentially further the divisions of haves and have-nots.

But Soros didn't just work in finance; he worked in finance in such a way that it broke countries' currencies. Perhaps, then, it is more accurate to say that if speculation itself is not at odds with an open society, the system as it existed then and exists today, which allows one person to make and keep as much money as Soros was able to make and keep, and in which Soros participated, certainly is. Because of his money, Soros—whose fund could push a country off of an economic course and who was literally rich enough to loan Russia enough to pay back wages—was too powerful to operate in one sense as a citizen of the market and in the other sense as a citizen of the political sphere. His sense of political citizenship impacted his market decisions (or at least was perceived by some of his colleagues as impacting it), and his market decisions had profound political consequences.

SOROS WAS KEENLY AWARE THAT society valued money. And so, too, was he aware that by having made money in such vast amounts, by being perceived as the person who broke the Bank of England, he could raise awareness for his philanthropic work.

"I had always wanted to get a hearing for my ideas, and for most of my life I didn't succeed. It was only after the sterling crisis that I became a public figure and it has really changed my position in the world," he said in his 1995 book. Until 1992, he even had a hard time getting an op-ed on the subject of Eastern Europe in the *New York Times*.

"It was my killing on sterling that gave me a high profile," he said in the same *Soros on Soros* interview, adding, "I think that's a commentary on the values that prevail in our society."[48]

And Soros intended to use his high profile for a particular cause. An ocean away from New York and a continent apart from London, there was a war going on, and he was going to use his new, dizzying fame to try to bring the world's attention to it.

CHAPTER 4

The Humanitarian Exception

George Soros considered humanitarian aid, or rather the need for it, a failure; he believed that a society that required humanitarian aid was a society that had broken down because people had not done what they should have done, or because other courses of action had not worked.

That meant that Soros and Open Society, generally speaking, were not in the business of providing water or electricity, but rather of providing scholarships and funding cultural foundations and civic organizations. The idea was to try to foster the kind of societies that would ensure access to water, food, and shelter. He wanted to stop the bleeding before it started, not to try to slap on expensive and often ineffective bandages.

But in the early 1990s, he made an exception. That exception was Sarajevo, the capital of Bosnia and Herzegovina, during the war in and against Bosnia. In the violent dissolution of Yugoslavia, in which conflicts that history had tried to push to the side came crashing to the front and politically manipulated ethnonationalism threatened to overtake multiculturalism, Soros made an exception in the form of $50 million of humanitarian aid.

YUGOSLAVIA HAD EXISTED FOR DECADES. It was a unique geopolitical entity, an exception to U.S. president Woodrow Wilson's rule of self-determination: other ethnic groups that had lived in polyglot, polyethnic empires before the First World War were now living in independent nation-states—except for much of the Balkans (except Czechoslovakia). Immediately after the war, the country was known as the Kingdom of Serbs, Croats, and Slovenes; then, a decade later, as the Kingdom of Yugoslavia. After World War II, a Communist government took over, and the Kingdom of Yugoslavia became first the Federal People's Republic of Yugoslavia and then the Socialist Federal Republic of Yugoslavia, which was itself made up of constituent republics—Serbia, Slovenia, Croatia, Macedonia, Montenegro, and Bosnia and Herzegovina. The Federal People's Republic of Yugoslavia and the Socialist Federal Republic of Yugoslavia were ruled by Communist leader Josip Broz Tito, who served until his death in 1980.

When Tito died, there was "really nobody able to take on his mantle, in part because he didn't think he would die," Dženeta Karabegović, a Balkan expert in the sociology department of Salzburg University, told me over Skype. (I was sitting in Sarajevo; she was, as her Twitter biography suggests she often is, traveling.) "There was never anybody groomed to take over."[1]

"The sort of one-party system, this whole Yugoslav system, operated on his personality," Karabegović said. And when he died, in the place of someone ready to take charge, Yugoslavia got several untested leaders.[2] (In fairness, other scholars note that the whole thing could not have been totally dependent on Tito, since it hung together for over a decade after his death.)

The Humanitarian Exception

There were hints of conflicting nationalisms before Tito died, but they were resolved through, as historian Mark Mazower put it, the power of the Communist Party and the power of Tito himself. Within the larger Communist Party, Mazower wrote in his book *The Balkans: A Short History*, the Bosnian branch of the party was the most hard-line in any of the republics, and "became increasingly important in supporting the federal leadership against the centrifugal tendencies operating from the grass roots"—specifically, Serbian and Croatian nationalism. Notably, the Bosnian Party included Bosnian Serbs. In the Bosnian War of the 1990s, Bosnian Serbs and Bosniaks would kill and die over who belonged to what country, but, according to historian Marko Attila Hoare, in 1945, Bosnia's prime minister, parliamentary president, and the head of Bosnia's Communist organization were all Serbs who identified Bosnia as their home. There were nationalisms within Yugoslavia, but they were not neatly divided along nation-state lines.[3]

Within Yugoslavia, Tito created "new" official national groups as part of his elaborate system of balancing nationalisms and nationalities and nations; among those groups were Bosnian Muslims, who were first officially recognized as a nation in 1971 (this year is somewhat debated; researcher Xavier Bougarel wrote that most put the date of recognition in 1968).[4] There obviously were people in Bosnia who were Muslim before then, but the group only became an official nation—something you were officially part of or apart from, depending on your perspective—at that point.

"Overnight, democratic rights and freedoms replaced censorship and dictatorship," Misha Glenny wrote of the fall of Communism after Tito's death in his book *The Balkans: Nationalism, War, and the Great Powers*. "But throughout Eastern Europe, the outgoing communist bureaucracies devised ways of adapting to the new conditions, preserving their privileges against the challenge of political or economic competition . . . In Yugoslavia, aggressive nationalism was the trump card. Milosevic [that is, Slobodan Mi-lošević, Communist turned revolutionary opportunist and ruler of the constituent republic of Serbia] reinvented himself as a Serbian chauvinist."[5]

Milošević was the leader of the official Serb republic of Yugoslavia, and he understood that his nationalism needed an international backer. The same was true of Franjo Tudjman, leader of the official Croat republic. So the two set out, separately, to secure support. Milošević, who, according to Glenny, was ideologically sympathetic to neo-Stalinism, sought military assurances from Russia; Tudjman, meanwhile, had an eye toward mobilizing the Croatian diaspora, but also to get support from Croatia's World War II ally, Germany.[6]

The Yugoslav Wars broke out in 1991, when Slovenia and Croatia voted for independence from Yugoslavia. Germany was a staunch supporter of Croatian independence, while the French and British worried over what else would come out of this geopolitical Pandora's box. The United States and its then-president, George H. W. Bush, maintained that this was a European concern. By the start of 1992, it was obvious that Yugoslavia as it had been was no more. In January of that year, international peacekeepers arrived in Croatia.[7]

In the War Childhood Museum in Sarajevo, I watched a video clip—one of several that played on a loop featuring people talking about their memories of the war—of an articulate woman with a short blond bob who was born in 1974. She said that people believed that war, even if it came to Bosnia, would not come to Sarajevo. After all, it was cosmopolitan, it was cultured, and, more than that, it was a place where people of different ethnicities and religions and backgrounds lived together.

"Until the last moment," Glenny wrote in his book, "Bosnians from all three communities [Bosnian Serb, Bosnian Croat, and Bosniak] cherished the illusion that there would be no war. This was not naivety but the knowledge that if war did break out it would be merciless."[8]

In February and March of 1992, Bosnia and Herzegovina—which is made up of (predominantly Orthodox) Bosnian Serbs, (predominantly Catholic) Bosnian Croats, and (predominantly Muslim) Bosniaks—voted for independence. The president, Alija Izetbegović, who had first opposed the concept given simmering neighborhood tensions and Croatian and Serbian designs on the territory, eventually gave in to the idea of an independent Bosnia, and stated, "The time has come for Bosnia-Herzegovina to become a free, sovereign state." The leadership of Bosnia declared independence, with encouragement from the United States, on April 5, 1992.[9]

Before the vote, Serb leaders had warned that a referendum could lead to violence—Bosnian Serbs, they said, wanted to remain in a Serb-led Yugoslavia. After the declaration of independence, Bosnian Serb paramilitary forces, backed by Belgrade, the seat of Serbian power, attacked Sarajevo, shooting at and shelling the city. They attempted to bring about two-thirds of the country under their control (despite the fact that Bosnian Serbs made up roughly one-third of the population), expelling Bosniaks to create contiguous land for rural Bosnian Serbs in a late twentieth-century episode of ethnic cleansing.[10]

In 1993, Bosnian Croats, who until this point had joined with Bosniaks to hold what were now the front lines, began a war within a war, fighting with Bosniaks for their own piece of what was left of the country. After a terrible, fatal winter for the country between 1993 and 1994, the United States convened a meeting of ministers from NATO member countries, who said Bosnian Serbs must withdraw their heavy artillery around Sarajevo in ten days.

Seven days into that, Russian President Boris Yeltsin announced Russia would send troops to Sarajevo to make sure the Bosnian government wouldn't take advantage of the absence of Serb guns. Moscow had previously refused to send troops, and Yeltsin's announcement was unexpected. The Russian announcement lowered the temperature around the NATO ultimatum, and Bosnian and Serb government forces turned their weapons in at U.N. collection points. Sarajevo got some months of, if not respite, then relief. The Americans and Germans seized on the moment to convince the political forces claiming to act on behalf of Bosnian Croats and Bosniaks (Tudjman and Izetbegović, respectively) to form a federation.[11]

But while reconciling matters, at least temporarily, with Bosnian Croats may have provided some respite for the Bosniaks, it did not bring an end to the war. In 1995, U.N. Protection Force troops, who were meant to protect "safe areas" designated by the United Nations, failed to do so in Srebrenica, a town in the very east of Bosnia; there, Bosnian Serb forces killed as many as 8,000 Bosniak men and boys.[12] Five decades after World War II and the promise of "never again," Europe witnessed the largest massacre since the Holocaust.

By the time the war was over in December 1995, roughly 100,000 had been killed in Bosnia. Eighty percent were Bosniaks.[13] According to some estimates, as many as 50,000 Bosniak women were raped during the course of the war.[14]

SOROS GOT INVOLVED IN BOSNIA in the same way that he got involved in philanthropy—through the people he happened to know.

Nobel Prize winner and then–political consultant Lord Mark Malloch-Brown first met Soros in the late 1980s while working on a campaign occurring half a world away from Bosnia. Malloch-Brown was then involved in the (ultimately successful) campaign to oust Augusto Pinochet from power in Chile. Malloch-Brown was "desperate to find some people to resource . . . and to travel down there [to Chile]," he told me in his aristocratic British accent over the phone from the United Kingdom.[15]

At the time, Soros was on the board of Human Rights Watch, which was then run by Aryeh Neier, cofounder of the organization. Neier introduced Malloch-Brown to Soros.

"Your phone number looks like—are you in Long Island?" Malloch-Brown asked when I called him. I live in Washington, D.C., but my 516 area code is an immediate giveaway as to where I grew up. I assured him that I am familiar with Long Island's geography and he began to discuss his first meeting with Soros in Southampton.

"I went out to his home in Southampton and spent an evening where I thought we would be talking about Chile, but actually . . . [had] extraordinary first exchanges sitting at dinner with him and his then wife." Soros "rather magisterially" asked Malloch-Brown about personal risk factors in Thailand and the Thai stock exchange, because Malloch-Brown had lived in Thailand in the late 1970s and early 1980s while he was the United Nations High Commissioner for Refugees.

They did eventually turn to Chile. "I saw immediately what a sort of passionate person he was about personal freedom and human rights," Malloch-Brown said.

Soros's support for the "no" campaign against Pinochet was "modest"—he ended up backing some focus groups, providing outside funding to do research and analysis for the "no" campaign. But the two men became friends and, a few years later, Soros reached out to Malloch-Brown, who he knew had worked in the humanitarian space as well as for the United Nations.

In 1993, "He called me up and said, 'I want to make this human-itarian commitment to Sarajevo.'"[16]

THERE ARE A FEW THEORIES as to why Soros chose this particular moment to become involved in humanitarian relief. Malloch-Brown previously noted publicly that Soros was coming off years of success in Central and Eastern Europe.[17] After the collapse of the Berlin Wall, his foundations across the region were trying to transition societies to democracy (Soros was also much more public than ever before, having just significantly contributed to the "breaking" of the Bank of England). Malloch-Brown also made the point that Soros's humanitarian aid was coupled with a political strategy—high-profile advocacy for greater international attention to and action in Bosnia. "It bought much more than just bed and blankets," he said.[18]

Soros himself said in 1995, "It is clear that people in the West failed to understand what the Bosnian conflict was all about . . . It was a case of Serbian aggression and the use of ethnic cleansing as a means to an end . . . it was a conflict between an ethnic and a civic concept of citizenship." It was a test of the very notion of an open society.[19] Soros had seen the threat of nationalism ready and waiting to swallow Central and Eastern Europe following the dissolution of the Eastern Bloc. Nationalism was harnessed for political purposes and was taking over Yugoslavia, which had been the most open and arguably multicultural country behind the Iron Curtain. An ethnic concept of citizenship means that those who can participate in society are predetermined, decided by blood. A civic concept of society means that participation is not determined by ethnonationalism, but by the full participation of all citizens. A civic society is an open one. It was the one that Soros wanted very much to preserve.

The Humanitarian Exception

Twenty-four years later, I asked Soros why he decided to make this the exception.

"I decided to stay out of humanitarian relief work because I wanted to concentrate my efforts on preventing humanitarian catastrophes from occurring. Bosnia was the first instance where I was personally involved and the international community clearly failed to prevent a humanitarian catastrophe," he responded. "I could not stand by and watch the Serbian army engage in the ethnic cleansing of the Bosnian population."

AT FIRST, MALLOCH-BROWN THOUGHT SOROS'S money should go to Sarajevo through the United Nations.

"My first and rather bad idea was to give the bulk of it [the money] to the U.N. High Commissioner for Refugees, an organization I'd worked for," Malloch-Brown told me. "They had access. They were able to move across the line between the city and outside. I felt they would, despite being a U.N. agency, be much better placed to put the aid into Sarajevo than a nongovernmental organization. I also felt, because they had a protection mandate, they would be able to be a louder voice in protecting the refugees."

Malloch-Brown told me that he went to the High Commissioner and said that, given that this would be the first very large private-sector donation, it needed to be treated with "real attention," and that the donor expected high-quality reporting on how the money was being spent. It couldn't be treated "like just another check from the government."

However, "we very quickly discovered that actually UNHCR was hobbled by the politics," Malloch-Brown said. The major powers were split in their support for different ethnicities—or at least, between the Croats and Serbs, as there was "really insignificant support at that stage [for] the Muslims." Rather than acting in the spirit of an institution dedicated to protecting common humanity, the members of the United Nations Security Council had picked their favorites in the conflict.

Later, when I asked Malloch-Brown if he—if we—should have qualms about one private citizen who is not a part of any government or necessarily accountable to anyone being able to get involved in humanitarian aid and awareness to such an extent, he pointed to the episode with UNHCR. "[Soros] was much more interested in a high level of strategic interaction of UNHCR over how his money was used," Malloch-Brown said. Soros wanted to see how the money was spent; governments, by comparison, were more content to "write a check," no questions asked. Soros at least wanted oversight and accounting to make sure the money was going where it would help the most.

Did Malloch-Brown have concerns about funding from an outside and unaccountable party? No, he did not, because, paradoxically, Soros was holding international institutions to a higher standard than elected governments were. Those governments, though, were ultimately accountable to their voters, whereas Soros was not.

Since Soros was not content to write a check and leave matters at that, "I quickly realized this [going through the UNHCR] had been a big mistake . . . George persuaded me to go and get the money back," Malloch-Brown said, half-laughing to himself, "on the grounds that they really couldn't spend it effectively. To my amazement, we did get it back, or a significant portion of it."[20]

And so the group—Soros, Malloch-Brown, Neier, who in 1993 left Human Rights Watch to become president of Open Society— then dispatched Lionel Rosenblatt, who at the time was president of Refugees International, and Fred Cuny, an American engineer with vast experience in aid work, to come up with initiatives that would make a difference on the ground.

Rosenblatt started up the political advocacy component of the work. The group brought on several other high-profile individuals who included Morton Abramowitz, the former U.S. ambassador to Thailand whom Malloch-Brown had known from his time in that country; Paul Wolfowitz, former diplomat and undersecretary of defense for policy; and the Aga Khan, the imam of a denomination within Shia Islam who is also a British citizen and businessman. In time, the political advocacy work became a high-level lobbying effort, putting pressure on governments around the world to do something to stop the slaughter.

They had what Malloch-Brown described as "very lucky public relations." Peter Jennings of ABC, for example, happened to be in Sarajevo as a bomb went off in the market and was able to broadcast that news out to the world, and to governments who were reluctant and unsure of how to act.[21]

Not everyone felt, or feels, similarly warmly about the foreign journalists who were in Sarajevo. At the old Ashkenazi synagogue in Sarajevo, I met with a man named Jakob Finci, who had helped 3,000 people escape the siege and flee to safety during the war, and who went on to run the country's Open Society Foundation when the war was over. After wryly explaining that somehow the only people who know what happened to Bosnia are not Bosnians, but rather foreign journalists, all of whom seem to have written books about it, he told me a joke. We were still sitting at the table in the middle of his spacious office, one wall lined with a seemingly infinite row of different types of menorahs. The joke goes like this: Two foreigners meet in the streets of Sarajevo. One asks the other when he arrived. Yesterday, the second foreigner replies. And when do you leave? Tomorrow, the second foreigner answers. And what are you doing here? I'm writing a book, the second foreigner says. It's called *Bosnia: Yesterday, Today, and Tomorrow.*[22]

I asked Finci how he squared this impression of foreigners,

and particularly foreign journalists, with his impression of Soros. Wasn't he also a foreigner, an outsider, someone dropping in to try to assess the present and influence the future?

But Soros's role, he told me, was "positive." And when I asked how that could be, he told me that Soros and his team "pushed everything in the hands of Bosnians." He did not parachute in to personally dictate relief efforts; he found talented people who wanted to rise to the occasion, and he gave them the money that helped them do that.

.

POLITICAL LOBBYING WAS ONLY ONE part of Soros's effort.

It was Abramowitz who brought in the aforementioned Texas engineer Cuny—the two had been in Turkey at the same time. And it was Cuny who figured out how to use Soros's money in Sarajevo to make a considerable impact on the people actually living there.[23]

"He worked wonders in restoring the supply of natural gas and building an underground tunnel beneath the airport to allow supplies to be brought in. He reinforced the resilience of the civilian population by providing seeds for them to grow vegetables on their terraces and small plots," Soros wrote to me.

"His most brilliant move," he added, "was to establish a water purification plant by having modules flown in by plane and installed into a well-protected road tunnel in the side of a mountain."

Cuny observed that people were going to old wells to collect water, from which they came back slowly, weighed down by jugs, making themselves easy targets for snipers on the surrounding hills. And so he built a water purification plant in the city—but under a hill, protected from shelling. He had the parts made in Texas, where he was from, and had the actual assembly timed so that the parts could be quickly moved from the trucks they were in to the tunnel under the hill. He also made smaller water plants on the hills, for those who couldn't get to the main plant, and had Jordanian troops guard them. He worked with UNHCR and with the Open Society staffers, but anyone and everyone I asked assured me that it was Cuny who was the brains behind this part of the operation.

Soros came to visit Sarajevo in November 1993. Beka Vuco, then regional director for Open Society, accompanied him on the trip. She recalled at an event in 2017 on the subject of Soros's contribution to Bosnia that she asked the man driving them to the hotel if he could slow down. She was informed that he could not; he had to drive faster than the rifles pointing down at them.[24]

Soros was there for the opening of the water purification plant, but local authorities weren't giving permission to turn it on, claiming that the water wasn't safe, despite tests that said it was. "Either somebody was making a lot of money selling water or the government wanted to continue having people killed by snipers while waiting for water in order to have pictures on TV generating sympathy for the city's plight," Soros later wrote. After threatening to make the incident public, the plant was opened for business.[25]

Soros's visit also coincided with the destruction of historic Mostar Bridge outside of Sarajevo.[26]

It was Bosnian Croat General Slobodan Praljak who ordered the destruction of the bridge and, by doing so, harmed the Bosnian civilian population physically (dozens of people, including at a nearby school, were killed) and psychologically (a bridge that had existed for hundreds of years was blown up and thousands were trapped on one side of the city). In 2017, Praljak had his war crimes sentence of twenty years upheld at a U.N. tribunal in the Hague; seconds after the decision was announced, he declared that he rejected it and that he was not a war criminal. Then he drank a vial of poison and died.[27]

The Influence of Soros

THE U.N. TRIBUNAL IN THE Hague is a legacy of Soros's money in Bosnia; the tribunal likely would never have existed without Aryeh Neier's commitment to the cause and Soros's money. The International Criminal Tribunal for the former Yugoslavia was a United Nations court that was responsible for prosecuting the war crimes committed in the Balkans in the 1990s. Its mandate lasted from 1993 until 2017.[28]

Before he left Human Rights Watch, Neier, in 1992, invoked the Genocide Convention—the agreements that originated in the nineteenth century, and were updated after World War II, that are supposed to govern wars and conflict. Neier wrote that what was happening in Bosnia was a violation of the Geneva Convention, and therefore could be considered war crimes. After becoming the president of Open Society in 1993, he was able, with Soros's help (and financial approval), to do more than write about it. He was able to push for the establishment of a tribunal to deal with what he perceived as a breach of international humanitarian law.

Bosnian Serbs used concentration camps during the war in Bosnia. Neier believed that the use of camps called for the establishment of a war crimes tribunal. At Open Society, Neier asked for, and was granted, $2 million of the $50 million spent on Bosnia for human rights. He used the money to establish the International Criminal Tribunal for crimes committed in the former Yugoslavia (ICTY).

The United Nations established a commission for such a tribunal but didn't give the commission any money. Open Society, through Neier, gave money from the $2 million, which was matched by the MacArthur Foundation. The commission published five volumes on war crimes committed in Bosnia.

Madeleine Albright, who became U.S. ambassador to the United Nations in 1993, "grabbed hold of the issue," championing it, Neier recalled. By May 1993, the United Nations Security

Council approved a resolution for the establishment of an international criminal tribunal for the former Yugoslavia.

It was shocking to me, listening to Neier's recollection, which he recorded at the Open Society event on Bosnia a few years ago, that this was how the tribunal came to be set up. It was shocking that the United Nations did not independently think that maybe there should be some group, or body, or *thing* to address what was happening in Yugoslavia, that so shortly after *never again* the international organization couldn't privilege international humanitarian law enough to fund something like that. And it was shocking to me, although at this point it probably shouldn't have been, that this is how it works: that if Soros had said "no" to Neier, there just wouldn't have been an international criminal tribunal for Yugoslavia.

Initially, the tribunal didn't function, as it was not empowered to make the accused appear before it. In fact, the first case happened by accident—one of the accused, Duško Tadić, happened to be spotted in Germany, and was arrested by German police officers and brought before the tribunal in 1995.

It was only after Clinton's reelection, and, arguably more important in this case, the election of British Prime Minister Tony Blair and the arrival of his foreign minister, Robin Cook, that people were found and arrested in the region—no mean feat, given that they were often in enclaves quite sympathetic to their former causes.[29]

The people who were tracked down and tried before the tribunal were ultimately the people responsible for some of the most gruesome crimes committed in the Balkans in the 1990s. Ratko Mladic, commander of the Bosnian Serbs and known as the "Butcher of Bosnia," was convicted in 2017—twenty years after he had first been indicted.[30] Milošević was turned over to the ICTY in 2001.[31] He was found dead in his cell in 2006. And Radovan

Karadžić, political leader of the Bosnian Serbs during the war, was arrested in 2008 after hiding from the ICTY's indictment for thirteen years. He was found guilty of the majority of the counts of the indictment in 2016. In 2019, an appeals court in The Hague upheld his sentence of life in prison.[32]

Aside from the former-Yugoslavia-specific tribunal, Open Society also provided funding for groups that campaigned for the International Criminal Court. President Bill Clinton signed on to the convention that established the International Criminal Court, but never presented it to Congress for ratification. In 2002, George W. Bush authorized its "unsigning," effectively erasing the U.S. signature. In 2018, President Donald Trump's then–national security advisor, John Bolton, threatened ICC prosecutors and judges who might look into abuses committed by Americans and vowed, "We will not cooperate with the ICC. We will provide no assistance to the ICC. We will not join the ICC. We will let the ICC die on its own."[33] The United States was not only passively undermining the ICC by not participating in it, but was actively working to undercut the institution established to hold people accountable for war crimes, genocide, and crimes against humanity.

Aryeh Neier got Soros to buy in, and Soros got the United Nations to buy in, but the United Nations, evidently, did not get the United States to buy in. It is as yet unclear whether the ICC will be destroyed by the United States of America.

THERE IS ANOTHER INSTITUTION, LESS maligned by the Trump administration, that, today, also serves as a reminder of the money Soros spent twenty-five years ago.

The idea was born as the violence in Bosnia was ending. "As the conflict started to wind down in Sarajevo and peace was on the horizon, I flew with Mort Abramowitz to Sarajevo,"

Malloch-Brown told me. On their departure, the whole journey, the work with Fred Cuny, and the high-level political lobbying seemed like a success. On their way back out of Sarajevo, sitting in a British Hercules, a Royal Air Force transport aircraft, Abramowitz and Malloch-Brown turned to each other "and said, 'god, we should do this again. This really worked.'"

They worked to create the International Crisis Group, an independent nongovernmental organization dedicated to preventing and resolving deadly conflict. The International Crisis Group was started in part with Soros's seed funding and was meant to replicate the success of the two-pronged approach in Bosnia: the provision of high-impact humanitarian relief on the ground and advocacy for political change at a high level.

But they ultimately could not replicate the Bosnia model due to personnel changes. Malloch-Brown, who was initially going to stay on the board, was recruited to, and left to work for, the World Bank. To remain on the board of the Crisis Group was a conflict of interest, and so Malloch-Brown stepped down. Fred Cuny, who all had thought would be the operations director, acting as the catalyst for more effective aid responses, disappeared and was likely executed while he was in Chechnya in April 1995. "That side of the organization," Malloch-Brown said—the side that figured out how to bring parts from Texas to let people drink clean water in Bosnia, the side that had troops guarding people hydrating on the hills, the side that kept the lights on in hospitals— "died with him." (In any event, Malloch-Brown said the "aid community was not very open to outsiders telling them how to do things better.")

Then the third president of the International Crisis Group, Gareth Evans, a former Australian foreign minister (the first director died, and the second, former Médecins Sans Frontières International Secretary-General Alain Destexhe, was described to me by Malloch-Brown as a "slightly incompetent Belgian") was the one under whom "the thing [ICG] really, really took off."

"His whole heart and appetite was the political side, the analysis side," Malloch-Brown said. It's that part that has been the foundation of the International Crisis Group ever since.[34]

When I think of the International Crisis Group, I think of the way in which I have encountered it as a journalist—I have turned to its experts and used their analysis with some frequency. I do not think of it as a high-flying political lobbying group. But that is how it started, and it started because Soros happened to be invested in a cause. It would not have begun without Malloch-Brown's tenacity, or Cuny's ingenuity. But mostly it seems that it would not exist without George Soros's money.

SOROS'S WARTIME WORK IN THE Balkans was not limited to humanitarian aid: Soros established an Open Society Foundation in Sarajevo during the war. Like other legacies of Soros's wartime involvement, it still exists today, serving as a reminder of the money spent long ago. And like other legacies of Soros's wartime involvement, it also reminds us of what money was not able to buy.

Originally, Soros did not think that the Balkans needed Open Society. Yugoslavia was the multicultural Communist country, and was—compared to, say, Hungary—open. But in the early 1990s, when nationalist voices began speaking more loudly, he changed his mind.

At first, he intended for there to be one Open Society Foundation for Yugoslavia, directed by a woman named Sonja Licht.

In the 1980s, Licht, born in what was then Yugoslavia, had a variety of professional connections in Hungary. She was familiar, she told me over Skype from Serbia, with a variety of people in what she called the Budapest Circle, a group of sociologists and philosophers critical to the dissident movement in Eastern Bloc Hungary. And so she knew of Soros, and of the Soros Foundation in Hungary—her first involvement was when she and her husband received Soros stipends to study at Brandeis, the private university in Massachusetts.

Her relationship to Soros changed in February 1990. Soros convened the heads of various Open Society Foundations and guests from other regions for a meeting in Dubrovnik, the Croatian city pressed up against the Adriatic Sea. Licht was the representative for what was then Yugoslavia.

She and Soros spoke about the possibility of starting a foundation in Yugoslavia. When he was finally convinced that one was necessary, in 1991, he wanted Licht as its director.

At first, Licht was meant to start a foundation that would work hand in hand with the government, not unlike the first Soros Foundation in Hungary in the 1980s. The idea was somewhat limited—they were to give out fellowships to students from Yugoslavia to Central European University and other institutions of higher learning.[35]

Licht remembers June 17, 1991, well. Soros was in Belgrade, and they went together to see different people, "including Mr. Markovic [Ante Marković, the socialist reformer leader of Yugoslavia], and then I personally understood for the first time that there would be a war for sure." So evident was Marković's desperation that Licht could tell the country was falling apart.

The day was also memorable because Soros and the government signed the contract for the establishment of an Open Society Foundation.

It was also around this time that serious fighting began between Croats and Serbs, and Licht forgot about the foundation.

"When your country's falling apart . . . nothing else seems real or important," she told me.

She was involved in the peace movement, in trying to stop the fighting and killing, and it wasn't until the fall of 1991, she said, that she remembered that she was supposed to be running a foundation.

"I told him it was not possible anymore," she said, even though she had already assembled a board comprised of regional intellectuals, many of whom were leaders in the Association for a Yugoslav Democratic Initiative, which called for "Yugoslavia's transformation into a federal, democratic community."

"Either we close down the whole thing that didn't even start or he considers creating foundations in all the parts of Yugoslavia," she told Soros. There could no longer be one foundation for all of Yugoslavia, because Yugoslavia was falling apart. If Soros wanted to do this and be philanthropically involved in a way that helped more than it hurt, he would have to set up foundations in each of the factions.

So Soros opened more foundations. The Open Society in Belgrade started running in the winter of 1991–1992. Licht ran it until 1999.[36]

The foundation in Bosnia and Herzegovina began in 1993. A professor named Zdravko Grebo had learned of Soros's intention to set up foundations in the region. He wanted to speak to Soros. A week after he managed to get through to the New York headquarters—rather improbably, given that Soros was not waiting by the phone to receive a call from wartime Sarajevo—he received a fax. "As you already know, I am in the process of opening the Open Society Fund–Bosnia and Herzegovina," the November 1992 letter read. "I would like to appoint you to the position of Executive Director of the Open Society Fund–Bosnia and Herzegovina. I expect future projects of the foundation to be designed to help the suffering people of all ethnicities overcome the devastating situation in your country."[37]

The Humanitarian Exception

The idea of no one ethnic group benefiting from the money was important to Soros. In 1992, Finci—the man who told me the joke about foreign journalists in Sarajevo—went to meet with Soros in New York. Finci was president of a Jewish humanitarian organization and asked Soros for $50,000. As Finci understood it, he told me, this was the first time a Jewish organization successfully received help from Soros. Soros's opinion of Jewish organizations was informed by his time in London—that he was able to scam them did not leave him with a high opinion of such groups.

"You can hardly say there is any Jewish conspiracy," Finci quipped.

Soros gave the money to Finci, who told me that Soros explained that he wanted the money to be distributed to other ethnic groups, too. Finci assured him that he would see to it that that happened.[38]

THE FIRST OPEN SOCIETY OFFICE in Sarajevo was in a single room in the president's building. Today, it is several rooms in a walk-up building nestled next to cafés and a few feet from the country's central bank on a main Sarajevo street.

I went there to meet with Dobrila Govedarica, a tall, elegant woman with a halo of red hair, who became executive director of the organization after 2000; shortly after our meeting began, she called in Hrvoje Batinić and Dženana Trbić, both of whom have been with Open Society in Sarajevo since the war. Batinić is slender and wore his hair cropped close to his head; he seemed serious, but then, we were talking about war. Trbić wore a white, floaty blouse, and smiled warmly while she spoke. We sat around an oval-shaped table on seafoam-green swivel chairs, the noise from the road outside loud enough for my tape recorder to pick it up. The bookshelf on the wall behind them contained, I noticed, a 2011 tome on

Soros's philanthropy that contains a chapter on his philanthropic efforts during the war.

The Bosnia and Herzegovina Open Society Foundation played a rather unusual role during the war for a nongovernmental organization and spent part of the humanitarian aid money in a manner that is often not considered humanitarian aid at all.

The Open Society staffers at the time (with the help of UNHCR) brought newsprint into the country so that people could run newspapers. They put on cultural events. They provided scholarships to students so that they could finish their studies abroad (one such student, I was proudly informed by Govedarica, was Ivan Barbalić, who went on to become the Bosnian ambassador to the United Nations).[39]

Open Society even gave out various writing prizes over the course of the war, to reward those who produced their own art even while their city was under siege.

In our meeting, Trbić told me she still has one of the awards. She hurried out of the room to get it, then came back holding a small but heavy silver square. It's so heavy because they made the awards out of the printing press plates, she explained. There is an image of a typewriter in the top right corner. The one she showed me is the award for the *najbolji roman*—the best novel—of 1995. It was meant to go to a Muhamed Kondžić. Trbić has it, she said, because Kondžić died before he could receive it. It sat between us for the rest of the interview, the prize that Kondžić won and couldn't accept.[40]

Batinić told me the story of his first meeting with Soros, where he tried to impress upon this big spender from New York the importance of providing money for cultural causes and events.

"I first met him in September of '93. That was my first trip outside of Sarajevo," Batinić said.

It was a project coordinators conference, and Grebo insisted that he, Batinić, attend. "I went there . . . for the first time, I was in Macedonia. Such a peaceful place."

There was a dinner for Soros, and Batinić attended. Soros heard someone from Bosnia was at the conference. He was sitting with the executive director of the Macedonia foundation. But when he heard that "a guy from Bosnia" was there, he asked that Batinić be transferred to his table (temporarily stealing Macedonia's thunder).

"I remember . . . part of my mission was to explain to him . . . that we should put much stress on the cultural life. And that we want as much money as possible for cultural activities."

It felt, Batinić said, "like we were living in a concentration camp, or like, in zoo. Kind of a zoo. Savages butchering each other. That was the outside perception for many people. They didn't know the story of . . . what was at stake for us domestically. And we wanted to correct that." He wanted to show them "this may sound naïve—that we are people who go to theatres and watch movies, read books, etc."

It didn't sound naïve to me. But it still made me sad, just as it had when Batinić told me that my entire line of questioning asked them to put into words feelings that I could never understand. Batinić had been asking, back then, for the wider world, for Americans and Canadians and so-called Western Europeans to understand something that they couldn't—that the people they were watching kill each other also went to birthday parties, and liked good food and drink, and had interests outside of war.

"I told that to Soros and he looked at me and said, 'Let me tell you something. That idea that you will attract big media and everything. The focus of international media on Bosnia is directly connected to blood on your streets and squares and where people are being butchered. That's what attracts their attention. As soon as that stops, you are not of primary interest to the big media companies. But of course I will give you . . . you may do all these things. But don't delude yourself.'

"He was in fact, bitterly, in a bitter mood explaining to me the logic of corporate media. And the whole world in which he was making his money and spending his money this way. He was aware of his paradoxical situation."[41]

It was not only, I thought, that Soros came from the place where corporate media zeroed in on foreigners only when they started to kill each other. Soros was not just aware of the problem; he was actively participating in it. Of course he knew the attention was connected to the bloodshed. Wasn't that why he had asked to speak to Batinić in the first place?

EARLIER IN THE INTERVIEW, I had asked if it was problematic that a man from Soros's rarefied world—a billionaire with so much money, accountable to no one, unelected by any people to any government—could come in and give so much money and have such an impact during a war.

The three of them looked at me as though I had switched from asking about Soros in English to talking about sandwiches in Portuguese.

"But that is great?" Govedarica half-asked, half-answered, as though she couldn't believe that this was the question I'd presented her. "If there were more people like him, it would be easier to live in Bosnia."[42]

It was the people who were "not interested in Bosnia surviving," Batinić said, who were unhappy that Soros was pouring support into Sarajevo.

Govedarica and Batinić are, of course, Open Society employees, and therefore particularly unlikely to say that Open Society money was bad for Bosnia. But they are not the only ones who responded as though my question was one more relevant to intellectual debates back stateside than it was to the people on the receiving end of the money.[43]

"Honestly, even right now, if I'm thinking about a place like Syria or Iraq, and somebody's willing to put up fifty million dollars—what ordinary Iraqi is going to be like, 'I don't know about the ethics of this'?" Jasmin Mujanović, a political scientist and the author of *Hunger and Fury: The Crisis of Democracy in the Balkans*, told me over the phone while waiting for repairs at an automotive shop somewhere in North America.

It's fine for people in the global north and donor countries to talk about the structural and institutional mechanisms of donation, he said, "but I don't know that you're going to find a lot of places on Earth . . . where they're having those kinds of debates."[44]

THERE WAS ANOTHER ANSWER, TOO, to the question of whether Soros's outside and outsized influence should be interrogated, which was this: Soros himself was, by and large, not the one calling the shots. He had to approve what was spent, but he mostly asked if whoever needed the money could find another donor to match it. He was involved, but that involvement was by finding local actors and trusting them to use his money well.

"I really believe it is not a one-man show," Sonja Licht told me. "It was at the beginning. There was this man with a vision and this need to do something in his own country. Where he deeply belonged to although he left it as a youngster. He did have, and has until this very day, kind of a missionary part of himself. He really would like to do something that would make at least part of the world we are all living in a better place. And he enjoyed doing it as an individual." But then he brought on a board, she said, and that board evolved into subboards (Licht, for example, stepped down as director of Serbia's Open Society in 2003, but is still a member of Open Society's Roma board).

What is also unique, she said, is that "the pillars were the local foundations. In the local foundations, you had local people running the show . . . I dare to say that I don't know one single organization that has such a developed local network."[45]

Finci, who went on to be the Bosnian ambassador to Switzerland and is now president of the Jewish Community of Bosnia and Herzegovina, said largely the same thing: "He never intervened."[46]

Trbić echoed the same sentiment. Soros, she said, "has trust in people to do what is best for that particular context."[47]

But this is as much another question as it is an answer: it is Soros, with all of his money and all of his power, who is picking people—like Licht, like Finci, like Trbić—who are then in turn empowered to do what they think is best.

"I used to say he has wealth which is bigger than the GDP of Bulgaria, yes? It seems to me, then, as a critical social scientist you would want to look at how he uses that wealth . . . The kinds of figures that he's supported who have tended to run the local Open Society Foundations [are] given an awful lot of autonomy, which is a really good thing, at least he went to local elite actors," Paul Stubbs, the British sociologist based in Croatia, told me back in 2017.[48]

Still, the local actors Soros trusted, who mostly had a similar (nostalgic, left-leaning) way of looking at the world, Stubbs argued, both to me and in his writing, were given power to enhance their own personal agendas.

In some cases, they were given power to advance their personal agendas not because they believed in the concept of an open society, but because they were able to convince Soros that they did. In 1991, Macedonia (now called North Macedonia) declared its independence; Greece was scared that the new country had greater territorial aspirations. In 1992, Soros, on a visit to Macedonia on the heels of a trip to Bulgaria and believing that Macedonia was the last place in the Balkans committed to existing as a multiethnic state, announced he was adding funding to the Open Society in that country. As Connie Bruck described in her 1995 *New Yorker* profile, he did not go to Greece to get the Greek view, and overlooked concerns of Albanians, Macedonia's largest ethnic minority, who believed that, despite what the Macedonian government may have told Soros, they were being discriminated against. Soros poured money into the country, and also empowered a person who, at least in Bruck's view, was not as committed to the idea of open society as he had led Soros to believe. "The executive director of the Soros foundation in Skopje, Vladimir Milčin, maintains that he, too, is committed to the principles of an open society. But it is difficult to reconcile a dedication to pluralism with the demagogic passion that Milčin exhibits on the question of Macedonian ethnic identity," Bruck wrote.[49] Under this view of Milčin, he could be seen as the type of person Stubbs and the anthropologist Janine Wedel have described in writing as a flexian—someone who knows how to speak the language of democracy, or openness, or whatever else to the person or people who want to hear it in order to get money and power.

Also troubling was that, in the early 1990s, the local actors running Open Society Foundations in the Balkans weren't necessarily following set procedures, and they weren't necessarily transparent[50] (though Finci stressed to me that during his tenure, from 1996 to 2000, every dollar was accounted for and published),[51] meaning local actors were able to spend money without anyone necessarily checking how they were spending that money. Stubbs quotes one respondent on the foundation in Serbia as saying, "It was not possible to be transparent in a normal way. But somehow I think the most important proof that we were doing things right was that we were never accused of financial wrongdoing."

Given that this was happening during a war, the fact that books were not kept perfectly straight is understandable; but that doesn't make it right.

INTELLECTUALLY, IT SEEMED WRONG TO me that one man from abroad could have such a large role in determining who in a society was able to have a voice and a platform and tremendous sums of money with which to execute an agenda. This is one paradox of philanthropy; that, even in the giving, it reproduces inequalities, reinforcing who has the means to give and who must beg to receive. George Soros was not from Bosnia, or the former Yugoslavia, and yet he had power and influence in the society, and the certain set of people whom he was elevating were of a certain mindset and background. He put everything in the hands of Bosnians, but what if the Bosnians in whose hands he put everything misguided him, or were wrong? And what about the Bosnians in whose hands he didn't put everything? And who is George Soros to decide that this is the issue on which humanitarian aid and international attention should be spent? Why was George Soros essentially an actor in a civil war across the world? Who appointed him to give humanitarian aid?

But, then, it also seemed wrong that global inequality is so great that the badly needed money was concentrated outside the country and region, and it was. It seemed wrong that there is such a thing as a donor country, and there is. It seemed wrong that 100,000 people were killed in a war, and that as many as 50,000 were raped, and they were. It seemed wrong that anyone should need to have as their agenda "try to seem a little more human while we're being slaughtered, so we are not seen as savages by the broader international community," and they did. It seemed wrong that the accountable governments, including the United States, France, Germany, the

United Kingdom, and Russia, spent months hemming and hawing and handing one another blame during a war, and that is what happened. It seemed wrong that the inequality between my country, the mighty and bloated United States, and Bosnia and Herzegovina continues to this day; that, in 2017, the gross domestic product, or GDP, of the United States was $19.39 trillion, while the GDP of Bosnia was $18.17 billion (the population of the U.S. is roughly 100 times that of Bosnia; the GDP is over 1,067 times larger).

None of that made me any more comfortable, intellectually, with Soros being in a position to contribute $50 million toward humanitarian aid during a war. But my intellectual concerns could not have mattered less to the people I was speaking with. Were they supposed to turn down the money on principle? Go back in time to give back their jobs, turn out the lights in their hospitals, unpurify their water, submit to being filmed on television killing each other and dying without a sense that the cultural cavalry was coming? Is that what I was asking them to do?

In that moment in that office, as I thought about the ethics of wealth and the fallacy of philanthropy, it seemed wrong for me to turn back to Govedarica and say, "Actually, it isn't great and I don't know that local actors should have been able to get money from one man from abroad for textbooks and scholarships and newsprint and clean water because in a more just society no one man from abroad would have the money to be able to provide for all that." So I didn't.

THAT PEOPLE WERE TREATED LIKE animals in their own country by prying outsiders is not the only criticism of foreign behavior during the war. Some say that the war raged on longer than it should have specifically because it took other countries so long to get involved. Originally, Western leaders took to presenting the war as an inevitable result of old ethnic tensions. In 1993, British Prime Minister John Major said, "The conflict in Bosnia was a product of impersonal and inevitable forces beyond anyone's control."[52] America's own unwillingness to move similarly came out of President Clinton's belief that the war was not caused by opportunistic leaders, but by ancient hatreds. Clinton's understanding of the region was apparently informed by Robert D. Kaplan's *Balkan Ghosts*, which he interpreted to mean that the people of the region had never gotten along and the roots of this conflict were stuck in the soil of history, leading the U.S. president to pull away from the notion of "lift and strike" (lifting an arms embargo to supply Bosniaks while striking Serbian supply lines).[53]

The nationalist movements did not begin with Tito's death but with political leaders who wanted territory and, more important, power and used nationalism to get what they wanted.

The talk of the inevitability of the war prevented Western leaders, at least for a time, from acknowledging the part that they could play in ending it.

"Undoubtedly, there was a great deal of obfuscation by Western governments which were determined not to get involved," Soros said in 1995. Leaders talked of old hatreds, he said, "ignoring the fact that they had lived together for 400 years."[54]

Some suspect that, for Europeans, the religion of Bosniaks was as much an issue as the imaginary inevitability of conflict in the Balkans. "They were 'actively cleansed' at the beginning of the war on the pretext that they were religious Muslims, even fundamentalists," wrote Slavenka Drakulić, the Croatian journalist and essayist, in her book *Café Europa*. "Of course, this was not true, merely a justification for what both the Serbs and the Croats wanted to do: to scare people away from 'their' territory. It is astonishing, however, that the European states, too, behaved as if the Muslims in Bosnia were religious." Muslims in Bosnia are Slavic, she wrote, and "were given Muslim nationality in the mid-seventies by Tito in order to maintain the balance between the Serbs and Croats in Bosnia."

"For some reason, however—was it fear of the rise of Muslim fundamentalism in Europe, combined with the very convenient theory of the 'ancient hatred' of the peoples in the Balkans—it was taken as read that the Bosnian Muslims were about to establish a Muslim fundamentalist republic in the heart of Europe . . . So the Bosnian Muslims were not helped by the European states," Drakulić wrote.[55] This argument could be read as implying that Bosniaks would somehow have deserved to be left to die if they were indeed religious Muslims. Perhaps the fact that European states, too, saw the majority of the victims of the war as "other" contributed to the slowness with which they responded.

As Glenny recounts in his book, the British and French, who had contributed the majority of peacekeeping efforts to the United Nations, saw lift and strike as American cowardice—their men and women weren't actually being put at risk. Russia didn't want unilateral Western intervention in Europe and certainly didn't want it before some sort of security arrangement had been established. And thus the so-called great powers accused one another of culpability while the war raged on, and they set up six safe areas to be guarded by U.N. troops, one of which was Srebrenica.[56]

The establishment of the Bosnian-Croat Federation in 1994 also came with a new plan by representatives from Britain, France, Germany, Russia, and the United States. There would be two sections to Bosnia: the Bosnian-Croat Federation, which would make up 51 percent of the country, and also a Serbian part, Republika Srpska (literally, Serbian Republic).[57]

By December of that year, the ceasefire was collapsing. U.S. Assistant Secretary of State for European (and Canadian) Affairs Richard Holbrooke had become the man taking responsibility for

Bosnia. His assistant, Robert Frasure, managed to strike a deal with Milošević, who was growing frustrated that sanctions on Serbia over Bosnia were hurting his economy, in early summer 1995. The two came to an agreement, but Milošević insisted that, if Serbia (which was, at the time, Serbia and Montenegro) failed to comply, sanctions could only be reimposed by the U.N. secretary-general—that is, not an independent commission of three U.N. member states, as the United States wanted.

Washington rejected the deal. Srebrenica was attacked in July.[58] This, to Soros, was a major failing of the multilateral institution.

It was not the only failure of foresight by an outside institution or country. That August, Croatian forces launched an offensive against two Serb strongholds in the country, leading to an exodus of 150,000 Serbs from Croatia. Operation Storm was carried out by Croatia with the support of the United States. As Glenny noted in his book, European diplomats—among them Carl Bildt, former Swedish prime minister and the European Union's man on the former Yugoslavia—wondered whether Tudjman's cleansing of Croatia didn't set a precedent for Milošević to do the same of Albanians in Kosovo; before the millennium was up, they would be proven correct.

In the course of Operation Storm, Croatian forces also caused territorial losses for Bosnian Serbs for the first time since the war started, which, coupled with the arrival of Serb refugees from Croatia and the obvious infighting of their political leaders, darkened matters for the Bosnian Serbs. Holbrooke now went back to Milošević (encouraged by Clinton, who was encouraged by his re-election campaign) with the plan Washington had killed earlier that summer. The Bosnian Serb leaders, however, still wanted to fight, and set off a bomb in Sarajevo's marketplace on August 28. NATO, in turn, bombed Bosnian Serb positions. Milošević did not try to defend the Bosnian Serbs—not because he was crippled by the foreign military interference, but because he wanted sanctions lifted and wanted to secure the Holbrooke deal.[59]

That November, Serbia, Croatia, and Bosnia-Herzegovina signed the Dayton Agreement. Bosnia-Herzegovina was, and still is, split into the federation and the Serbian republic. The Dayton Agreement, or part of it, continues to serve as the country's constitution, under which all places at all levels of government are allocated between Bosniaks, Croats, and Serbs. What that has meant in practice is that Finci, for example, who helped get 3,000 people of different ethnicities to safety during the war, can never hold his country's highest office because he is Jewish, and so not a member of one of the three major ethnic groups that need to be represented according to the law of the land (Finci, along with a member of the Roma community, Dervo Sejdić, took this up with the European Court of Human Rights, which agreed that the constitution and certain laws discriminate against minority groups, but Bosnian lawmakers have not done anything to change that).[60]

It also means that situations like the following arise: In 2016, Božo Ljubić, a Croat politician, argued that it was unconstitutional for the House of Peoples to be made up of delegates reflecting the proportion of the main ethnic groups living in different cantons, with at least one delegate from each ethnic group. Ljubić said that this violated Dayton, arguing that appointing Croats from majority-Bosniak cantons distorted Croats' rights to legitimate representation. The Constitutional Court agreed with him. Critics, however, said that the whole thing was a ploy for Ljubić's Croatian Democratic Union of Bosnia and Herzegovina, Bosnian Croats' largest political party, better known as the HDZ, to make certain regions into a one-party state, or at least to mobilize their voters.[61]

Dayton as constitution, in other words, has codified Bosnia as a state with legally entrenched ethnonational divisions. There is no appetite in the international community to change it. Nor is there desire among the political leadership of the country—the ethnonationalist system allows them to maintain their patronage systems.

The politician in the country who knows this best is arguably Milorad Dodik, who, as leader of Republika Srpska, threatened secession. He is now the Bosnian Serb president in the country's tripartite presidency. In addition to pushing the sort of ethnonationalist politics that Soros was so worried about, he is himself a Soros conspiracy theorist, arguing that criticism of his pro-Russia policies comes from civil society groups backed by Soros, as though he couldn't possibly have generated antipathy from citizens without outside intervention.[62] As it happened, while I was in Sarajevo, Dodik was in Hungary to meet with the world's most prominent proponent of anti-Soros speech, Viktor Orbán.

AT A MEETING IN MACEDONIA in 2000, Soros told Finci that he was moving on from Bosnia, taking considerable amounts of funding from the central foundation with him. There were other pressing matters to which he wanted to attend. Finci stepped down as executive director of Open Society in his country. He suspected that Soros, in addition to wanting to turn his time, money, and attention to other things, was disappointed by the side effects of Dayton, and by how, in the country in which he had fought to preserve an open society, ethnonational lines had become entrenched. The charitable reading is that, as time passed from the war and life got better, Soros's money was less necessary; a cynical reading is that, as in South Africa and China, when things didn't go the way he'd thought they would, Soros pulled his money out.

Govedarica, one of the people I met in the OSF office in Sarajevo, took over and has been executive director in Bosnia since 2000. She later clarified that they do still get money from Open

Society. "Of course," she wrote in response to the email I sent her clarifying that they still do get OSF money. "That's how we exist. We are part of the OSF family." But there was a large budget after the war because so many needs had to be met. "As the situation improves, the money decreases."

Open Society in Bosnia and Herzegovina then, per its 2002 report, shifted so as to focus on a limited number of initiatives—education, youth participation and development, law and local governance, and the treatment of the Roma, arguably the most vulnerable minority in the country and in Europe more broadly.

Trbić and Batinić are still there, and still working toward a more open society in Bosnia and Herzegovina. But there is a sense that, for all of the good that the money during the war did, the thing that they were fighting for is gone.

"I think that today he's disappointed in Bosnia," Batinić said of Soros just before I got up to go. He paused for a beat, then added, "We all are."[63]

CHAPTER 5

Rocking the Vote

In the 1990s, much of Central and Eastern Europe was, in fits and starts, becoming more democratic, more open, and moving closer to the transatlantic community—that is, toward European Union and NATO membership. It was less than a decade after the dissolution of the Eastern Bloc, but many countries in the region appeared to be making great strides from their past into a European future.

And then there was Slovakia, which was descending quickly into authoritarianism.

By the end of the decade, Slovak civil society had decided to do something about it, mobilizing voters to reclaim a role in Slovak democracy. It was a massive movement, driven by Slovaks themselves—but funded by public and private Western European and U.S. sources.

Soros was one of those sources, but he was not the main one. And yet, when those in power—specifically, the prime minister, Vladimír Mečiar, and forces that backed him, like progovernment media—were looking for someone to blame for the challenge by civil society, they looked squarely at Soros. His actual work in the country was spun out of proportion and refracted from reality. In its place, people in power presented lies infused with antisemitism. It was one of the first times that the leader—not a fringe figure or a fading star, but the leader—of a country blamed Soros as a campaign strategy, choosing to paint Soros as a nefarious foreigner with outside influence threatening the sanctity of his own nation, so as to bolster his own political future.

But it would not be the last. Those looking for examples of how Soros conspiracy theories emerged should not overlook Slovakia. As its people fought to find their way into democracy and Europe, their prime minister tried to hold them back by blaming Soros.

THE CZECHOSLOVAK DISSIDENT MOVEMENT, LED by playwright Václav Havel, was one of the most renowned dissident movements in the Eastern Bloc. In 1977, a group of writers and dissidents from Czechoslovakia signed a petition saying that their government should respect human rights. The document became known as Charter 77, and it was a watershed moment. Many of those who signed the document went on to become prominent dissidents in the 1980s and even in the Velvet Revolution, through which Czechoslovakia reclaimed its political independence from one-party rule in 1989.[1]

Though the dissidents were intellectually independent, they received outside financial support. The Charter 77 Foundation, which funded the Czech and Slovak dissidents of Charter 77, was launched in Stockholm in the late 1970s.[2] Soros, working with Czechs and Slovaks in exile, was, by his own admission, their main source of support.[3]

Slovakia was, in general, the junior partner in Czechoslovakia. Of the 241 original signatories of Charter 77, only six were Slovak.[4]

There were far more Czechs than Slovaks in most positions of power in the country (and more Czechs than Slovaks in the general population, too), which partially explained this imbalance but they also, traditionally, had had less say in how the country was run than their Czech counterparts—and many were less invested in it, believing instead in the Slovak national cause.[5] And when the Eastern Bloc dissolved, as much as Havel, who went from writing dissident plays to being the country's first president, tried to keep Czechs and Slovaks working together, the relationship between the two dissolved.

The "Velvet Divorce"—the peaceful dissolution of Czechoslovakia into the Czech Republic and Slovakia—took effect in 1993. There were originally meant to be two legislative leaders: the Czech Václav Klaus and the Slovak Vladimír Mečiar, of the People's Party—Movement for a Democratic Slovakia (LS-HZDS), a populist Slovak party. Mečiar ran on a campaign of standing up to Prague and fighting free-market reforms. He wanted looser ties between the two republics; Klaus wanted more centralization. In July 1992, the two decided, without a referendum, that it would be better for the future of both countries to create two separate states. And so, in 1993, without a verifiable popular mandate, Mečiar became the prime minister of an independent Slovakia.[6]

The Slovaks were therefore transitioning out of socialism and also transitioning into independence. Even with a leader committed to democratic norms and values, the country would likely have struggled to create accountable institutions and an effective bureaucracy and develop and implement economic reforms.

Slovakia, of course, did not have a democratic leader. They had Mečiar.

MEČIAR CAME TO POWER BY way of free and fair elections in 1992, but, almost immediately, he began manipulating institutions and consolidating power. The state administration was politicized; the Hungarian minority was ostracized, while parliament passed legislation requiring the use of the Slovak language for official use. The government interfered with the media, firing those it deemed insufficiently loyal from government-run television. The process of privatization was rendered clientelistic, and state-owned companies were sold off to Slovak officials and Mečiar allies. Mečiar himself refused to give up ownership of the largest industries owned by the state. And Mečiar's security services were involved in kidnapping Slovak President Michal Kováč's son (the president was Mečiar's political opponent, and, conveniently, the head of the security services was a close Mečiar ally). In 1994, Mečiar was briefly ousted in a vote of no confidence, but then won parliamentary elections later that year and created an alliance with the far-right party (the Slovak National Party, or SNS) and extreme anti-reform leftists.[7]

It wasn't just that the situation inside the country was deteriorating; Slovakia's domestic political situation was changing its foreign policy orientation. Other Central European countries—the Czech Republic, Hungary, and Poland—were on track to join the European Union and NATO. But with Mečiar leading the government, Slovakia was not. In 1995, German Chancellor Helmut Kohl gave a speech calling for European Union enlargement, suggesting Hungary, Poland, and the Czech Republic as candidates. "Recent events in Slovakia have led Western Governments to complain with unusual force that this country is failing to live up to European standards of democracy," the New York Times dutifully reported that year, noting that Bratislava-based Western diplomats said Mečiar's government was "seeking to consolidate its power with undemocratic tactics." The European Union delivered a formal complaint about human rights abuses, the United States urged Slovakia's government to place "greater emphasis" on tolerance, and the European Parliament adopted a resolution that said Slovakia's government pursued "politics which show no respect for democracy, human and minority rights and the rule of law."[8]

Soros joined Western governments in sounding the alarm. "The Czechs have undoubtedly benefited from the separation from Slovakia, but the Czechs' gain has been Europe's loss," Soros said in 1995. "Mečiar is trying to align Slovakia with Russia. His ambition is to become the first outpost of a new Russian empire. If he succeeds, it bodes ill for Europe: Slovakia will become a dagger pointed at the heart of Europe."[9]

Madeleine Albright, the then–U.S. Secretary of State who was herself born in Czechoslovakia, went a rhetorical step further and famously dubbed Slovakia "a black hole in the heart of Europe."

There was, however, a saving grace for those in Slovakia who opposed Mečiar, even while its institutions became more firmly secured under Mečiar's thumb and media became politicized: civil society.

Soros was not the only source of funding for civil society, but he was a major one. In 1992, a chapter of Open Society Foundations— then the Open Society Fund—was officially registered in Slovakia. The Open Society Fund in Bratislava provided support for, among other things, NGOs and scholarships for Slovak students to study and travel.[10]

"There were hundreds of students on stipends going to, you know, foreign lands. There were publications of humanities, history books, social affairs books, foreign policy books, security studies, sociological studies published with George Soros's money," Jan Orlovsky, the current head of Slovakia's Open Society, told me in his Bratislava office over tiny cups of coffee. (The foundation is no longer part of the larger Open Society; by 2012, the Central and Eastern European foundations were made to become independent, though they could still apply for funding from

OSF. Orlovsky, however, appeared to me to still be a true believer in Open Society and its mission.)[11]

In 1994, a voluntary advocacy group of sixteen elected NGO representatives was founded. The group was called the Gremium of the Third Sector. The emergence of the Gremium of the Third Sector coincided with increased governmental pressure on civil society and came about thanks to long-term grant-making programs launched by, among others, Open Society.[12]

Open Society was not the only foundation in Slovakia at the time, but it "is the largest foundation in Slovakia's modern history," wrote Pavol Demeš in 2012. In the 1990s, Demeš had been the spokesperson for the Gremium of the Third Sector, that NGO collective. "The ruling elite's attitude toward Soros and [Open Society] has served as a relatively reliable indicator of the character of governance in Slovakia over the past two decades."[13] In other words, those governments that were unfriendly to rule of law also happened to be hostile to Soros and his foundation, because civil society, however nebulous a concept, is threatening to those who would rule over society without its active participation.

"Basically, between 1992 when our foundation was constituted until 2015 there was forty-five million dollars [of Soros's money] spent in Slovakia on six thousand plus different kinds of events, programs, projects, and I don't know how many hundreds of people who were able to travel and see the world," Orlovsky said.[14]

In February 1998, there were 14,400 civil society organizations—groups that were dedicated to holding their government accountable to rule of law and involving people in their own democratic process—registered in Slovakia.[15] But even with all of those NGOs and civil society groups, the government was becoming increasingly illiberal, and it was unclear what could be done about Mečiar leading into the 1998 Slovak parliamentary elections.

"There seemed to be no hope. Opposition was fragmented,

media was oppressed. Civil society was strong thanks to help from Western democracy, and specifically the United States," Marek Kapusta, now a consultant in Slovakia, told me. "Everyone knew . . . this was really [an] extremely important milestone."[16]

But within that less-than-auspicious framework, there was a movement coalescing. From the perspective of civil society actors, it would be a campaign to save the civic soul of Slovakia. It would also mark one of the first times that Soros's philanthropic actions would be significantly manipulated by a person in power to achieve political ends.

KAPUSTA HAD PARTICIPATED IN VOTER drives in Bosnia after the war in 1996 "as a volunteer in Eastern Europe that would help [the Organisation for Security and Co-operation in Europe] to organize elections after the war so there would be conditions for political reconciliation and refugees to come home."

The experience changed him, he said, and "after that I started to actively organize trips to Bosnia . . . I really managed to build quite a substantial team of Slovaks that went to Bosnia. Every other mission was bigger and bigger and bigger. We had a pool of people that were experienced, that were well trained, that were motivated to participate in elections. And then," Kapusta said, "I got a phone call."

The call was from a U.S.-based foundation—the Foundation for a Civil Society, now known as the Pontis Foundation; Open Society was a funder, providing $5,300 for a Rock the Vote bus tour. "They told me they viewed [Slovakia's 1998 elections] as important and they wanted to build turnout."

And so Kapusta got involved in the Slovak Rock the Vote campaign, modeled after youth-focused campaigns in the United States of the same name.[17] The Rock the Vote campaign was only one part of the push from civil society—funded and with know-how from abroad—to increase voter turnout. Most of the campaigns were organized under an umbrella movement called Civic Campaign OK '98.

"OK stands for civic campaign [in Slovak]," Demeš told me. "This ethos that we created—it will be okay in '98 because we citizens will step in."[18] The framework for OK '98 was discussed and adopted by Third Sector's founding NGOs in January 1998. In March of that year, over fifty civic leaders issued a statement about the upcoming election.

"Slovakia is currently at a critical stage in its development. Citizens feel that their votes cannot alter developments in society. For this reason, it is enormously important that we take responsibility for our own future in the coming elections," they wrote. "We declare that, in the case that anyone attempts to disrupt the democratic process in Slovakia, we will make use of our constitutional right to resist these attempts, together with representatives of trade unions, churches, local governments and other democratic forces."[19]

The idea was that if people were informed and involved, things would work out for Slovakia; if they didn't get involved, they wouldn't be able to prevent the descent into a more authoritarian society. The organizers faced a broadly cynical society. Two months before the election, over 50 percent of the population believed Mečiar would win again. Mečiar seemed to control everything, and the population had descended into apathy; how could those who hadn't take their country back?

OK '98 managed to gain the attention of around 70 percent of Slovakia's citizens and included education and information campaigns as well as media and election monitoring. Women, seniors, and members of the Roma population—a historically marginalized and politically disenfranchised minority in the country—were targeted during the campaign to encourage voting.[20]

The campaign was driven by Slovak volunteers—but Western Europeans and American public and private sources provided both financial support and knowledge. Open Society provided funding, too.

"I think the role of OSF was trying to provide some kind of umbrella to some of these activities—most of the meetings of these different players who were participating in the framework of those activities took place in OSF," Rasťo Kužel of MEMO 98, a media-monitoring project established ahead of the 1998 elections, told me, later adding, "The foundation [for a civil society] was basically built thanks to Soros."[21]

While Open Society funded various 1998 campaigns—Soros himself wrote in 2003, "My foundations contributed to democratic regime change in Slovakia in 1998"—it was by no means the main funder.

"As far as I can recall—of course I knew about Soros Foundation, they were very prominent and a very important donor in the country at the time," Kapusta said. "But I don't remember them being actively involved at the beginning" of Rock the Vote. "I think eventually the Soros Foundation . . . supported our campaign with a grant amounting around ten thousand dollars."[22]

Rock the Vote was inherently political, although it wasn't partisan. "I think that was the first seed when organizations like OSF were seen as political, not as civil society organizations," Orlovsky said.[23]

Kapusta said the Rock the Vote campaign received between $150,000 and $160,000. So $10,000 from Open Society was hardly a major donation. Most of the funding, Kapusta said, was from public, not private, sources.

And it wasn't just that Open Society wasn't central to the campaigns—the campaigns weren't central to Open Society, which was, for the most part, spending its money in Slovakia elsewhere.

Nevertheless, when it came time for Mečiar to lash out in response to OK '98 and the efforts by civil society to increase voter turnout, he pointed his finger directly at Soros and Open Society. It was one of the first times that the head of a government used a conspiracy theory about George Soros as cover for his illiberalism, and that a person in that position blamed Soros for his citizens' discontent. Though the people of Slovakia could not know it, it was to be the first of many.

AT THE TIME, SOROS CONSPIRACY theories, like the one pushed by István Csurka back in the early 1990s in Hungary, were, for the most part, not the sort of thing that prime ministers participated in. There were exceptions, like Milošević and Tudjman, both of whom lashed out at Open Society. And there were some government officials in Central and Eastern Europe in the early 1990s who cast various antisemitic aspersions on Soros and CEU. For the most part, though, it wasn't what heads of state did.

Mečiar's case is significant because he was the leader of a European country who decided to use his platform and power to go after Soros and Open Society to discredit expressions of discontent and to prevent political change. In hindsight, it looks like an aspiring authoritarian was perfecting the handbook for his illiberal heirs; at the time, Mečiar attacking a Jewish-American philanthropist was one more piece of evidence that he didn't quite belong to the European club and was trying to keep his country from fully joining the Western, democratic, liberal European family of nations; attacking Soros was not, at the time, how things were done.

Mečiar, who wanted to consolidate power and who relied on popular complacency, perceived Soros, a person funding and encouraging civil society in Slovakia, as a threat. In 1995, Soros suggested Slovakia was not yet ready for EU or NATO membership because of Mečiar's authoritarian leanings. That same year, Mečiar went on the offensive, attacking Soros. "Ignoring the millions in scholarships and medical equipment Mr. Soros has given Slovakia, the Government moved to declare him persona non grata," a *New York Times* article from that August read. "Mr. Meciar pursued the attack last week by awarding a top journalism prize to an anti-Semitic magazine that regularly runs cartoons of Mr. Soros wearing a yarmulke."[24] A yarmulke itself is not an antisemitic symbol, but to put one atop the head of a secular Jewish man so as to smear him in the eyes of citizens is an antisemitic act.

In 1998, Mečiar's HZDS, as well as the SNS, attacked Americans for meddling in Slovakia's internal affairs, but the American most targeted by Mečiar and company was George Soros.

"These allegations, [the] labeling started first on the state television. We were called CIA agents funded by Soros. Particularly the newspaper of the then ruling party . . . it really had very negative articles about us," said Kužel, the head of MEMO 98. To a degree, the idea that Americans were meddling in internal affairs and that Soros was contributing to the campaign to democratically check Mečiar was grounded in reality.

"I mean, we were benefiting basically from all US donors' assistance. I don't mean only financial. Slovakia didn't have—there was no experience with activism, with NGOs. It was very important to bring this type of ideas, this type of activities to Slovakia," Kužel admitted.[25]

Even so, while Open Society did provide some funding, support for civil society, and meeting places for organizations, the idea that Soros was orchestrating Mečiar's ousting was fabricated in order to render the Slovak citizens mobilizing for change illegitimate. And yet Mečiar clung to and tried to propagate that notion.

In part, Mečiar picked Soros as an adversary because Soros was a known entity; not only had he broken the Bank of England six years earlier, but, for over a decade, he had poured money into Central and Eastern Europe through his foundations. The Slovak foundation had been in Slovakia providing money and support for civil society since 1992. But Open Society and Soros supported human rights and an open society—concepts still distrusted by some in Slovakia, who, again, were just getting used to the idea of living differently. (Support came for more mundane projects, too. Kapusta, who was director of Slovakia's Open Society for five years in the 2000s, noted that Soros also provided funding for computers in Slovakia's Ministry of Health and the first internet connections to Slovak primary schools, but "of course this is not what people talk about.")[26]

But it wasn't just that he gave a lot of money to various causes. Soros wasn't the average philanthropical-minded billionaire; he had an ideology that he actively pursued.

"If you look at all other donors—they were very neutral. And leaders of these foundations were rather invisible. People didn't care who's the president of this foundation or that foundation," Demeš said, citing the Rockefeller and Ford Foundations as examples. Soros, by comparison, didn't just want to quietly write a check. He was meeting political leaders and sometimes challenging them, and writing books, one of which was titled *Underwriting Democracy* and dealt with his adventures in trying to open Central and Eastern Europe.[27]

"I think it is very unusual [for a] philanthropist . . . he wanted to be heard and wanted his views of life to be applied to countries, particularly countries that went through reform processes, in Central and Eastern Europe," Demeš added.[28]

"The only people who were against George Soros at the time were the politicians who were running the country. Because they felt, we don't need any different views. We are the consensus," said Orlovsky. Mečiar's vision for Slovakia was that of a majority-ruled nation-state, whereas Soros, per Orlovsky, "said, no, nation-states were the plague of this part of the world. This is stupid."[29]

Mečiar wasn't making up that Soros was philanthropically involved in the country; he was. Mečiar wasn't wrong in his conviction that Soros had a different vision for how Slovakia could be; he did. Mečiar wasn't even lying when he said that Soros was helping those who were trying to make that vision a reality; he was. The lie was that, in Mečiar's portrayal, it was Mečiar versus Soros, and not Mečiar versus the people of Slovakia, who had their own agency and agenda but were aided by Soros and Open Society, among others.

It also helped that Soros, being Hungarian-born, U.S.-based, and, critically, Jewish, was practically ready-made for manipulation in Slovakia's collective imagination. "Just imagine a kind of average Slovak voter, where you combine a Jew, a Hungarian, and a wealthy businessman. This is a bogeyman," said Daniel Milo, a senior research fellow at the Bratislava-based GLOBSEC Policy Institute. "You could not create a more cartoonish type of bogeyman."[30]

Some Slovaks were, and are, suspicious of Hungarians, the largest ethnic minority in their country; some Slovaks were, and are, suspicious of anyone too fully in the thrall of capitalism; and some Slovaks were, and are, deeply suspicious of Jews. As elsewhere in the region, the complicated and in many cases tragic history of the Jewish people (or any minority group, for that matter) is seen as of secondary importance to the plight of the main ethnonational group, concerned as it is with its own painful path. To grapple with the fate of the Jewish people would be to admit their own complicity in it, and it can be difficult to hold the dual identities of victim and oppressor in one's national narrative. In

2019, only 32 percent of Slovaks saw Holocaust denial as a problem, and only 20 percent considered antisemitism a problem;[31] this despite the fact that a neo-Nazi party was sitting in the Slovak parliament.[32]

"The fact that Mr. Soros is Jewish, that's also adding to this kind of stereotype," conceded Kapusta.

THE ATTACKS ON SOROS WEREN'T enough to save Mečiar. He may have thought that fearmongering or making people think that those mobilizing in the streets were there solely because of outside influence would keep him in power; it did not. "This [the successful voter mobilization] was really the first time for us," Kapusta said, referring to Rock the Vote and other movements of 1998. "And that's why it worked so well. Mečiar completely underestimated potential impact of this."[33]

Eighty-four percent of Slovakia's voters turned out in the 1998 elections. Mečiar was ousted.[34]

Slovakia did not make it into NATO in 1999 with the Czech Republic, Hungary, and Poland, but it did manage to join in 2004. The black hole of Europe wasn't a black hole at all; it was a country full of people who decided, in 1998, that they, not Mečiar, would determine the direction in which their country was headed.

The 1998 elections also made it clear that Soros was a tempting imagined adversary for powerful political leaders who were losing their strong hold on their country.

Mečiar could have lashed out at anyone—his actual political opponents, EU officials, Madeleine Albright. But he didn't focus on those running against him and risk building up their stature or profile in the process. He didn't focus on institutions or individuals who were empowered to control his country's political future. He focused on Soros. And though he lost power, he won the creation of a powerful bogeyman.

Just over a week after the elections, a progovernment newspaper published a cartoon of Demeš in which the Third Sector spokesperson was lounging back and smoking a cigar emblazoned with the word "Soros."[35]

CHAPTER 6

To Baltimore

Originally, George Soros focused his philanthropic efforts on those societies he thought needed to be opened, not on countries that could already be considered open. For its first decade, Open Society Foundations (then the Open Society Institute) focused on what was happening abroad, not on the United States.

But that changed when the Iron Curtain fell and the Cold War faded into history's rearview mirror. "By 1995, I felt that we had done enough on the first point of our agenda, opening up closed societies, so that we could pass on to the second, making open societies more viable," Soros wrote in 2011. "The activities of the Open Society Foundations were concentrated in foreign countries; it was time to do something at home."[1]

The "something" at home was focused in part on reforming U.S. drug policy—and, with it, the U.S. criminal justice system. In the 1990s, that meant trying to make room in a political space that was primarily occupied—by members of both parties—by people who disagreed with Soros and Open Society. Soros believed that drug addiction was a medical issue that was being treated by politicians as a criminal one to the detriment of society.

Soros's early work on drug policy and criminal justice, which was centered in Baltimore, Maryland, encapsulates Soros and his approach to philanthropy: he committed early on, with foresight and political courage and conviction, to something because he believed it was right, and because he believed that the mainstream way of thinking about the matter was myopic and politically cowardly.

But his early work on drug policy and criminal justice reform, and what came out of it, also raises some of the central tensions of philanthropy: Does philanthropy forever reinforce who is in a position to give and who is in a position to receive? Can those who are not vulnerable reform a system for those who are? And can those in positions of power be trusted to reform a system sufficiently?

IN LATE FEBRUARY 1996, SOROS invited eight distinguished individuals to his Bedford, New York, estate to discuss what he and Open Society might do in the United States. The eight, according to Michael Kaufman's biography of Soros, were Open Society's president, Aryeh Neier; Bard College President Leon Botstein; philosophers Alan Ryan, T. M. Scanlon, and Bernard Williams; political theorist Seyla Benhabib; professor David Rothman of Columbia University; and Ethan Nadelmann, a former Princeton professor who had written on the folly of treating drug addiction as a criminal issue instead of a medical one. The guests talked in part about socioeconomic divisions in cities, rising prison populations, failed drug policies, and the lack of support and resources for families and communities most affected by drug policies.

The "war on drugs" was declared by President Richard Nixon in 1971. The Drug Policy Alliance (Soros, it should be noted, is on the board—the Alliance is the outgrowth of the center Nadelmann founded back in the early 1990s) points to an increase in the size of federal drug control agencies and a push for mandatory sentencing as battles Nixon won early on in the war.

It also points to Nixon aide John Ehrlichman, who later admitted, "You want to know what this was really all about? The Nixon campaign in 1968, and the Nixon White House after that, had two enemies: the antiwar left and black people. You understand what I'm saying. We knew we couldn't make it illegal to be either against the war or black, but by getting the public to associate the hippies with marijuana and blacks with heroin, and then criminalizing both heavily, we could disrupt those communities. We could arrest their leaders, raid their homes, break up their meetings, and vilify them night after night on the evening news. Did we know we were lying about the drugs? Of course we did."

In 1977, President Jimmy Carter was inaugurated after campaigning on a promise to decriminalize marijuana. But parents across the country were worried about teen marijuana use, and so that particular campaign promise was left unfulfilled.

In the 1980s, President Ronald Reagan expanded the war on drugs. Reagan's wife, Nancy, had her famous "Just Say No" anti-drug campaign. Los Angeles Police Chief Daryl Gates, who said that casual drug users should be shot, founded the D.A.R.E. education program (D.A.R.E. stands for Drug Abuse Resistance Education; when we learned it in my elementary school in the 1990s, the curriculum included a song in which D stood for "I won't do drugs" and A for "won't have an attitude," which is the entirety of what stuck with me from D.A.R.E.).

The problem with "Just Say No" is that programs that would have made drug use safer—like those that provided access to clean syringes—were seen as enabling drug use, not potentially saving lives. And so those programs were cut, and more people died. From 1985 to 1989, the percentage of Americans who believed drug use was the number-one issue grew from 2–6 percent to 64 percent. The next year, that percentage dropped significantly, but as the Drug Policy Alliance put it, the policies that created that fear remained in place even after the interest waned.

While Nixon started the war on drugs and Reagan dramatically expanded it, to present this as a Republican issue would be unfair and untrue. It wasn't just that Republicans were tough on crime and believed drug use should be criminalized; it was that this was mainstream political thought.

Consider, for example, President Bill Clinton's administration. The Democratic president, who admitted to smoking marijuana but claimed he didn't inhale, and who campaigned on treatment instead of incarceration, rejected a U.S. Sentencing Commission recommendation that would have eliminated the difference in sentencing for powder cocaine (a drug for rich white people) and crack (associated with use by black people). He rejected Health and Human Services Secretary Donna Shalala's recommendation to end the federal ban on syringe access. The 1994 Crime Bill, which Clinton signed into law, increased incarceration, and also encouraged states to build prisons in which those sentenced served at least 85 percent of their sentence.[2]

It wasn't only Bill Clinton. In 1996, his wife, Hillary, who would go on to be a New York senator, secretary of state, and Democratic presidential candidate, said, "We need to take these people on, they are often connected to big drug cartels, they are not just gangs of kids anymore. They are often the kinds of kids that are called superpredators. No conscience. No empathy. We can talk about why they ended up that way but first we have to bring them to heel."[3] And Joe Biden, a Democratic senator from Delaware, partly authored the 1994 law, in addition to other punitive legislation in the 1980s. When he ran for president in the 2008 Democratic primary (ultimately losing the nomination to Barack Obama, for whom he would serve as vice president), his campaign touted the 1994 law as the "Biden crime law."[4] (In 2019, Biden, a candidate for the Democratic nomination once again, unveiled a crime policy at odds with the 1994 bill; his new plan would decriminalize marijuana, get rid of mandatory minimum sentences for nonviolent crimes, and discourage the incarceration of children, among other measures.)[5]

On both sides of the political aisle, drug use was seen as a criminal issue, not a medical one, and even as the prison population swelled—according to the Drug Policy Alliance, the number of people in prison for nonviolent drug offenses increased from 50,000 in 1980 to over 400,000 in 1997—more incarceration was still seen as the answer by high-profile, powerful politicians.[6]

Soros, even before the Bedford convening, had already recognized the need to right what he saw as the wrong of America's drug policies. Soros authored an article in 1988 (advocating for the creation of an international currency) published in the same issue of *Foreign Policy* as an article on drug policy, which he read with interest. He contacted its author, the aforementioned Ethan Nadelmann, who, in 1993 and with Soros's financial backing, established a center whose mission was "harm reduction," or "an alternative approach to drug policy and treatment that focuses on minimizing the adverse effects of both drug use and drug prohibition."

In 1996, after the Bedford meeting, Soros brought the work of reforming U.S. drug policy in-house. Open Society's American programs were established, and Gara LaMarche, who had worked for Neier at the American Civil Liberties Union and Helsinki Watch, was brought on to be the director in New York.[7]

In 1998, an office—the only U.S.-based Open Society field office—was also opened in Baltimore, a city that was as impacted as any by America's failing drug and criminal justice policies. It was not a coincidence that Baltimore's mayor had a mind to do things differently.[8]

The Influence of Soros

KURT SCHMOKE BECAME THE FIRST African-American mayor of Baltimore in 1987. Shortly thereafter he became the first mayor of a major U.S. city to openly challenge the idea of treating drug addiction as a criminal matter. He called for decriminalization of drugs and said that a public health issue should be handled by public health authorities. At the time, drug addiction was handled across the country by law enforcement and prosecutors.

"During the course of the five years that I was the chief prosecutor, I came to feel that there were more people that were hooked on drug money than hooked on drugs," Schmoke told me over the phone in August 2019. "The whole drug war started more and more to remind me of the way we tried to become an alcohol-free America back in the 1920s."

Then a good friend of his—a police officer by the name of Marty Ward—was killed while working undercover. Ward was wearing a wire. "I had to listen to him die over and over," Schmoke said. "It just struck me that the man who shot and killed Marty was more interested in money than he was in getting high." Schmoke wanted to reduce the appetite for drugs. And the way to do that, he realized, was not through the criminal justice system, but through public health.[9]

It makes a certain amount of sense that mass incarceration and the failings of the criminal justice system would be addressed through drug policy, Nicole Porter, director of advocacy at the Washington, D.C.–based Sentencing Project (which has received money from Open Society), told me over the phone in August 2019. In the 1980s and 1990s, "we were in the midst of the drug war," she said. The language around crack use in particular fed into "the general conversation around the war on drugs, increasing drug use . . . so many people thirty years ago, twenty-five years ago got prison terms."[10]

Mass incarceration was justified by the war on drugs. Ending mass incarceration meant fighting a battle against the war on drugs.

Schmoke and his team managed to set up a needle-exchange program, following which HIV incidence among drug users who participated was down 70 percent compared to those who did not. His team also changed how drug treatment centers were operated after the city's health commissioner, Peter Beilenson, pretended to be a drug addict to experience firsthand how horribly those who went to the centers were treated.[11]

Beilenson joined the mayor's team in 1992, served as health commissioner until 2005, and "worked on changing the semantics of his drug policy from legalizing to ethicalizing," he told me in August 2019 over the phone from California, where he now serves as director of Sacramento County's Department of Health Services. Schmoke, he said, was "very prescient."

In some senses, Baltimore was an unusual choice to be Open Society's only American field office. "It's not usually an out-front city," Beilenson said. "We don't have a lot of Fortune 500 companies. We get movies late."[12]

But Baltimore had Schmoke, and Schmoke had Ethan Nadelmann. Nadelmann reached out to Schmoke after Schmoke's first public comments about the need to consider an alternative to the war on drugs. He gave Schmoke information on efforts to change the war in the United States, Europe, and Canada. "I developed a good friendship with Ethan," Schmoke said.

Nadelmann invited Schmoke to a dinner at Soros's apartment. There were, in Schmoke's recollection, some ten to twelve people there. "We talked about drug policy and a number of other urban issues," Schmoke told me. But they didn't talk about Baltimore in particular.[13]

In 1998, Baltimore was the only major American city that looked at drug abuse as a public health matter, as opposed to (or, rather, in addition to, since drug-related arrests didn't stop) a criminal one. And so Soros and company chose it as the location for the only U.S.-based Open Society field office. Under the leadership of

Diana Morris, previously executive director of the Blaustein Philanthropic Group and a program officer at the Ford Foundation, the Open Society Institute–Baltimore focused on addiction, lack of support for Baltimore's inner-city youth, and, as Chuck Sudetic, author of *The Philanthropy of George Soros*, put it, "the criminal justice system's overreliance on incarceration."[14]

THE OFFICE FIRST TRIED TO draw attention to the idea that treatment was a cost-effective way to keep people and communities alike healthy, and then tried to raise funding for treatment.

It also helped support programs that had already been established, whose leaders saw the issue in a manner similar to Soros. Beilenson, individuals at Johns Hopkins University's public health school, and the University of Maryland Hospital's Christopher Welsh, a psychiatrist, worked together to use the city's needle-exchange program to train drug users to recognize an overdose and inject other users with Narcan, a drug that can stop overdoses.[15]

The program, Welsh told me over the phone in August 2019, had gotten started independent of Open Society, which was "roped in" later on. Now, he explained, programs like the one they were working on are more common, but "when it was initially started—it was actually very unique . . . when it first started, it was its own thing." Open Society helped bolster it at a time when, in the political mainstream, such programs were seen as promoting heroin use. In actuality, the Baltimore program was saving lives—the number of overdose deaths in the city was down to the levels of the mid-1990s by 2008.[16]

"That was something that had an impact nationally. We showed that you could decrease the spread of AIDS without increasing drug use," Schmoke told me. "It still, unfortunately, didn't change federal drug policy as much as we'd hoped," he added, but "it did have an impact in paving the way for other cities to do innovative programs without fearing people labeling them as being soft on crime, soft on drugs."[17]

Even so, Welsh expressed frustration to me that the program didn't grow the way it should have. The city's model program run by the health department was widely copied. But the health department was also "subject to all the politics and red tape of the health department," Welsh said, also noting that the program was frozen for a while because those in power were worried about the optics of it.[18]

IN ADDITION TO MAKING TREATMENT more accessible and reducing deaths by overdose, the Open Society Institute–Baltimore worked to put forth alternatives to incarceration, on which the criminal justice system heavily relied and which predominantly affected African-American men (who were also less likely to be released on parole than white men).

For example, the Open Society Institute–Baltimore gave grants to George Washington University and the JFA Institute (which works with federal, state, and local government agencies and with philanthropic organizations to assess criminal justice practices and propose policy solutions) to encourage Maryland to reform the state's parole system. It funded the Maryland Public Safety Compact, a program signed off on by community organizations and the state to shorten the prison stay of some felons and to work with them on drug addiction and treatment. It gave tens of millions to after-school programs so that children would have somewhere to go in the early evenings.[19]

Open Society also gave grants and fellowships to individuals and local advocacy groups for smaller projects that worked, if not directly on drug policy, then on alternatives to incarceration. One of the first fellows, Lauren Abramson, worked to design for Baltimore a reconciliation process based on work done with New Zealand's Maori people. Participants in the program come together to discuss the event over which they disagree, talk about how the situation has impacted them, and work to come to a solution.[20]

"We were trying to show that there's a different way to do justice," Abramson told me over the phone in August 2019. "We were asking the current system to forgo their cases, which is kind of like their bread and butter . . . In many ways, we were up against the prevailing system." Soros's money, she said, was "a good infusion for Baltimore." Soros is obviously rich and powerful; he is also obviously white. He was, with this project, coming into a community that was predominantly poor and nonwhite.

I asked Abramson what she made of the money coming from someone with outsized, outside influence.

Her criticism was with philanthropy more generally, she told me. "There's issues around philanthropy in this country that are separate . . . Wealthy people should be taxed." (Actually, she noted, "one of the first people I heard talking about a critique of philanthropy in the United States was somebody OSI brought into Baltimore to talk about it.")

"It's to me a separate issue in some ways" from Open Society and Soros in particular, which she saw as a boon to Baltimore. "I can see a lot of programs in the city that were seeded by this community fellowship program."[21]

"It would be one thing if it were paternalistic and imposing requirements," Peter Beilenson, the health commissioner at the time the Open Society–Baltimore started, told me when I asked him the same question.

"It was much more along the lines of . . . it opened the playing field for trying new things. Did he have an outsized influence? Yes. Particularly for someone from outside Baltimore." But, he added,

"We were able to do a lot of things that we would not have been able to do."[22]

Schmoke said largely the same: "It was clear to me that he recognized that his investment by itself wasn't going to solve the problem." But the idea was to set up a group that could serve as a catalyst for people interested in drug policy and how it "affected urban life."[23]

There's also the reality that people working to reform drug policy and the criminal justice system need to eat. "It is work that needs to be funded. The people doing this work have to support themselves and eat. The way to do that has been to raise money through philanthropy," Nicole Porter said. "We do live in a capitalist country . . . These are the realities that activists and community advocates are bumping up against."[24]

IN 2000, OPEN SOCIETY HELD its national board meeting in Baltimore. Soros spent the earlier part of the day telling reporters that his sidekick, Stanley Druckenmiller, the man who had run his hedge fund, Quantum, for twelve years, would be resigning. Quantum was down 21 percent for the year that year. After his press conference, Soros headed to Baltimore, where he went to the Living Classrooms Foundation and chatted with four sixteen-year-old boys, asking about how much money there was in drug running.

He then spoke with Beilenson, who told Soros what he had told the other visitors earlier in the day. The city, now under a new mayor, Martin O'Malley, had not found the funds needed to expand the pilot programs Open Society was funding. Beilenson had asked for $25 million in state aid. Maryland's governor had approved $8 million.[25]

(Beilenson, for his part, remembers the day "very clearly."

Soros, he said, was "quite personable. I was kind of surprised.")[26]

When, during that visit, O'Malley toasted Soros, saying, "I just want to say that you had the leadership and courage to invest in this city when others were not wise enough," and mentioned in his speech the governor's partial funding of drug treatment, Soros said, "I wish to express my disappointment at the grant that the mayor referred to. I am less of a politician than he is . . . we have shown that there is a way of dealing with the problems of drugs that had not been tried at the time. If we could get 60,000 people into treatment we would have real statistics. There has to be a systematic approach to the problem."[27]

The incident works as a representation of the shortcomings of philanthropy in the criminal justice reform space. Donor money is a start, and it allows advocates and activists to do what they wouldn't otherwise be able to do. "The elected officials by themselves can't solve the problem," Schmoke told me. "This is a multifaceted issue. It needs all hands on deck. It was very helpful that he made the investment that he did."[28] But philanthropy alone can't get governments at the local, state, and federal level to work in tandem. Philanthropy alone isn't enough to reform police departments. Philanthropy alone can't address the racist underpinnings of the U.S. criminal justice system. It alone can't get people to change popular attitudes. "Even today, there continues to be a disproportionate response to crime," Nicole Porter, from the Sentencing Project, told me, adding, "even something that might be relatively minor might elicit the general response of, throw the book at somebody." But philanthropy alone can make political actors think that they've done something, when in fact what they're toasting is a grant that's but a third of what was requested.

Confusing the celebration of small steps with meaningful change continues to be a problem, said Jonathan Blanks, a research associate in the Project on Criminal Justice at the Cato

Institute, a think tank founded as the Charles Koch Foundation and distinctly libertarian in bent (criminal justice being one of the issues on which libertarians and liberals have found a way to work together). Coalitions, funded in part by philanthropists, provide cover for politicians, and can get some momentum, but it only goes so far. Take the First Step Act, he told me, sitting in his office in front of a sign that read I'D RATHER BE DIVISIVE THAN INDECISIVE. The First Step Act, aimed at federal criminal justice reform, was passed in 2018. It sought to address punitive prison sentences at the federal level by allowing earlier release. It was touted by some as a major breakthrough.[29] In reality, Blanks told me, it's "a drop in the bucket." The vast majority of people in prison in the United States are not in federal prison. The act is only what its name says—a first step. But it is not clear when the next step will be taken, or what it will be.[30]

"I think back then, I thought we were about reforming that system," Abramson, the woman who brought the Maori reconciliation process to Baltimore, told me. "I've realized that system—I don't think can really be reformed. It has to be changed." Later, she clarified via email that she didn't mean the system isn't working—it's working exactly as it was designed to work. "Reform won't fix it," she wrote. "It needs to be redesigned so that it can provide equal access to fair justice that focuses on healing and accountability."[31]

IN 2019, INCARCERATION IN MARYLAND dropped to its lowest point since the 1980s. Experts credited 2016's Justice Reinvestment Act, which aimed at sending nonviolent offenders from prison into drug treatment and other programs, as well as a reduction of arrests in Baltimore City that's taken place since the early 2000s.

I asked Soros if, looking back on his work in the drug policy space and debates on the subject now, he considered himself ahead of the curve.

"My view has always been based on the recognition that drug addiction is an insoluble problem. You cannot eradicate drug use and only a fraction of drug users become dangerously addicted. The war on drugs caused more harm than drug use by itself. We advocated the principle of harm reduction," he wrote. "I am heartened to see today that the principle is widely applied—this is doubtlessly due to the work that advocates have done over decades to address misconceptions and build greater understanding about the drug issue. Clearly, we were ahead of the curve. But due to ill-conceived policies, including those of the Trump administration, we have a worse drug addiction crisis than ever before. So, our work is hardly over."

It's true: the work isn't over, in criminal justice generally or drug policy specifically. Incarceration is still racialized. As of January 2019, 71 percent of people in Maryland prisons were black.[32]

But, then, the way the United States—including those in the highest positions of political power—thinks about criminal justice is still racialized, and racist. Language around addiction has changed in large part due to the opioid epidemic—the victims of which are largely white. "I've been pleased to listen to elected officials—many elected officials—at the state, local, and national level who've talked about these issues more," Schmoke told me, adding, "I recognize that all of that unfortunately has to do with the opioid epidemic and the recognition by public officials that this is not just an inner-city problem of people of color."[33]

And where people of color, and in particular black Americans, are concerned, the criminal justice system is still violent and unforgiving—police killings are a leading cause of death for young black men in America. The language that is used to describe predominantly black communities is still violent and unforgiving, too.[34] In 2019, President Donald Trump, while attacking Representative Elijah Cummings for criticizing the president's immigration policies, tweeted, "Rep, Elijah Cummings has been a brutal bully, shouting and screaming at the great men & women of Border Patrol about conditions at the Southern Border, when actually his Baltimore district is FAR WORSE and more dangerous. His district is considered the Worst in the USA. . . . . As proven last week during a Congressional tour, the Border is clean, efficient & well run, just very crowded. Cumming District is a disgusting, rat and rodent infested mess. If he spent more time in Baltimore, maybe he could help clean up this very dangerous & filthy place."[35]

This is directly antithetical to the concept of an open society. A society in which one group of people is disproportionately more likely to be locked up and killed by the people meant to keep peace therein, a society in which some people in power dismiss out of hand the concerns of others who would participate in it, is hardly a society in which everyone has an equitable chance at participation.

I asked Nicole Porter what we get wrong, still, not just about drug policy, but about mass incarceration. The U.S. criminal justice system was designed, she told me, to "socially control formerly enslaved residents; checking liberty [and] criminalization of behavior evolved and expanded to strengthen and reinforce that control."

"If the country and if advocates don't work to undo that underlying feature of the United States criminal justice system, and don't work to engage directly with it and find solutions that directly confront that racist, racialized punishment," she said, "then we won't be genuinely undoing mass incarceration in the United States."[36]

SOROS CONTINUED, AND CONTINUES, TO fund advocates in the drug policy and criminal justice space. The Open Society Institute–Baltimore is also still up and running, and, separate from his foundation work, Soros has backed progressive prosecutors in their district attorney races—individuals who vow to reform the criminal justice system from within.[37] This is an indication that Soros, too, recognizes that drug policy in and of itself is not enough, and that criminal justice more broadly needs to be reformed. It has also been fodder for his critics, who argue, as Michele Hanisee, the president of the Association of Los Angeles Deputy District Attorneys, did in 2018, that Soros is attempting to "buy the criminal justice system" to push his agenda of radical reform.[38]

Back when he got involved in Baltimore, Soros was more rarely accused of trying to buy politicians to push through his reforms. But that was about to change. His philanthropic foray into U.S. policy decisions was, it turned out, a prelude to his entry into the American political sphere: specifically, the 2004 U.S. presidential election.

CHAPTER 7

The Elections of 2004

For the first two decades of his time as a philanthropist, Soros remained largely nonpartisan. That is not to say that his work was apolitical; anything about the way in which people in society live can theoretically be considered political. Democratic participation, civic efficacy, greater voter information—these are not apolitical concepts. But they do not belong to one political party or group. And Soros was not in the business of privileging one political party over the other. That may be why, in the 1990s, George Soros and his philanthropic efforts were mostly positively received around the world. There were exceptions, of course, but he was broadly seen as a benefactor, provider, and progressive; he was perceived as helping move society forward in a nonpartisan manner.

The turn of the century brought a turn of fortune for Soros on both sides of the Atlantic, not in terms of pecuniary position, but in public perception. It was, he would learn, one thing to be a progressive philanthropist, and quite another to play politics. Soros wanted to personally open society. In 2004, he was perceived as the personal antagonist to those who he thought threatened to keep it closed, including some very high-profile politicians; their conviction was only strengthened by Soros's newfound involvement in partisan politics.

THROUGH HIS FOUNDATIONS, GEORGE SOROS had been involved in philanthropy in the United States for nearly a decade. In the run-up to the 2004 United States presidential election, however, he became involved politically in a distinctly personal and partisan way. His political involvement was his own; it was not through Open Society. But his involvement in partisan politics impacted the way some people perceived his philanthropy.

The September 11, 2001, attacks by al-Qaeda killed nearly 3,000 people; Soros watched the towers fall on television during a trip to Beijing. "I was coming from Mongolia," he recalled in 2004. "And my son called me and told me, 'Switch on your television.' And I actually saw the second plane crash into the tower. So it's—even though you are in Beijing, it's like being there, so it has the same impact."[1]

The attacks marked the starting point for then-President George W. Bush's war on terror, which included ignoring the United Nations charter and invading Iraq to oust Saddam Hussein[2] over weapons of mass destruction that it was later proven he did not possess; torturing suspected terrorist ring leaders; and passing the Patriot Act, which authorized, among other things, indefinite detention of immigrants and broad new surveillance policies. "Every nation, in every region, now has a decision to make. Either you are with us, or you are with the terrorists," the president declared, speaking to Congress nine days after the attack.[3]

Soros decided he was against Bush. He believed that Bush—with his war on an amorphous concept, his imposition of a particular understanding of the American way of life on others, and his with-us-or-against-us mentality—posed a tremendous threat to the work of his life: a more open society.

Getting Bush out of the White House, Soros said in 2003, became the "central focus" of his life.[4] In July 2003, he convened Democratic activists and two political strategists, Mark Steitz and Tom Novick, at his summer estate in tony Southampton, Long Island.[5]

There had been a fundraising dinner several weeks prior, during which "apparently Mr. Soros went off talking about the importance of beating George Bush," Novick told me over the phone from his office in Portland, Oregon.[6]

Since 1994, Novick has worked for M+R, a national public affairs firm. When Soros was bashing Bush at the fundraising dinner, Novick had recently completed a study on how donors' money had been used (effectively and otherwise) in the 2002 midterm elections. He got a call from some people asking him to stop by when he was in Washington, D.C. It turned out they worked for Soros and wanted to know if Novick could put together a plan for how Soros could contribute effectively to defeating Bush. Six weeks later, he and Steitz (who had been contacted by others in Soros's world for his connections in Democratic Party circles) were at Soros's Southampton home to present that plan.[7]

The plan, it should be noted, was not for Open Society, which is a philanthropic foundation. The plan was about how Soros himself could throw money—and a lot of it—into the political arena.

There were three central tenets to the plan. The first was that, whenever an incumbent president looks weak, as Bush did, "everyone has an idea about how they can beat him." But people splitting money between "20 or 30" different ideas wasn't going to be useful. Someone "putting down a marker with sizable resources [was] sending a message that this was a place to place a bet," Novick said.[8]

And where was that place? The second key part of the plan highlighted that new campaign finance laws—for which Soros had actually pushed, having given $18 million to groups that supported campaign finance reform since the late 1990s—meant donors couldn't give unlimited amounts to the Democratic (or Republican) Party, but could give money to independent groups. Presumably, Soros had supported campaign finance reform because the involvement of big money in politics makes it more difficult for full and equitable democratic participation, and thus an open society. Pushed by Jane Mayer in her *New Yorker* interview about the perceived hypocrisy of his spending large amounts of money on politics after backing reforms to keep big money out of politics, Soros said, "This is the most important election of my lifetime. These aren't normal times. The ends justify every legal means possible."

And the third and final section of the plan was on voter mobilization.[9] In 2001, Karl Rove, Bush's deputy chief of staff, had, per Novick's earlier study, experimented with highly targeted voter mobilization to get the vote out in their favor.[10] So Soros decided they should do the same.

A highly polarized electorate, an opponent who was going to use targeted voter mobilization to get out the vote, and limits on what could be given to the actual party (and candidate, who, in July 2003, was as yet unknown) meant that the strategists and activists concluded that it would make the most sense for Soros to give his money to independent groups dedicated to getting out the vote across America.

"This in some sense was classic Soros—he was early on the direct voter contact, data-driven . . . the metrics-oriented things that Obama would later be known for," Steitz, a senior principal at TSD Communications, the communications strategy firm he founded back in 1993, told me over the phone.[11] "I was just astonished at how interested he was in every detail."[12]

Soros donated $5 million to MoveOn.org, a liberal activist group[13] (though MoveOn's founder, Wes Boyd, warned him not to become a distraction—Soros was not, after all, the main act of the 2004 campaign, and did not want to become a sideshow).[14] He pledged money to America Coming Together, a group intended to mobilize voters in seventeen swing states.[15] The November elections were, for him, "a matter of life and death." He gave to the Center for American Progress, which was, at the time, a new think tank established to counter Washington's influential conservative policy institutions.[16] Altogether, Soros spent roughly $27 million to defeat Bush and help elect his opponent, John Kerry, then a senator from Massachusetts.[17] The aforementioned 2004 *New Yorker* article on his spending was titled "The Money Man." Jane Mayer conducted an interview with Soros over lunch at his Southampton estate, "on the brick patio of a Mediterranean-style pavilion; the velvety green lawns were dotted with magnificent specimen trees, meticulously tended flower beds, and lily ponds."[18]

"It was hard to feel too worried in those surroundings," Mayer wrote.[19] Evidently, Soros managed.

IT WASN'T JUST THAT SOROS poured millions of dollars to mobilize voters with the express purpose of defeating Bush. There were, after all, other big spenders. Between the primaries and the general election, a total of $880.5 million was contributed to presidential campaigns in the 2004 election, and Bush, in the end, raised more than Kerry ($367,228,819 to $328,479,256, respectively).[20] The 2004 presidential election was the most expensive in history up to that point. Soros was not the only billionaire backing a horse in that race—Texas oilman T. Boone Pickens, for example, donated $2 million to Swift Boat Veterans and POWs for Truth,[21] the group that challenged the narrative of Kerry's war

service, and bombastically offered an additional $1 million to any-
one who could disprove his group's attack ads (he reneged on that
promise).[22]

"We—I should say I, and I was chief strategist—I mean, there
were so many entities on each side that were spending money to
defeat the other person," Matthew Dowd, who led strategy for
Bush's 2004 campaign, told me in the spring of 2019, speaking by
phone from central Texas. There was the actual Bush campaign;
there was the Republican National Committee; there were third-
party donors; and there was the same thing, including Soros, on
the other side.[23]

"It was never, 'Uh-oh, what is Soros doing,'" he said. "It
was—we would add up every week the amount of money being
spent by various Democratic or progressive organizations and
make a comparison."[24]

"The only concern was how much was he spending and how
much others were spending."[25]

Soros himself saw what he was doing as a counterbalance to
Republican spending. "I don't oppose other views, even right-
wing ones," Soros told Mayer in that interview, "because I think
in an open society a variety of points of view should be heard. But,
by giving this money, I was trying to level the playing field. The
Republicans have so much more money, the debate had become
lopsided."[26]

To counter one side's money in politics, then, Soros gave
money—and quite a lot of it—to the other.

I asked Novick if there was a discussion about the tension in
this idea—wanting to balance out money in politics and opening up political debate by having one man give a lot of money. If
you're concerned about money in politics, how does having one
person pump more money into politics help matters? And if the
idea was to increase political participation, isn't there an irony in

the grassroots effort springing from such concentrated wealth? Did anyone talk about that?

"Not necessarily," he said. "This really was more of a business proposition."

Soros's thought, per Novick, was, "If I have resources, or we can gather resources, is there something that can be done to beat George Bush?"[27]

Soros believed that this was the most important fight of his life, and that it wasn't about the principle of money in politics, but about beating George Bush. I do not doubt that he was sincere in that belief. Nor do I doubt that there were other very wealthy people on the other side of the political aisle who told themselves the same thing—that there wasn't time to worry about the principle of money in politics or fairness, because they had to keep George Bush in office at all costs.

I gave this example to Anand Giridharadas, the author of *Winners Take All: The Elite Charade of Changing the World*. I told him how Soros had pushed to make money in politics fairer until he decided the time had come to throw his money into it. I asked him what he thought of that.

"This is what it looks like," he told me, "to depend on the whims of rich people."[28]

SOROS WAS NOT, HOWEVER, JUST spending. He publicly and repeatedly proclaimed that Bush and what he stood for needed to be defeated.

He went so far as to publish a book. The general point of *The Bubble of American Supremacy: The Costs of Bush's War in Iraq* was that those surrounding Bush had used the attacks on September 11, 2001, as a pretense to invade Iraq, something they had wanted to do for a decade, and had cost the United States credibility in the process of doing so, all while espousing values that were directly antithetical to those of an open society. It wasn't the case that Soros was opposed to any American military intervention; he had supported NATO's military intervention,[29] which did not have U.N. approval, in the former Yugoslavia in the late 1990s (NATO airstrikes continued until Yugoslav armed forces withdrew from Kosovo). But he saw the war in Iraq as different. He saw it as wrong.

In Soros's telling, the story of the Bush administration begins before the president took office. It begins in the 1990s, with a certain segment of the right (dubbed "neoconservative" by Soros and others) calling for a more aggressive foreign policy.

In the 1997 mission statement of the conservative institution the Project for the New American Century, future Bush administration officials—including Vice President Dick Cheney, Secretary of Defense Donald Rumsfeld, Deputy Secretary of Defense Paul Wolfowitz, and Senior Director of the National Security Council for Democracy, Human Rights, and International Organizations Elliott Abrams—wrote, "We aim to make the case and rally support for American global leadership." The Project for the New American Century urged invading Iraq as early as 1998.[30]

Soros argued that this group had wanted to wage war at the very beginning of George W. Bush's presidency—but couldn't because the 2000 election went to the Supreme Court, which decided against a Florida recount and so (liberals believe) handed Bush victory, meaning that the president didn't have a mandate to begin a war, and because the United States didn't have a clear enemy. "September 11 removed both obstacles in one stroke. President Bush declared war on terrorism, and the nation lined up behind its president," Soros wrote.[31]

In imposing its view of freedom on both the American people and a foreign country, "the supremacist ideology of the Bush administration is in contradiction with the principles of an open society because it claims possession of an ultimate truth."[32] The Bush administration's thinking, Soros said, was that the stronger know better. Soros saw this as a uniquely Republican coupling of religious and market fundamentalism. "The two groups feed off each other—religious fundamentalism provides both an antidote to and a cover for the amorality of the market. Market fundamentalists and religious fundamentalists make strange bedfellows, but they have been held together by their success: Together they came to dominate the Republican Party."[33]

Soros had not, prior to the George W. Bush years, spoken or written so negatively about the Republican Party. He had been critical of what could be considered the Republican Party's financial policy—speaking out about what he called "market fundamentalists" who believe the market knows all and should be followed at all costs—for quite some time. But he had been pushing for specific policies; he had not cared so much about which party was in power. That changed with George W. Bush. Soros saw a party wrapping itself around money, a crucifix, and an American flag. He did not see it as simply another political force, but as something that had to be stopped.

What's more, the Bush administration, in Soros's view, wanted to use its strength to make everyone adhere to American thinking. The National Security Strategy, he noted, made mention of a "single, sustainable model" for any nation's success. This was impossible, Soros argued; there was no one model that worked for every nation.[34]

"When President Bush says, as he does frequently, that 'freedom' will prevail, in fact he means that America will prevail. I am rather sensitive to Orwellian doublespeak because I grew up with it in Hungary first under Nazi and later Communist rule."[35]

"President Bush equates freedom with American values. He

has a simplistic view of what is right and what is wrong: *We* are right and *they* are wrong," he wrote. "This is in contradiction with the principles of an open society, which recognize that *we* may be wrong."[36]

There was something else, too. In Soros's view, Bush, in the way he had reacted and responded to the attacks of September 11, 2001, had allowed the American people to harness their grief into rage that could be released onto others. The United States had, he argued, fallen into the trap of morphing from victim into perpetrator. (In yet another example of Soros's Jewish identity having nothing to do with support for Israel, Soros added that the most famous and tragic example of victims becoming perpetrators was Israel, a state established after the unthinkable persecution of the Jewish people that was the Holocaust, and that now, per Soros, bullied Palestinians into victimhood.[37] This was not the first time that Soros had said that his idea of Judaism and of what it meant, and means, to be a Jewish person was not tied to support for Israel; he had mentioned his disinterest in Zionism before, and had previously said that he was interested in universal suffering and humanity. But here he was writing not only that he wasn't interested in Israel, but that it was a perpetrator of violence, and that the United States was, too.)

President Bush, Soros had come to believe, was the main threat to the very idea of an open society. He needed to be defeated, and Soros would say, again and again, in writing and in interviews, that he would work tirelessly to defeat him.

It wasn't that he liked partisanship—on the contrary, he said, he was deeply uncomfortable with it. If this were an ordinary election, he would not have thrown this kind of money behind one side. But this was not, in his mind, an ordinary election.

"I used to be rather balanced between the two main parties, seeing some good and some bad in each and leaning only slightly toward the Democrats," Soros wrote in his book. "I did not use to consider it a matter of life and death which party won the elections. I do now."[38]

DOWD DENIED THAT SOROS'S WORDS or self-appointed role in the campaign were of particular import to the Bush camp.

"Our campaign [was] solely focused on, how are we gonna get our message across and what is the contrast with John Kerry," Dowd said. "The hardest part of the campaign, the hardest part, [was] how do you stay on message."

There were some, he acknowledged, who wanted to go after Soros.

"There's always people in a campaign who could get distracted," Dowd said without specifying who those people were. "George Soros might do something, they announce some five million [dollars], some people in the campaign get all caffeinated about it."

But those people were brought back to heel, he said. "We stayed very, very, very disciplined."

That's largely because Dowd didn't believe that voters actually cared about George Soros. "Just because somebody does that doesn't mean you should go after that person if it doesn't work for what you want to accomplish," he said. "You go duck hunting, there's a lot of decoys. Doesn't mean you shoot at every decoy."[39]

OUTSIDE OF THE CAMPAIGN, HOWEVER, there were plenty who were ready to aim and fire.

The Republican opposition "responded. Aggressively. And in George they had an opponent that I think they kind of quickly realized worked with their base," Steitz said.[40]

The 2004 election was understood at the time as a major battle in the culture wars. Issues were not just economic or political; they were moral. The war in Iraq was not just a war on Iraq; it was a war on terror. A piece of legislation that, objectively, infringed on civil liberties had "patriot" in its name. Countries were either with or against us; who constituted "us" remained undefined yet understood.

The candidates themselves played into this nicely. Kerry was from coastal Massachusetts, married to the widow of the heir to a ketchup fortune; the president was a good old boy from Texas (who was Yale-educated and whose father was from Connecticut and had been president, but a good old boy from Texas nonetheless).

From a particular kind of right-wing perspective, Soros was an even more effective counterpart to Bush than Kerry was. Kerry, over the course of the 2004 campaign and when in front of certain audiences and groups, played up his Christianity and love of hunting. Soros lived in New York, worked in finance, was an émigré and so could not play up an all-American background, and not only was Jewish, but reminded his one nation, under God, that church and state are meant to be separated. "Our concern about Islamic fundamentalism is that there's no separation between church and state, yet we are about to erode that here,"[41] he said. The causes that his foundation had been supporting in the United States for nearly ten years—criminal justice and drug reform, for example—were decidedly on one side of the culture war. And so partisans on the other side of the war lined up to fight him.

"Part of the issue is that Republicans always have the 'we are the party of the wealthy' problem to get off their neck and having George to attack may have helped them on this front," Steitz said.

"Here's a wealthy financier with a foreign accent—implicit, Jew—who is trying to influence elections. I think that portrayal helped them in several ways."[42]

The *Wall Street Journal* called him "the new Daddy Warbucks of the Democratic Party." Bill O'Reilly, then of Fox News, called him a "far-left radical bomb thrower" and "sleazoid"[43] (O'Reilly and Fox parted ways in 2017 after multiple allegations of sexual harassment against him).[44] Perhaps most notable was Dennis Hastert, then Speaker of the House, who, in late August 2004, went on *Fox News Sunday* and said, "You know, I don't know where George Soros gets his money. I don't know where—if it comes overseas or from drug groups or where it comes from." Asked for clarification from host Chris Wallace, Hastert said, "George Soros has been for legalizing drugs in this country. So, I mean, he's got a lot of ancillary interests out there . . . I'm saying I don't know where groups—could be people who support this type of thing. I'm saying we don't know. The fact is we don't know where this money comes from." Hastert, some speculated, was borrowing these talking points from political activist and failed presidential candidate Lyndon LaRouche Jr., whose campaign literature read, "Years of investigation by LaRouche's associates have answered that question in grisly detail: Soros's money comes from impoverishment of the poor countries against whose currencies he speculates, and from deadly mind-destroying, terrorism-funding *drugs*." LaRouche had been pushing anti-Soros theories since the 1990s, but LaRouche was a fringe figure and convicted felon; Hastert was the Speaker of the House of Representatives.[45]

Soros, for his part, denied that he was part of a drug cartel and demanded an apology.[46] (Hastert would eventually go to prison for illegally structuring bank withdrawals to pay off a student he had sexually abused; he was released in 2017.)[47]

Rob Johnson, the man Soros brought onto the fund shortly before shorting the pound, told me that the attack surprised Soros, both because it was ludicrous and because people believed it.

"George was in shock because philanthropic grantees started sending him checks back . . . he didn't believe anybody could believe that," Johnson said.

The experience was, for Soros, a "pivot point," Johnson said. Soros "started to prepare for being demonized. That was a big change in the level of his political sophistication."[48]

Novick, on the other hand, said that the attacks weren't wholly unexpected.

"I think they [Soros and his team] were certainly cognizant that the more public his role was, the more attacks they would get," he told me.[49]

"Anybody that raises their head up in a prominent way and spends vast sums of money in order to achieve their goal brings it on themselves. That's true wherever you are," Dowd said. "You brought that heat onto you."

Still, he said, "One may disagree with the path that he wants to have—George Soros is only doing this out of a sense of good will and care from the world. George Soros isn't doing this for personal gain." The difference between Soros and the Koch brothers, he said, referring to Charles and the late David Koch, businessmen heavily involved in funding right-wing politics and pushing particular policies, was that the Kochs could be seen as benefiting from some of what they spent their money to push. If the Kochs spent to support politicians who would push deregulation of certain industries, for example, they stood to have "huge personal benefits." "I think it's very hard to say that about George Soros." The causes behind which Soros was throwing his money, in other words, were not going to help enrich Soros (in the monetary sense, at least—one could argue that being a political backer makes one powerful, and that in itself is enrichment). The money that Soros was giving away was not going to make more money for Soros.

It's one thing to say that now, I noted, fifteen years after the election. Did he think that way about George Soros during the 2004 campaign?

"*I* always did," Dowd said. But then, he added, he, like Mark

McKinnon—Bush's chief campaign media advisor—was a former Democrat. In fact, in 2007, Dowd publicly broke with Bush, telling the *New York Times* that the president he had helped reelect needed to face America's increasing disillusionment with the war in Iraq.[50]

IN ANY EVENT, FOR SOROS, the ire of right-wing media, scorn from the Speaker of the House, and even $27 million constituted a small price to pay to achieve his goal of defeating Bush.

"I am confident that he will be rejected at the polls," Soros wrote, adding as a footnote, "I have made an unconditional prediction once before, in 1997, when I predicted the imminent collapse of the global capitalist system. Later I had to eat my words. On this occasion, I shall do everything I can do to ensure that the inevitable actually happens."[51]

The inevitable turned out not to be inevitable after all. On November 2, 2004, Bush won reelection.

"My line was, we built the best field goal kicking team ever, but the quarterback's gotta get you close enough," Novick said. The get-out-the-vote and voter registration made the race closer than it would have been, he said, adding, "Obviously, we didn't win."[52]

I asked Soros if he regretted his involvement in the U.S. presidential campaign in 2004. His side lost, after all, and maybe it put his philanthropic work at greater risk.

"No, but it gave me many enemies," he wrote. "I believe the best defense is counterattack. This keeps me busy."

IT WASN'T ONLY RIGHT-WING AMERICAN conspiracy theorists like Hastert and O'Reilly who started talking about Soros in 2004. That same year, Soros's involvement in an election half a world away from the United States would eventually incur the wrath of another world leader, and perhaps the most famous conspiracy theorist of all: Russian President Vladimir Putin.

In the early 2000s, the country of Georgia was ruled by Eduard Shevardnadze. Back in the 1970s and 1980s, when Georgia was part of the Soviet Union, Shevardnadze had been Georgia's ruler on behalf of the Communist Party. Now, in the twenty-first century, he was post-Soviet Georgia's president.

Shevardnadze was ostensibly pro-Western. Still, he continued to do things Soviet-style. Nepotism, connections, and corruption, all Soviet holdovers, were still very much a part of life in Georgia.[53]

A rising star of Shevardnadze's own party, Minister of Justice Mikheil Saakashvili, tried to work with the speaker of the parliament, Zurab Zhvania, to implement an anticorruption program, which Soros cheered on—but which was, to his disappointment, not properly implemented.

"The [anticorruption] program itself was well formulated and ambitious," Soros recalled, "but could not get off the ground. Every time I visited Georgia, President Shevardnadze made a gesture of support, but he could never deliver because the main source of corruption was the Ministry of Interior, and his life literally depended on the security services."[54]

In 2001, Saakashvili resigned from Shevardnadze's government, declaring that it would be "immoral" for him to stay on.[55] Later that same year, he began his own party, the United National Movement.[56]

"I expressed my support for them by giving them the 2003 Open Society Prize on behalf of the Central European University," Soros wrote several years later, which is to say that he threw the support and prestige of the university he founded behind Saakashvili.[57]

In 2003, Georgia held parliamentary elections. Saakashvili competed against Shevardnadze. Shevardnadze claimed victory, but

Saakashvili—and independent observers—said the election had been rigged. Tens of thousands of people took to the streets. Eventually, Saakashvili and his supporters stormed parliament, the final act in the so-called Rose Revolution. Incredibly, in late November, under pressure from protesters, Shevardnadze resigned. An interim president was put in place. In January 2004, new elections were held. Saakashvili won an overwhelming majority.

And so, it seemed, had Soros—the person who he believed would open society, whom he had personally championed and whose election he had supported, was president.

"The people believed the exit poll, not the official results, and there was a revolution. Saakashvili became president," Soros wrote. "I was elated and did whatever I could to help him succeed."[58]

Soros had long been involved in encouraging a democratic spirit in Eastern Europe, and even in fostering democratic change. But his work in Georgia and with Saakashvili, more than with any other politician he'd supported abroad so far, was arguably his most direct involvement in a political uprising to date.

"I DON'T KNOW WHY THERE are moments he would pick to get very involved," Paul Stubbs, the British academic based in Croatia, told me. "Georgia was a strange case of nationalism and neoliberal, U.S.-inspired economic reforms."[59]

Before these events in Georgia, in 2000, Serbians had had their own revolution, through which they nonviolently ousted their brutal authoritarian leader, Slobodan Milošević. Open Society played a role there, too; along with the Washington-based Freedom House, the British Foreign Office, and various Western European governments, Open Society helped support projects meant to get out the vote.[60]

The Georgian Rose Revolution is sometimes said to resemble

the "Serbian model."[61] And it did, but not because Saakashvili simply noticed and admired Serbians from afar. The Georgians received money to learn how the Serbians pulled it off.

Soros, according to political analyst (and later an informal advisor for the party formed in opposition to Saakashvili) Lincoln Mitchell, paid for exchanges through which Georgian and Serbian activists and politicians could gain knowledge about what made the Serbian "Bulldozer Revolution" so effective.[62] Prominent Georgian activists were then able to train many more Georgians in the Serbs' techniques. Georgians convinced their independent television network to air a documentary about the Serbian revolution twice a day every day for ten days in November 2003. Georgians borrowed the Serbs' slogan—*Gotov je!*, or "He's finished!"—and applied it to Shevardnadze.[63]

It wasn't just that Soros helped the Georgians talk to some Serbs. Georgia's Open Society Foundation helped fund the exit poll that countered the official results.[64] What's more, Open Society Georgia, the Georgian arm of Soros's foundation, helped build up those who would work with Saakashvili to take over. Alexander Lomaia had been the executive director of Open Society Georgia Foundation; he then joined Saakashvili's cabinet.[65] Soros also donated several million dollars to a capacity-building fund established by the United Nations Development Program to help set up an anticorruption fund to supplement government employees' salaries to eliminate the temptation to seek illicit financial gain.[66] Soros did not orchestrate the Rose Revolution, but he and his money did help create the conditions that let the revolution bloom.

Soros himself denies that he was any sort of puppeteer pulling the strings behind the Rose Revolution. "I'm very pleased and proud of the work of the foundation in preparing Georgian society for what became a Rose Revolution, but the role of the foundation and my personal [role] has been greatly exaggerated," he said at Open Society Georgia's tenth anniversary commemoration. "I think you here must know more than anybody else that the Rose Revolution was entirely the work of Georgian society." The mission of the foundation, he insisted, was not to prepare for revolution.[67]

The main beneficiary of Soros's involvement appreciated his generosity, at least at first. "George Soros did a very good job in many places—he was supportive of the Rose Revolution, young groups," Saakashvili told me back in the fall of 2017. "It's obvious that, at that moment, he was a natural ally."[68]

After he won his election, Saakashvili did work to create a more transparent society, cracking down on corruption and crime. Georgia's identity, he insisted, was with the West, and Saakashvili used a horde of lobbyists to make Georgia's case in Washington. He also tried, albeit unsuccessfully, to get his country into NATO, the Western military alliance that dates back to the Cold War. He became close with President George W. Bush, who hailed Saakashvili's Georgia as a "beacon of liberty."

Saakashvili himself, however, proved not to be the beacon some had hoped he would be. In 2008, he took much of the international blame for the Russo-Georgian War; there is a debate as to how much fault is his as opposed to Putin's, but it was Saakashvili, after all, who moved on the capital of South Ossetia, despite warnings from the United States and allies in the Bush administration (the United States did not envision itself going to war with Russia over Georgia).[69]

And the fact that Saakashvili created a less corrupt society did not necessarily mean that he intended to maintain an open one.

Saakashvili "came in with such a huge mandate," Marc Behrendt of Freedom House told me. "He could have done anything that he wanted. Instead, he did whatever he wanted."[70] Behrendt pointed to the judiciary, which he described as the only successful reform of the Shevardnadze period. Saakashvili dismantled it and put his own people in.[71]

"Many good people hoped that he would provide a leap forward in modernization, as emblemized by the Revolution of the Roses," former Saakashvili ally Tedo Japaridze told me via email. Indeed, Japaridze was Saakashvili's first foreign minister but served only briefly. However, he said, "as Saakashvili was nearing the end of his first term it became abundantly clear that he was using his authority to create an unshakable power fiefdom within Georgia." At one point, Japaridze said, he and his wife stopped using their cell phones, afraid that Saakashvili was trying to monitor him.[72]

"My foundation in Georgia spoke out against this lawless behavior, and in the absence of a new parliamentary opposition it became the most vocal critic of the new government," Soros wrote. At first, he acknowledged, they gave Saakashvili the benefit of the doubt, but eventually they became vocal and critical. "Saakashvili in power turned out to be much less of a paragon of open society values than he was in opposition."[73]

Soros has come to concede that he should not have championed Saakashvili as forcefully, or gotten as closely involved in Georgia's politics, as he did. It is wholly possible that Saakashvili would have been elected president without Soros's support, but the reality remains that he came to power with it, and that Soros's money and influence helped propel to power a man who changed the course of history for his country and region. Soros was well intentioned in his support of Saakashvili, a man who he believed was genuinely committed to the same things as he was, but the best of intentions can have unintended impacts. And even if Saakashvili had been the leader Soros had thought he was going to be, should Soros have had a role in helping him become president?

There is at least one very prominent world figure who believes that the answer to that question is a decisive "no": Russian

President Vladimir Putin, who once vowed to string Saakashvili up "by the balls."

Even while his foundation was criticizing Saakashvili's government, "I was accused by the Russian media of being Saakashvili's paymaster," Soros wrote, noting that Putin advised Central Asian republics to close down Soros's foundations—and although in the end they did not do so, those foundations did come under pressure.

"The painful lesson taught me to keep a greater distance from the internal politics of the countries where I have foundations." George Soros, political supporter, may not have been at odds with George Soros, philanthropist, but the former did, as it turned out, put the latter's work at risk.[74]

From Soros's perspective, he was encouraging elements within a country that wanted something better—more open, more transparent, more forward-looking—for themselves. He did not install some outside leader; Saakashvili was Georgian, as were the thousands of people protesting, and if someone went from running a local foundation to helping run the country, so much the better.

But from Putin's point of view, Soros, in 2003, rooted out Shevardnadze and put in his place someone who not only tried to disentangle Georgia from Russia, but threatened Russia with the expansion of a Western military alliance. Georgia had once been part of the Soviet Union. Saakashvili wanted to make clear that, for Georgia, the Soviet Union and the Soviet way of working was a thing of the past. For Putin, who called the dissolution of the Soviet Union a geopolitical catastrophe, that was unacceptable. The fact that Open Society had also been involved in Ukraine, where, from 2004 to 2005, protesters also ousted a president who had come to power in an election fraught with fraud, could hardly have mitigated the negative attitude Putin may have had toward Soros.[75] (Open Society, like various U.S. government agencies and other American and European NGOs, did work to create conditions for free and fair elections in Ukraine—for example, by helping to fund exit polling—and Soros had been funding various civil society groups in Ukraine for a decade. He had even said in the 1990s that he had given so much to Ukraine because he knew that a robust Ukraine meant that Russia could never again be imperialist.[76] But to describe the revolution first as Soros-funded was and remains a quick, easy way to discredit and dismiss the agency of local leaders and protesters.)

Putin had long been suspicious of Western leaders' promises of cooperation with Russia. He thought that they cared little for international norms when it came to respecting what Putin insisted was Russia's sphere of influence, its neighborhood, and its business. The Rose Revolution confirmed those suspicions. In 2005, the same year that Soros stood in Tbilisi and stressed that it was Georgians themselves who brought about this change to their country and society, Putin gave his own take on the Rose Revolution. "We are against solving political issues through unlawful ways. Let's speak of Georgia's case: the West actively supported [Georgia's ex-President Eduard] Shevardnadze there. Why was it necessary to ouster him through revolution? And if it was necessary, then the question emerges of who the West supported and why? All issues should be solved through legal means and in constitutional frames," Putin said in Paris.

It would prove to be the first of many times that Putin accused the West, through Soros, of illegally undermining other countries. In 2015, the Open Society Foundation was banned from Russia, ostensibly for being a security threat. In July 2018, Putin stood next to President Donald Trump at a summit in Helsinki and compared those in Russia who had allegedly meddled in the U.S. 2016 presidential election to Soros. "You have a lot of individuals in the United States—take George Soros, for instance—with multi-billion capitals, but it doesn't make him—his position, his posture—the posture of the United States. No, it does not," Putin said.[77]

PUTIN DID NOT MANAGE TO cause Saakashvili bodily harm, but he did outlast him in office. Saakashvili won reelection in 2008, but in 2012, his party lost to Georgian Dream, an opposition party formed by a mysterious billionaire named Bidzina Ivanishvili. The election came a month after a video of prisoners being beaten was released to the public.

By the time I spoke to Saakashvili in 2017, he had done a stint as a Brooklyn exile; been told to return to Georgia to face prosecution; renounced his Georgian citizenship to become a citizen of Ukraine to become governor of Odessa; and fallen out with the Ukrainian government and lost that citizenship, too (he has since had it reinstated). When I spoke to him, he was in Budapest, Hungary, taking advantage of his close personal friendship with Prime Minister Viktor Orbán.

Sitting in the capital of Soros conspiracy theories, Saakashvili showed little loyalty to Soros. "When [Soros] starts to play politics, he's not that good," he told me.[78] Perhaps he said this because he was in Viktor Orbán's Hungary; perhaps it was because Soros had grown critical of Saakashvili, and Saakashvili appreciated election monitoring and support for government salaries more than he did the criticism that came with it. In either case, he believed that the man who had supported his political revolution should stay out of politics.

On this point, Saakashvili and Vladimir Putin agreed.

Soros, meanwhile, expressed disappointment in the man he had once tried to encourage and support.

"The real lesson I learned in Georgia," Soros wrote, "is that helping countries in transition is a difficult and thankless task . . .

Still, there is a more subtle lesson to be learned. It is dangerous to build systemic reforms on a close association with one particular government. Systemic reforms need broad public participation and support. That is what makes them irreversible."[79]

THERE ARE CERTAIN PARALLELS BETWEEN Soros in the United States and Soros in Georgia in 2004. In both cases, he stuck his neck out, spending time, energy, words, and money on something in which he believed. In both cases, he attracted criticism because of it, some of it from high-profile and powerful figures, much of it borne out of conspiratorial thinking.

In both cases, Soros saw a problem with a political system and tried to spend a lot of money—an outsized amount of money for the U.S. political process at the time, and certainly an outsized amount of money for Georgia, where it was supplementing salaries—to fix it.

Soros concluded that reforming the system—of a country, of a way of thinking, of a political era—requires broad public participation and support. But what does it say of the system itself, and how broad can the support possibly be, if one man has enough money to buy public participation—to get out the vote, to encourage people to move on, to pay public servants? Is the fact that one man, however well-intentioned, can spend $27 million in an election to try to maintain an open society helpful or hurtful to the openness of that society?

In 2004, the tension between Soros, a man who had become incredibly wealthy by working within the system, and Soros, a man who wanted to fix the system, was once again laid bare. That was true in the case of the election of George W. Bush; it was true in the election in Georgia; and it was true in the case of globalization, about which Soros was vocally critical around the same time and which he saw as connected to the American political campaign. Soros's issue with Bush largely revolved around the president's foreign policy and the role the United States was playing in the world; globalization was inextricably a part of that role.

In his book on Bush, Soros wrote critically of globalization, "The objective of the Reagan administration in the United States and the Thatcher government in the United Kingdom was to reduce the ability of the state to interfere in the economy, and globalization served their purpose well." Other countries joined in the globalization game, he wrote, to attract and keep capital. But globalization also hurt the ability of the state "to provide public goods for its citizens by interfering with the most convenient and copious sources of revenues, namely, the taxation of incomes and profits while reducing or eliminating customs duties at the same time."

He continued: "There is a growing inequality between rich and poor, both within countries and among countries. Admittedly, globalization is not a zero-sum game: Its benefits exceed the costs in the sense that the increased wealth produced by globalization could be used to make up for the inequities and other shortcomings of globalization and there would still be some extra wealth left over. The trouble is that the winners do not compensate the losers either within states or between states."[80]

Which is true. As is the fact that George Soros was surely a winner of globalization. He made money all over the world; he made some financial decisions that caused other, average people to lose large amounts of money; and private equity funds he controlled used an offshore law firm, Appleby, to manage what a 2017 article published by the International Consortium of Investigative Journalists described as "a web of offshore entities, including an investment in one company engaged in reinsurance, or insurance for insurers." That same article quoted Brooke Harrington, a Copenhagen Business School professor, as saying that the offshore industry makes "the poor poorer" and exacerbates wealth inequality—the same inequality Soros bemoaned in his book.[81]

There are two possible ways to look at this. The first is that Soros is at best paradoxical and at worst hypocritical. He wanted money out of politics, but not his money; he wanted a more open political process, but wanted to be one of the people dictating the future of politics; he wanted systemic change in other countries but thought it could be paid for by him, a person not of or from those other countries.

The second is that Soros is unafraid to criticize even that which has been good for him if he believes it should be changed. "He's been awfully consistent on the rules needing to change in ways that would not have benefited him," as Mark Steitz put it to me.[82]

Though it was not fully examined, this was the tension that ran through Soros's involvement in the 2004 election in the United States—and in Georgia, a country in which both the negative and positive effects of globalization are felt.[83] Still, even with this dissonance, and even while partisan involvement in the United States and political support for Saakashvili in Georgia seemed to have unintended effects, 2004 was also the year in which Soros's philanthropic work seemed to be paying off dividends, as it was the year of the single largest expansion of the European Union. Ten countries were admitted that year, including seven from the former Eastern Bloc—the Czech Republic, Estonia, Hungary, Latvia, Lithuania, Poland, and Slovakia.[84] These were countries into which Soros and his foundation had poured millions for decades in the hope that they would one day be able to move out from behind the Iron Curtain and into a more progressive, open society.

In 2004, it looked like the story of Soros in Central and Eastern Europe would have a happy ending after all. For a few years, it did.

CHAPTER 8

United We Fall

There was a sense, after various Central and Eastern European countries finally got to join the European Union in the early 2000s, that the work had been done. Soros had not originally intended to keep funding all of his foundations forever. The idea was that the foundations wouldn't need to exist forever, and either they would close after society had been opened or they would spin off and run independently. These countries were in the formal family of European nations now. It was Brussels's turn to take over—to ensure the countries abided by the rule of law and had robust democracies and civil societies and a space for multiculturalism.

"If I think of what was the predominant thinking, especially after the accession of 2004 . . . oh, our work is done," Goran Buldioski, codirector of the Open Society Initiative for Europe, told me over a WhatsApp call in July. "We were all joking, 'Oh, soon we will be without a job.'"

There were dark spots across Central and Eastern Europe, to be sure. There was rising economic inequality between those who could increasingly consider themselves elites and those who even more increasingly could not, and there was a widening socioeconomic gulf between the capital cities and the countryside. Still, Buldioski said, "Everyone was feeling we are profiting . . . there were fewer critical views."[1]

But not everyone was profiting—or, at least, some were acutely aware of profiting less than others. There would be more critical views, and those views would turn into votes.

It wasn't the end of history. It was the beginning of a new chapter of it, one for which, it turned out, civil society wasn't entirely prepared.

IN 2011, OPEN SOCIETY DECIDED to change its relations with its seven Central and Eastern European foundations, which it had set up to help with the transition to democracy. The foundations became fully independent entities. They still received substantial funds from the Open Society Foundations, but the expectation was that, going forward, they would develop their own sources of support. Organizations in the region could still apply for grants from the local foundations or from Open Society, which is, to this day, a major funder of work in the region. But individual Open Society Foundations in the region fully supported by the main Open Society, with their overhead and staff and work fully paid for—that was finished. The change came into effect in 2012.

The idea, Laura Silber, Open Society's chief communications director, told me back in 2017, was that these countries were in the EU now—that is, in a democratic and open environment in which OSF's support was less crucial, as there were now more developed sources of funding.[2] The theory was that the countries were not democracies in transition anymore, but members of a club that ostensibly valued human rights and human dignity, democracy, equality, and the rule of law—all ideas that Open Society had worked to promote in the region. There were other parts of the world that needed more of Open Society's attention now that Central and Eastern European countries had acceded to the European Union.

And Open Society did spread out farther in the world. In 2005, Open Society began work in Pakistan, where it first spent $3 million on earthquake relief and has since spent $40 million on programming. It began working on disability rights worldwide, a program on which it has spent $10 million since 2007. The program goes after discriminatory laws and practices that inhibit the equal inclusion of people with disabilities. An office was opened in Tunisia in 2013, following the popular uprising there in 2011.[3]

It also expanded its human rights portfolio. Kenneth Roth, director of Human Rights Watch—the organization through which Soros first became interested in participating in the human rights space as a board member back in the 1980s—told me over the phone in July 2019 from Geneva, where he was spending the summer, that their advocacy and donor base had been focused on North America and Western Europe, and that he, Roth, thought that needed to change.

"I kind of outlined this plan of going global" to Soros, telling him, "'You're the only person I know who has both the means and the interest to be our lead donor.'

"I needed somebody to give ten million dollars a year. I asked, 'Would you be willing to do this for five years?' And he came back to me and said, 'I'd be willing to do it for ten.'

With that money, Human Rights Watch stepped more fully into advocacy and media outreach, sending out reports on their findings and giving extensive interviews to reporters to bring more attention to their work than before. It also expanded its work into Brazil, South Africa, Kenya, Lebanon, Thailand, Australia, and

Japan, and built a donor base that is split 50/50 between the United States and the rest of the world.[4]

Soros, two decades into his philanthropic work and having seemingly accomplished his mission in the former Warsaw Pact countries, wanted to expand throughout the world. And he did.

But he also contracted what he had been doing in Central and Eastern Europe.

When I asked Aleksander Smolar, the head of the Polish Stefan Batory Foundation, about the restructuring of Open Society funds in the 2000s, he corrected me. "Restructuring," he said, wasn't the word. Open Society reduced the funding, and numerous organizations had to close down. He stopped himself, and noted that his organization was not one of the ones that had to close and was doing very well.[5]

Some organizations figured out how to exist in this brave new world, and funding grants from the Norwegian government in particular were useful to fill in the gap left by Open Society. But others didn't figure it out and were not able to survive.

Marta Pardavi is the cochair of the Hungarian Helsinki Committee, an organization that receives funding from Open Society. Pardavi is one of the most high-profile Hungarian civil rights advocates. We met on a very hot day in June 2019 at an outdoor café.

Pardavi explained that some organizations lost not only their funding from Open Society, but also their EU grants because EU grants require cofunding—they'll only fund a program or project if that program or project is also getting funding from somewhere else—which had come from Open Society in the past. That meant that when Open Society pulled out their matching funds, the organizations lost that funding and the EU funding, too. And some of the organizations had never actually learned, or been taught, how to go out and raise money. There is work that some people feel could have been done, but wasn't, because the funding was gone or at least not as plentiful as it once was and they didn't know where to turn to replace it. Soros and Open Society had been especially generous in the region, but they were trying to change their role in this part of the world, and some people doing work in civil society were not able—and in some cases, could not imagine how—to keep doing that work without Open Society.

The cultural realm was hit, too—performances, literary journals, exhibits and openings. Soros and Open Society, she told me, were known, and were everywhere, in part because of their support for cultural life. When that was reduced, not only was there less cultural life, but what Soros and Open Society did, she said, was less understood, and seemed murkier and more mysterious.[6]

András Bozóki, who turned down a role in the first free parliament to be a professor at CEU, went on to be the Hungarian minister of culture in the early 2000s. What he noticed, he said, is that there was more cultural life in the 1990s. The money had just been there for it, and so the people who put on shows and played music and made journals never learned how to go out and get it.[7]

And there was also less money for them to go out and get in the mid-2000s, not because of Open Society, but because the world—and societies in it, both open and closed—was about to take a financial plunge.

THE EARLY 2000S AND MID-2010S were a tumultuous time for Soros personally. In 2005, he divorced his second wife, Susan Weber. In 2011, his ex-girlfriend, Brazilian Adriana Ferreyr, who was then twenty-eight years old to Soros's eighty-one, gave an interview to the *New York Post* in which she alleged that Soros told her that he was giving the $1.9 million condo she had picked out to another woman, and that he threw a lamp at her and tried to choke her when she "tried to reason with him." (Soros later said that it was Ferreyr who had attacked him; her $50 million lawsuit against him was thrown out.)[8] The other woman, whom Ferreyr said Soros described as a nurse and a travel companion, was the then–thirty-nine-year-old Tamiko Bolton.[9] In 2013, Soros married Bolton, a health and education consultant who, at the time, had recently advised on the development of an internet-based yoga education program.[10]

But if those years were tumultuous for Soros personally, so, too, were they an upheaval for almost everyone else. In 2008, the world economy crashed.

It began in 2007 with the subprime mortgage market in the United States, but then evolved into a U.S. banking crisis, which, since the world economy is interconnected, snowballed into a global financial crisis.

In his book on George W. Bush and the bubble of American supremacy, Soros had written that one problem with globalization is that, when something goes wrong, the have-nots are hurt more than the haves.[11] After the 2008 financial crisis, this was true both within and between countries. The crisis hurt the poor in individual countries, and it hurt poor countries.

Soros himself was not shaken by the financial crisis, for which he credited his philosophical outlook: his knowledge of fallibility and reflexivity, his keen eye for bubbles and busts. "My conceptual framework enabled me both to anticipate the crisis and to deal with it when it finally struck," he said in the opening of his Budapest lectures in 2009.

There was financial as well as philosophical skill involved, too. "George traded brilliantly," Rodney Jones, the economist who'd worked with Soros at the time of the Asian financial crisis, told me. "George hedged Quantum Fund in 2008 personally . . . [he] worked out quickly that asymmetries were at work again."

Soros felt that his success during the crash in 2008 meant that, as he put it in the Budapest lectures a year later, "My philosophy was no longer a personal matter; it deserves to be taken seriously as a possible contribution to our understanding of reality." That inspired him to give the Budapest lectures, but it also inspired him to establish the Institute for New Economic Thinking.

INET, founded in 2009, is, per its website, "a nonpartisan, non-profit organization devoted to developing and sharing the ideas that can repair our broken economy and create a more equal, prosperous, and just society." Soros, its cofounder, announced $50 million toward the project in the form of $5 million each year for ten years.

Rob Johnson—the man who joined Soros Fund Management from Bankers Trust shortly before the shorting of the pound—said that back in 2008 he and Soros talked about how the global financial crisis was not the end of "this kind of stuff." The global economy needed to be changed. Johnson said he and Soros believed that the Troubled Asset Relief Program that passed Congress in the wake of the crash was "buying everyone off in the way least offensive to the financial sector, and the population is paying for it."

Johnson recalled to me that Soros told him, "I grew up in a Hungary that was torn up by Nazi Germany, and it's my belief that the 1931 banking crisis destroyed order. I want to start a foundation about what's wrong with economics."

They convened about thirty people at Soros's Bedford estate for two days ("and a breakfast") and concluded that economics was further off course than they'd thought. INET was, and is, meant to fill the void. "George is essentially saying, this one could be so severe. These guys are so far off course," Johnson told me.[12]

Soros had long been critical of what he described as "market fundamentalism" and of unchecked deregulation. But critics of INET and its output argue that that isn't enough, and suggested that, for all its focus on debate, INET's products aren't sufficiently pluralistic in recognition of different approaches to economic thought.[13]

SOROS ALSO UNDERSTOOD THAT ECONOMIC calamity wasn't only an intellectual matter: for people on both sides of the Atlantic, it meant real, tangible hardship, particularly in communities that were already less well-off.

In Europe, those poor countries were predominantly in Central and Eastern Europe. Soros gave money—$100 million—to buffer the blow in the region by supporting nonprofits in June 2009. "The EU must do more in terms of providing support, including financial support," Soros said in an interview at the time. "The International Monetary Fund programs [launched in Hungary, Ukraine, Latvia, and about five other countries] are very severe in terms of cutting budgets. The EU must solidify support for EU values."[14]

But the EU didn't, or at least didn't sufficiently to stop the rise of the kinds of political sentiment that Soros was worrying about. People had sacrificed to join the EU. Joining the EU is expensive for aspiring countries; they need to implement a set of rules and regulations, and their laws and institutions need to fall in line. All of that costs money.[15] And some citizens don't necessarily immediately see a return on their countries' investment, despite all the promises made about how joining the EU is joining the future and how their lives—not just their countries' or their neighbors' but their individual lives—will be better. In part, that is because the integration process is driven by European and national elites,[16] and fails, some say, to fully involve or inform the citizens in the countries that are joining. In part, it is because these countries joined the EU roughly around the time of the global financial crisis.

Many voters in Central and Eastern Europe were tired of their elites. The EU elites had failed them and their own politicians had, too. And so they turned to politicians who spoke ill of the EU, and elites, and bureaucrats, and financiers.

"The system is actually broken," Soros said of the world

financial system in one of a series of speeches at Central European University in 2009. "And needs to be fixed."[17]

Soros believed that the post-2008 financial markets had been put on "artificial life support." He offered a series of changes that could be made to improve matters: He argued that financial authorities needed to keep bubbles from getting too big. Regulators may not be able to recognize bubbles, but they can at least receive feedback from markets and correct their mistakes. Availability of credit, he argued, needs to be checked by monetary tools and credit controls. Central banks could go back to limiting lending to particular sectors to keep sectors from "overheating." Banks that were bailed out for being too big to fail after 2008 need to be made to "use less leverage and accept various restrictions on how they invest the depositors' money." Regulators should check compensation packages of proprietary traders.

Soros's argument was that he had successfully foreseen the financial crash, knew the system, and had the recommendations to improve it.

The electorate of Central and Eastern Europe agreed that the system was broken. But they didn't want international reform. They didn't want financiers, whom they blamed for their ills, to offer suggestions. They wanted to vote for antisystem politicians.

In Hungary, that meant reelecting Viktor Orbán to power.

ORBÁN HAD ALREADY BEEN PRIME minister for a few years once before, from 1998 to 2002. He had flirted with conservative politicians across Europe—he'd won, after all, by beating the coalition that was the Socialists and liberal Free Democrats. And he established the House of Terror, a museum directed by Maria Schmidt, a sometime Orbán-confidante historian who controversially manages to consistently present Hungarians as the victims of history, not complicit in crimes against Jewish people but suffering themselves before others.[18] The museum presents German occupation and Soviet rule as equally terrible.

After 2002, the Free Democrats and the Socialists were back in power in a coalition, as they had been in the 1990s—after the Hungarian Democratic Forum, otherwise known as the conservative party that slandered Soros with antisemitism as he was launching CEU, and before Orbán won the first time.

Then the financial crash happened. In 2009, Ferenc Gyurcsány, the liberal prime minister, resigned, saying that his remaining in the role was rendering necessary socioeconomic reform impossible—he was, after all, in charge during the economic crash, and so was blamed for the country's ills. The man who replaced him, Gordon Bajnai, was quite effective, talented, and committed to reform. That, at least, is how Péter Balázs, who was the Hungarian minister of foreign affairs from 2009 to 2010, presented the situation to me in May 2019. Balázs and I met at the Prague European Summit, held in the Czech Ministry of Foreign Affairs; I interviewed him in an ornate room literally called the Gold Hall. I wondered if this sort of thing contributed to a general exasperation with elites.

Bajnai, in order to rein in the deficit, had made painful budget cuts. When Orbán won, unemployment was at 11.4 percent. The economy had contracted by 6.3 percent in the year prior to the election.[19]

Orbán came back to power, in Balázs's telling, simply because he had been out of power when the economy crashed. And Orbán was determined not to lose it again.

There is a photo of Orbán and Soros from 2010—the year that Orbán became prime minister again, and the year that Soros gave almost $1 million to help Hungary with an industrial sludge disaster. Soros is looking at Orbán and smiling. Orbán is looking down at the floor and grinning.[20] Looking at it now, one wonders if he knew then that he would turn on his onetime patron and Hungary's most famous benefactor, or if, that year, he was just happy to take the money.

CHARLES GATI FIRST MET GEORGE Soros in the 1980s. Gati, who is originally from Hungary, was a professor at Columbia University at the time, and back then Soros was still seeking advice on the best ways to give money. When I spoke to Gati in July 2019, he told me the two were never especially close. They'd go out for lunch occasionally, and once, on a stormy day when Soros's limo couldn't make it to the Council on Foreign Relations to pick them up after an event, Gati lent Soros $1.25 for bus fare (Soros never paid him back; Gati estimates that, with inflation, he's now owed $2.50). Gati doesn't feel that Soros gave sufficient credit for the success of his work in Hungary in the 1980s to his close friend, Miklós Vásárhelyi, who was Soros's right-hand man at the Hungarian Soros Fund. Gati and Soros grew further apart when Gati moved to Washington, D.C., in the 1990s—where he still lives and works as a professor at the School of Advanced International Studies at Johns Hopkins. That was where I interviewed him in an office seemingly as full of books as it was space to move.

Gati got invited to several Soros parties but found them "unpleasant occasions."

"He was married to his previous wife," Gati said, and "in front of everybody else said the most unpleasant things about her." One such incident is detailed in Kaufman's biography of Soros. At their turn of the century party, Soros toasted his wife, saying he'd always had a taste for ugly women (it was apparently a joke between husband and wife meant to lessen some of the tension that Soros's mother's dislike of Susan Weber brought into their marriage).

All of this is to say that Charles Gati and George Soros were friendly, but never especially close. Charles Gati was, however, close to another Hungarian: Viktor Orbán.

Back in the late 1980s, Gati, like Soros, supported Fidesz. Almost all of his friends back in Budapest supported the Free Democrats. I asked him why he, then, went for Fidesz. Gati explained that the Free Democrats were intellectual and Jewish, and he didn't think they'd be able to capture power. Fidesz had a better chance to win the countryside; they weren't Jewish.

I asked him when, in his years of knowing Orbán, did he realize that Orbán was not the liberal democrat that people—educated people, including Gati—had believed him to be.

He said he would tell me a story.

In 1992, Orbán, then a parliamentarian, came to the United States on an Eisenhower Fellowship. For the time that he was in New York, Gati said, Orbán stayed in the living room in the Gati family's 96th Street apartment.

And so, two years later, in 1994, when Gati was going around Hungary to see the different parties' campaigns, Orbán said that he would personally take him to his village to see the Fidesz campaign.

Orbán drove him out to a town called Szekesfehervar ("Hungarian is a beautiful language," I told Gati after he spelled out the name for me; he told me not to try to learn it). Orbán was driving quite quickly on the main road, and continued, in their cheap car, to go quite fast even though when they turned onto a less-than-well-paved country road Gati asked Orbán to slow down. He was scared; it was a bad car on a poor road, and Gati explained to his friend that he wasn't used to it. Orbán agreed, looked in the mirror, looked at Gati, and then sped up.

"He was testing me," Gati said. "I should have noticed at that time that he was a gambler."

He said that only five years later, during Orbán's first term as prime minister, he realized that his friend did not have the character he'd once thought he possessed. In 1999, Gati introduced Orbán at a stateside event (Gati believes it was at Freedom House). Orbán said, "I wouldn't know anything about Hungarian history without Professor Gati." But Gati hadn't taught Orbán Hungarian history.

"He was a politician who wanted to gain an audience," Gati said. And he was friendly, and he played, by Gati's own admission, to his vanity. "Other friends kept warning me," he said. But Orbán was dynamic, and smart, and had "political acumen."

Even so, by 2001—the year Orbán got a visit with Vice President Dick Cheney (President George W. Bush declined to offer the prime minister an Oval Office visit, reportedly at least in part because Orbán refused to denounce a far-right leader who said the United States deserved the September 11 attacks)[21]—the two men, Gati and Orbán, were no longer on speaking terms.[22]

I had one more question for Gati about Orbán. Was the anti-Soros campaign—the fact that Orbán ran his reelection campaign by attacking Soros, the fact that he was pushing Soros's university out of the country, the fact that parliament kept passing laws that conveniently targeted NGOs that had received funding from Open Society, the relentless attacks against a man who lives an ocean away—just a cover for his alleged corruption?

I asked because Bálint Magyar—the Hungarian sociologist who was minister of education before Orbán came to power and before he came back to power again—described Hungary, to me and in writing, as a mafia state. He says that Orbán's illiberalism is a distraction from the corruption through which he has reportedly enriched his family—in particular his father—and close friends.[23] There have been accusations that the Hungarian chief prosecutor is not investigating corruption charges against Orbán allies, including members of the prime minister's family. Award-winning Hungarian journalist Katalin Erdélyi said in 2019, "In the past years, it has become clear that there are a few businesspeople close to the government whose companies nearly always win the large public contracts. The investments are frequently overpriced, costing much more than initial estimates."[24]

Soros himself now uses Magyar's language to describe what's happening in Hungary. In March 2018, in his New York City apartment, Soros held a book launch that I attended for the writer and historian Paul Lendvai's biography of Orbán. At the very beginning of his opening remarks, Soros said that Orbán's most ardent "followers," his inner circle, were "afraid to lose their livelihoods" if Orbán lost the elections of 2018. "There are countries, Hungary in particular, which are stealing European money on a large scale," he later added, though he stressed that the Hungarian people "should not be punished for the sins of their government."

But Gati disagreed that it was all about money. "Deep down," he told me, Orbán's "number-one motivating factor is to show his father he is a big deal."

That means Orbán needs to stay in his job. It means it isn't enough to show he's as good as the liberals, the urbanites, "slick city boys who knew languages." People "like Bálint Magyar," whose father was a theatre director, who knew anyone who was anyone.

Orbán, Gati said, wants to show that he is the most anyone of all.

The goal, Gati said, is "defeating the liberals." The "means to that end is the mafia state. So that he and his Fidesz will live forever."[25]

Soros—the real Soros, the person who made money and gave it away—helped make Orbán somebody. He gave him and his Fidesz money. But Orbán could use Soros—a mythical version of Soros, someone accused of using his money to undermine everything Hungarians hold dear—to become somebody bigger and more powerful.

And there was another man, also an ocean away, who could show him how.

ARTHUR FINKELSTEIN WAS A NEW Yorker. He was Jewish. He was wealthy (asked by Ronald Reagan biographer Craig Shirley how his name was pronounced, Finkelstein reportedly said, "If I was a poor Jew, it would be Finkelsteen, but since I am a rich Jew, it's Finkelstine"). He was gay. And he was a powerful Republican political operative.[26]

In the 1970s, Finkelstein worked for Richard Nixon. In the decades that followed, he worked for various Republicans—according to some, half of all Republican senators in the 1980s were Finkelstein clients. He learned the effectiveness of pitting one part of the electorate against the other; he learned what happened when you harnessed fear: you could win.

Then, in the mid-1990s, he started to work for an Israeli politician by the name of Benjamin Netanyahu. When Netanyahu became prime minister, Finkelstein was hailed as having forever changed campaigning. Finkelstein kept Netanyahu on as a high-profile client through his (that is, Finkelstein's) consultancy firm, GEB International, along with his protégé, George Birnbaum (another Finkelstein protégé was David Cornstein, Trump's current ambassador to Hungary).

In 2008, Netanyahu introduced a still-out-of-power Viktor Orbán to Arthur Finkelstein, a man who would be instrumental in Orbán's return to power and in developing Soros conspiracy theories.

They first worked toward getting Orbán back into office. Birnbaum proudly told reporter Hannes Grassegger, "We blew the Socialist party off the table even before the election." This perhaps had more to do with the economy than the particular genius of Arthur Finkelstein: Hungarians were deeply unhappy with the government after the economic crash of 2008 and subsequent crisis. It was the world financial crash, one former Hungarian official told me on condition of anonymity back in 2017, that started to change things for George Soros.

The Influence of Soros

In 2012, with the Hungarian government rewriting the constitution, drawing criticism from the opposition, Finkelstein and Birnbaum realized that Orbán needed an enemy to maintain political energy and enthusiasm. The Socialists and Free Democrats were defeated, and Fidesz was co-opting the nationalist rhetoric of their far-right challenger, Jobbik. The enemy needed to be fresh, outside of the Hungarian political spectrum. They came up with Soros.

How? In Birnbaum's telling, the selection of Soros as bogeyman was counterintuitive. He wasn't a politician, he didn't live in Hungary, and he was already old. It was only Finkelstein's ingenuity that recognized Soros—a name everyone knew, a man blamed for Black Wednesday and seen as supportive of liberal causes—as the perfect choice.[27]

What this telling overlooks is that Finkelstein and Birnbaum didn't invent Soros the bogeyman; they reinvented him. István Csurka of the Democratic Forum in Hungary, Václav Klaus after the Czech Republic and Slovakia split, Vladimír Mečiar while losing his grip on power, and Mahathir Mohamad after economies in Asia crashed—they had all blamed Soros in the 1990s. Dennis Hastert, Bill O'Reilly, and Glenn Beck had turned the House of Representatives and Fox News on to him in the 2000s.

Finkelstein didn't discover the magic lamp. He just went back into the cave, retrieved it, dusted it off, and released a genie that has yet to go back in. Their rhetoric is slightly more subtle—Orbán is careful to not actually say "Jew," even while he was regularly accused of antisemitic tropes—but only slightly.

The difference, István Rév, the first CEU employee and now its archivist, explained to me in his office in Budapest, was that, while the conspiracy theories had been there, they'd never been embraced quite so wholeheartedly by the government. By the mainstream.

Now, with Finkelstein's old new idea embraced by Orbán, the

person in the highest, most central position of power was pushing the idea of Soros the bogeyman.

THE SOROS CONSPIRACY THEORIES STARTED slowly.

In 2013, *Heti Válasz*, a progovernment newspaper, ran an article criticizing NGOs funded by Soros. It argued that these organizations were controlled by Soros to strengthen civil opposition.

Conspiracy theories and rewritten realities weren't limited to Soros, although his persona was an integral part of them. A year later, in 2014, the Hungarian government had a memorial to German occupation erected under cover of darkness. It was meant not to atone for the Jewish victims of collaboration and occupation or the antisemitic laws that preceded World War II, but to honor the victims of German occupation. There was objection from Jewish leaders, who noted that Hungary had been Hitler's ally and that the Arrow Cross, the Hungarian fascist party that briefly ruled the country toward the end of World War II, had been actively involved in the persecution of Jews. The memorial still stands to this day, its presence passively by and large accepted by the city and the country. Across from it there is a smaller makeshift memorial with a sign protesting the historical inaccuracies of the official memorial. This, Rév told me, was where it started: Orbán's rewriting of history for Hungary's glory, and his, and the smaller, but still present, resistance against it. This was Orbán's second term—and Orbán's grip on control of national narratives was set to tighten.[28]

Rewriting history to stress Hungarian innocence went beyond one memorial: During President Barack Obama's administration, Hungarian government spokesperson Zoltán Kovács told Erika Schlager, an expert in international law at the U.S. Helsinki Commission, "While the greatest tragedy for Hungarian Jews was the

Holocaust, the greatest tragedy for the rest of the Hungarians was the signing of the Treaty of Trianon." The U.S. ambassador at the time, Eleni Kounalakis, tried to impart to Kovács that this was not helpful messaging for Hungarians. She later understood that it was the new national narrative; Hungarians weren't the losers of history but its victims.[29]

In 2015, the anti-Soros campaign shifted into high gear. When Russian opposition figure Boris Nemtsov was murdered, government television, at the behest of higher-ups, added to its report the allegation that Nemtsov was not working independently as a leading opposition figure, but was paid by Soros to challenge Putin. According to one state-backed journalist familiar with the matter who asked to remain anonymous, that was a surprise—Soros wasn't featured on television or in conspiracy theories as much back then. Whether the government was trying to gain favor with Russia, which banned Open Society in Russia that same year, or just saw a way to slip Soros and his nefarious deeds into a story, is unclear.

Then came the development that cemented Soros's status as bogeyman. The migration crisis in Europe started that year, and Soros, whose organizations helped, for example, to provide lawyers for asylum seekers, was blamed. The concept of Soros as bogeyman really gained momentum in September 2015—after the summer of migrants and refugees trying desperately to make it to safety from war in the Middle East, particularly from Syria. Soros was already responsible for undermining Christian civilization, for smuggling in migrants, for the corrosion of Hungarian society. And centrist parties elsewhere in Europe didn't speak up to counter it or push back or put a stop to the conspiracy theories, Balázs told me in that gold room, because they agreed. They also didn't like migrants, also weren't happy with German Chancellor Angela Merkel's decision to let them through to Germany. They were relieved someone was saying something. They didn't mind if Soros was blamed in the process.[30]

EVENTUALLY, BLAMING SOROS FOR ONE'S ills, real and imagined, caught on across Europe. When, in Romania in 2017, protesters took to the streets to stop political kingmaker Liviu Dragnea from pushing through laws that would let him get away with his own corruption, the protesters (as well as, incredibly, the dogs that accompanied them) were described on television as having been paid for by George Soros.[31] That same year, I interviewed two teenagers who were leading anticorruption protests in Slovakia. They said that some accused them of not really organizing the protests and asked if I could guess who the person on whose behalf they were apparently acting was. I guessed George Soros; I was correct (lucky guess).[32] Several months later, when the Slovak prime minister, Robert Fico, was called on to step down because corruption in Slovakia had led to the murder of a young journalist and his fiancée, Fico said that Soros was behind the calls for his resignation (he did eventually resign).[33] In 2018, Turkish President Recep Tayyip Erdoğan said that the man who was really behind the 2013 Gezi Park protests against an urban development plan in part of Istanbul a full five years earlier was "the famous Hungarian Jew George Soros. This is a man who was assigned to divide nations and shatter them. He has so much money and he is spending it in these ways."[34]

It took off outside of Europe, too. In 2018, Benjamin Netanyahu, through whom Orbán met Finkelstein, shared an article falsely alleging that Soros had cooperated with the Iranian regime.[35] One might think that Netanyahu, leader of the only Jewish state, would be opposed to smearing a Jewish person by accusing him of having invisible power and influence, reproducing a centuries-old trope. One would be wrong; Netanyahu was no friend to liberalism, which Soros was broadly seen as promoting, and, in any event, Soros, through Open Society, has supported organizations that opposed Netanyahu government policies, like J Street and Amnesty International (or, as Netanyahu put it, Soros "continuously undermines Israel's democratically elected governments by funding organizations that defame the Jewish state and seek to deny it the right to defend itself").[36]

That same year, at a press conference I attended following the Russia-US Helsinki summit, President Vladimir Putin said while standing next to Donald Trump that Soros's influence in the United States was somehow akin to that of Russian companies accused of meddling in the 2016 U.S. presidential election. (Trump did not push back on this accusation.)[37]

And the conspiracies took off again in the United States, and this time not from fringe politicians or right-wing talking heads. In 2017, six U.S. senators wrote a letter asking then–Secretary of State Rex Tillerson's staff to look into what U.S. funding was going to Soros-backed organizations. "Our skepticism about Soros-funded groups undermining American priorities goes far beyond Eastern Europe," a spokesperson for one of the senators, Mike Lee of Utah, wrote to me in an email that fall.[38] The main thrust of the letter—which was more notable than any particular action that came from it—was not that billionaires should not be involved in development abroad, but that Open Society in particular was pushing progressive values around the world, and that the senators did not feel that they should stand for that. Also in 2017, Connie Mack IV, a former congressman from Florida, lobbyist for the Hungarian government, and friend of Finkelstein, tried to smear Fiona Hill, a top National Security Council official, for having alleged ties to Soros; he was unsuccessful, but two years later, in 2019, Marie Yovanovitch, the U.S. ambassador to Ukraine, was pushed out of her position after similar allegations were made (in the fall of 2019, Hill would go on to slam Soros conspiracy theories as part of her testimony during the impeachment hearings held in relation to Trump's dealings in Ukraine after Yovanovitch was removed).[39] In 2004, Soros conspiracy theories were for the likes of Lyndon LaRouche and the angriest Fox commentators (and Dennis Hastert). Now, through a combination of foreign suggestion and deep fear of the other, they were being pushed by elected U.S. senators and having repercussions for people who had dedicated their professional lives to serving the United States.

And, in time, they were pushed by the president himself. In the fall of 2018, protesters demonstrated at the U.S. Senate, holding up signs against Brett Kavanaugh, who, after being nominated to a lifetime appointment on the Supreme Court, was alleged to have attempted to sexually assault Dr. Christine Blasey Ford in high school. Trump tweeted, "Look at all of the professionally made identical signs. Paid for by Soros and others. These are not signs made in the basement from love!"[40] When it was revealed that two women who confronted one senator, Jeff Flake, in an elevator worked for the Center for Popular Democracy, which does receive funding from Soros, the story became that Soros was behind the confrontation. "Look who was behind the Jeff Flake elevator set up," read one *New York Post* headline.[41]

It wasn't that the *New York Post* was wrong, exactly. Soros did provide money to the organization. Soros, through Open Society, does support NGOs that support people, some of whom do protest, around the world. But there was an agency given to Soros—and taken from the people actually protesting—that made it conspiratorial. It also gave it whiffs of that old antisemitic trope—that of the wandering Jew turning the good folk, subverting the nation to which he himself would never belong.

Nowhere was this trope as consistently on display as in Hungary.

The Influence of Soros

During his election campaign in March 2018, Viktor Orbán—who said before the campaign began that fighting Soros would be a major campaign feature—said, "We are fighting an enemy that is different from us. Not open, but hiding; not straightforward but crafty; not honest but base; not national but international; does not believe in working but speculates with money; does not have its own homeland but feels it owns the whole world."[42]

He never said the word Jewish, and the Hungarian government, then and now, denied there was anything antisemitic about invocations of Soros, offering reassurances that Hungary is experiencing a Jewish renaissance, even though, in fall 2017, parliamentarian András Aradszki delivered an address on "The Christian duty to fight against the Satan/Soros plan."[43]

Eventually, in Hungary, it wasn't enough to rhetorically attack Soros. If he was such a threat, then, surely, he had to be stopped, and his organizations did, too. In 2017, the Hungarian parliament passed a law similar to a "foreign agent law" that already existed in Russia, where Open Society was banned back in 2015.[44] The Hungarian variant, which passed 130–40, said that Hungarian organizations receiving more than $26,000 in foreign funding needed to register as "foreign supported" and disclose their foreign donors, or close down.[45] Open Society moved its offices from Budapest to Berlin in 2018; staff were apparently too scared to stay in Budapest after learning that people appearing to be state security operatives showed up at their homes.[46] The same year, in 2018, the Hungarian government made giving certain kinds of help to migrants illegal under what was literally known as the "Stop Soros" plan (NGO workers who helped migrants who weren't eligible for asylum to seek asylum risked jail time under the law).[47]

Some of the NGOs that came under pressure were left to feel that Open Society and Soros hadn't actually been there for them in their time of need. They were tagged as Soros-sponsored even though Soros and Open Society aren't nearly as present in the region as they once were. In 2017 in Bucharest, the head of what was once the Romanian Open Society, now the Serendinno Foundation, Gabriel Petrescu, who was fighting with Open Society over who owned the building out of which the organization works, complained to me that he has difficulty fundraising because he's associated with the organization.[48] Sándor Lederer, an anticorruption activist in Hungary, told me that same year, "NGOs' most important value, and why citizens trust them and believe them, is their credibility . . . The one thing to ruin this [is] to show they're only puppets of other interests."[49]

"Some NGOs might feel they were abandoned by this donor," Marta Pardavi, the cochair of the Hungarian Helsinki Committee, told me at that outdoor café.

You have to wonder, she said, given how much money Soros has given to Hungary, "Why don't you have more people saying this [what Orbán is doing] is unacceptable?"

In part, she said, it's because they are afraid. They are too intimidated to speak out. I had already seen this—there were organizations that had refused to speak to me when I reached out ahead of my trip in June 2019 after I explained why I was getting in touch; they apologized and asked me to please understand. And I did. They were already under pressure from the government, and I could appreciate why they would not want to bring more attention to themselves and drain more of their already limited resources by going out of their way to defend Soros or talk to me.

But it is also, she said, that there is a "detachment" that is perceived in the local NGO scene. Local actors believe that Soros has withdrawn from Hungarian society. And so they have withdrawn their support from Soros, staying silent.

To her organization, Pardavi said, Open Society "has been a useful, good donor." They've been supportive, they put them in touch with other, useful people, and they improved the work that Pardavi and her team were doing.

Before Open Society left, there was a farewell event. Pardavi told me that she made the recommendation that Open Society should put more money and support into Hungary and similar places. She said she hasn't seen that anyone's taken her up on that yet.[50]

I had, and have, some sympathy for these NGOs, which were set up to be attacked by a government because of an affiliation with a person and organization that, in some cases, wasn't even supporting them anymore. I could understand why they were frustrated.

But I wondered whether the answer to attacks on Soros could be more money and presence from Soros. If what Soros had learned—and relearned, and relearned—was that only society can open society, would more outside money help? Would it hurt? Would it matter at all? If these organizations were now in trouble because Soros had funded them and they hadn't learned to fundraise for themselves, and because his name was attached to them, it seemed difficult to conclude that more money and attention from Soros was the answer.

The idea had been that the European Union would do its part—why hadn't it? Why did the EU seem to really push back against Hungary once Orbán started attacking not only Soros, but also Jean-Claude Juncker, who, until 2019, was president of the European Commission? Why was it only then that the EU-wide party to which Orbán's Fidesz belonged, the European People's Party, suspended Fidesz? For years, while attacks on Soros—and, by extension, the NGOs that work on migrant and asylum seeker rights and transparency and government accountability—were ramping up, it hadn't.[51]

I asked Charles Gati if he thought this was somehow Soros's fault. If he, by leaving this part of Europe before it was ready to go on without Open Society, had ensured that it would devolve into a closed society.

"It's hard to judge," Gati told me when I interviewed him back in Washington. "How far do you go to fight a battle or a war that doesn't pay off?"

"I don't blame him," he said. "Enough is enough."[52]

Particularly because CEU, the one institution that was always meant to outlast Soros in Hungary, has mostly been forced to leave.

AT FIRST, ISTVÁN RÉV, THE CEU archivist, told me, they'd thought that CEU might remain untouched by the Hungarian government. It was, after all, an American institution, affiliated with Bard College in upstate New York. Students who graduate from CEU get U.S. and Hungarian degrees. Surely, it was one thing to cross NGOs, but another to go after a U.S. institution, particularly given Orbán's eagerness to develop closer ties with the new U.S. president, Donald Trump.[53]

Perhaps they should have known better. "CEU," Balázs said, "was a window to the outside world . . . Dictatorships are always afraid of criticism and knowledge."[54]

Those who believed CEU would remain under the government's radar were disabused of that notion in the spring of 2017. In early April, the Hungarian parliament voted 123–38 in favor of a measure that said that foreign universities could only remain in Hungary if they had a bilateral agreement with Hungary and the institution's "home country," where the university had to have a campus.

The measure was passed on the first day that lawmakers had the opportunity to debate it. The law was quickly and widely seen as targeting Soros's university and became known as "Lex CEU," Latin for "CEU law." (The Hungarian government denied that they were targeting Soros specifically, one spokesperson writing in an email, "Nobody stands above the law in Hungary. Any other interpretations are symptoms of political hysteria," which was blamed on opposition parties "having the support of self-styled nongovernmental international networks funded by George Soros.")

There were two parts of the law that were difficult for CEU to follow. The first was that, although it had an affiliation with Bard College and gave out U.S. diplomas, it didn't make much sense for a university dedicated to Central Europe to have a U.S. campus. The second is that, in the United States, agreements with other countries are made with individual states, not the U.S. government. CEU couldn't do what it was being asked to do.

Still, CEU tried. The rector, failed Canadian prime ministerial candidate Michael Ignatieff, was confident that he could drum up support from the United States. This was, after all, a U.S. institution. Ignatieff told me over the phone in 2017 that the Hungarian government, in making an example of an American institution, would run afoul of Trump's America First administration. Ignatieff also said that the law was unconstitutional—Hungarian basic law protects academic freedom. When we spoke, Ignatieff pointed out that the Hungarian Academy of Sciences had openly backed CEU, because the issue was bigger than any one university[55] (in hindsight, on this point, he was correct; in 2019, the Hungarian parliament put the academy's institutes under government control).

The Trump administration would later be blamed for not doing enough to support CEU. Cornstein, Trump's ambassador to Hungary, would blame George Soros in a *Washington Post* interview for bringing pressure from the Hungarian government upon himself. In fact, though, the Trump administration did try to save CEU, albeit not particularly publicly. Cornstein said that "resolving the CEU issue" was one of his main goals as ambassador in an interview in August 2018. Two months later, at a CEU event, Cornstein suggested that the Trump administration expected Hungary to resolve the issue in CEU's favor in exchange for everything else it had done for Hungary, including arranging meetings with key Trump officials and a general softening toward the Orbán government. "He just made it clear, and I mean surprisingly clear, that the U.S. has given several things to Hungary and it is time that they give something back," a person at the event told me. Trump officials told their Hungarian counterparts, albeit privately, that keeping CEU—which was, after all, a U.S. institution in which U.S. students were enrolled—open was a priority for the United States.[56]

Meanwhile, CEU was doing what it could to placate the Orbán government. In August 2018, CEU suspended its education programs for registered refugees and asylum seekers ("CEU has been forced to take this action in response to Hungarian legislation in respect of refugees and immigration which came into effect on August 24," an announcement on the CEU website read. "CEU's action follows advice from our tax advisors in respect of potential liability for a 25% levy on our immigration related programs. We are suspending these programs while we await clarification of our tax and legal situation").[57] That October, Hungary officially ended its recognition of gender studies as an approved master's program; a CEU spokesperson confirmed that that meant the end of Hungarian-accredited degrees in gender studies from CEU (the U.S. degrees were unaffected).[58] CEU signed a memorandum of understanding with Bard College to set up educational activities in New York State, hoping that that would be enough to allow CEU to stay in Budapest.[59]

And Hungarians, too, even those unaffiliated with CEU, took to the streets to march for the university. Thousands protested in Budapest.[60]

None of this was enough for the Hungarian government. The Bard agreement wasn't enough. And it was evidently not swayed by the U.S. government or by Ignatieff's public pleas—even as, more quietly, the university ended programs that set it apart in the first place.

The Hungarian government did not certify CEU to continue its operation in Hungary by the December 1, 2018, deadline. "CEU has been forced out," Ignatieff said in a statement. The university confirmed it would move to Vienna shortly thereafter; the Hungarian staff felt this was as much an end as it was a new beginning. Bozóki, the political scientist and former minister of culture, told me that it would just be a nice boutique university. Budapest and Vienna are different, he said. Maybe the U.S. board members just looked at a map, saw they were close, and thought it was the same. But it wasn't to him.[61]

Rév spoke with a sense of resignation, too. A university is like a tree, he told me. You can uproot it and replant it, but it won't grow in quite the same way. He had told me that CEU's battle in Budapest was existential. In Vienna, it wouldn't be.[62]

To say, as Bozóki seemed to, that it was all the same to the university's powers that be is not entirely fair. One member of the board of trustees, Kati Marton, is herself Hungarian-American. Her parents survived the Holocaust; her grandparents did not. Her family fled Hungary after the revolution in 1956, but she began going back in the 1980s. She does not remember, she told me, when she wasn't aware of George Soros (who insisted from the first, she said, that she call him George).

"That drama has absorbed a lot of his attention, and I have to say mine because we're both Hungarians," she told me over the phone in the summer of 2019. "It's more than merely—'merely' is a poor word here—about academic freedom. It's what's happening to our poor benighted homeland."

Joining CEU's board, she told me, "was the most exciting way for me to reconnect with the country that I was forced to leave.

What could be more meaningful than to be part of building a different kind of Hungary?" A cosmopolitan Hungary, a cultured Hungary, an open Hungary.

But Orbán, she said, had other ideas. "He's turning the country into his fiefdom and has really degraded all the things that my parents loved about the country."[63]

There is much pain felt by students, faculty, administrators, and even board members around the move. But the forced closure of an American institution—one the Trump administration had tried, however quietly and ineffectively, to save—did not bother the America First president too much. Orbán got his White House visit the following May, roughly six months after Ignatieff announced the university was forced out.[64]

Its existence in Hungary was, as István Rév put it to me, a fight from the beginning. That was why it was important that it be there, he had told me. But now the university in Budapest—at least the university as it had been, the robust, internationally renowned university that existed to serve as a counter to nationalism and small-mindedness—was no more.

I asked Soros if he felt that the European Union had failed to sufficiently take Open Society's place after Central and Eastern European countries joined it, and if he felt that what happened to CEU was a failure of the EU.

"I should think the lion's share of the responsibility for the closure of the Central European University rests with the Hungarian prime minister. From banning gender studies to deliberately targeting the CEU with unnecessary restrictions, he created a climate where it was impossible for the university to function in Budapest freely and with integrity," he wrote. But then he added, "Although some members of the European Union have been strong in condemning his actions, the structure of the European Union is deficient in tools to discipline member states that fail to abide by its constitution. I can see that the new leadership of the EU are firmly aware of the problem and I am hopeful that they will address it."

ON A SWELTERING DAY IN June 2019 in Budapest, I took the tram to just in front of parliament, its big mauve domes overlooking a square of tourists. I walked, my face coated with sweat, around the corner to a building nondescript but for one sign: it was the office of the prime minister.

I was there to meet not with Orbán, but with his spokesperson, Zoltán Kovács. Kovács is highly educated—he got his Ph.D. at CEU—and speaks excellent English. He can, and often does, twist any argument so that it is the other person who is in the wrong for so much as suggesting, for example, that attacks on Soros are anti-semitic, or that CEU was targeted, or that it shouldn't be illegal to help asylum seekers.

I waited in a small room for about twenty minutes and then was greeted by Kovács. We walked into his considerably more ornate office and sat around a table—Kovács; his chief of staff, Rajmund, whom I'd met once back in Washington and who set up the interview; and me.

I explained first of all that I was not writing a hit piece on Soros, but that I did want it to be fair, and so wanted the official view.

I asked when the government came to believe Soros was a threat. "It is and it was a process," Kovács said. He believed that Soros and his foundations and university became more overtly political during the first Orbán government. They took sides with the Free Democrats, and the Free Democrats had gone into government with the Communists, and that was why Orbán's government needed a new constitution.[65]

I thought of the reference to Communists a month later, reading Paul Hanebrink's *A Specter Haunting Europe: The Myth of*

Judeo-Bolshevism. "Throughout the twentieth century, the idea of Judeo-Bolshevism embodied threats to national sovereignty," he wrote. "Nationalists in many different countries across Europe imagined the Jewish Bolshevik as a malevolent agent who worked tirelessly to subordinate the nation, which they imagined as a monoethnic community, to an international revolutionary order that had no place for 'true' national belonging or 'real' national identity." I thought of who gets to be a part of the nation, and of what happens to those who happen to live in a nation-state when they're not of the predominant nationality, and of how seeing all Jews as Communist was an easy way to discredit Jews in a non-Communist country, just as seeing all Jews as insufficiently Communist was an easy way to discredit them in the Soviet Union.[66]

I asked what Kovács made of the theory that Finkelstein was responsible for Orbán's embrace of anti-Soros campaigns. He said it wasn't true. Finkelstein was "nowhere at the turn of the millennium," the date Kovács had said was the starting point. It was then, he said, that he was sitting in CEU's library building, still a student, completing a Ph.D., and someone approached him and asked if he was a fascist. That, he said, was a "sign of something going wrong." CEU today, he said, is completely elitist. Ignatieff thinks everybody who doesn't think like him is "stupid." Kovács didn't seem particularly hung up on the incongruence of his degree being from the university his government was pushing out. In fact, in his telling, it was at that university that he realized there were these forces at work in his country.

I pushed him on why, then, people said Finkelstein had come up with it. Finkelstein's whole approach, Kovács told me, was that "to express something clearly, you need contrast." From contrast, he said, comes conflict.

And his conflict, their conflict, with Soros was that Soros "made himself a political actor."

"He doesn't have a democratic mandate," Kovács said. He and his foundations were never elected. Fidesz was. It is their job to defend the borders. Those who were helping people cross illegally were going against the law and the democratically elected government.

This was their problem, he said, with Soros. "Soros's Jewish identity was never a topic." The issue was "his globalist approach to things."

The word "globalist" is often taken as an antisemitic code word for "Jew." Tying Jewish individuals to nefarious international agendas is nothing new; such famed antisemites as Adolf Hitler blasted Jews as "international elements." The word "globalist" got fresh support from the alt-right in more recent years: for example, when Breitbart, the right-wing publication formerly run by Steve Bannon, who was White House chief strategist in the first year of the Trump presidency, put then–National Economic Council Director Gary Cohn's name between two globe emojis. The Anti-Defamation League has argued that Jewish people should not be described as globalists. Still, in fairness, some argue that it is not antisemitic, and is meant only as an alternative to "nativist" or "nationalist."[67]

"He is the ideal person in many ways," Kovács later said, "to personalize the globalist phenomenon," again using a word often taken to mean "Jews."

I asked why, then, the claims of antisemitism kept sticking to Hungary. He said it went back to the interwar period, when Hungary couldn't switch sides and so was with Germany. (A similar argument is presented in the Hungarian National Museum. Hungary had to stick with Germany; it was the only hope they had of reclaiming the land lost in the Treaty of Trianon.) In the 1990s, he said the liberal party "was basically reinforcing that narrative." The narrative of Hungary's historical guilt, and that said that the Hungarian political right was antisemitic.

But their problems with Soros, he reiterated, had nothing to do with Jewishness. And what even is Soros's Jewishness? I offered that I did not think it was tied to a particular nation. He said yes, exactly, it is supranational. "Just look at his attitude, his relationship with Israel." Soros is for globalism and against sovereignty. That is the issue.[68]

(Soros, in *George Soros on Globalization*, had this to say on sovereignty: "The interests of the sovereign state do not necessarily coincide with the interests of the people who inhabit it.")[69]

I asked about the idea that Soros was an excuse to cover their own corruption. "Corruption," Kovács said, is one of those "code words which . . . belongs to political liberals and the left."

The people who really refuse to play by the rules, he said, are NGOs. And were we really meant to think that Soros was just giving all this money away? "I've never seen in my life any institution where money was not conditional, including Mr. Soros's own university, actually . . . You have to fall in line in Mr. Soros's empire, it's unbelievable. Especially if it's a politicized area, like human rights."[70]

And in a certain sense, Kovács is right about all that. Soros was never elected. The NGOs he supports to track corruption or help asylum seekers are not accountable to the general public. Soros does not believe in the will of the sovereign nation above all. Soros does have far more power than the average person, and his philanthropic work isn't bound by borders, and he did make his money as a speculator. All of that is true.

But it's only part of the whole truth. Because it's also true—I hope it's true, anyway—that a democracy has more than democratic elections, and that it also has rule of law, and a free media, and allows independent institutions to try to hold elected representatives accountable. It's also true that I'm not crazy, and that when I hear someone describe a person as belonging to no nation but wanting to control the whole world, there is a reason that I think, "Jewish." It's also true that human rights are not so much inherently political as they are politicized by governments that use—or, more to the point, deny—them to score points. It's also true that there's a reason that so many NGOs received funding from Open Society, and it's that they weren't getting that support from their own government. It's also true that terms like "sovereignty" are used all over the world to tell those from abroad who might happen to catch a glimpse of hideous human rights abuses to butt out.

Politics is contrast, and from contrast comes conflict. All you have to do is not care too much about who really loses from the battle and you can beat your opponents. You can win. And when I left Kovács's office that day, it seemed very clear to me that he understood that, and that, even then, when he was sitting with me for my little interview, he knew he'd already won.

OF ALL THE COMPONENTS TO Soros campaigns and conspiracies, there is one that stands out as the reason that they stuck. The reason that Soros conspiracy theories picked up steam around the world beginning in 2015 is that that was when they stopped being conspiracy theories just about Soros. Soros was a danger to society, but not just because he existed. It was because of who he was accused of helping: migrants and asylum seekers.

Soros was almost a perfect foil for politicians in Central and Eastern Europe, and even in the United States: He was a wealthy, Hungarian, U.S.-based Jew. But in 2015, he became the perfect bogeyman. He became more than himself; in trumpeting Soros conspiracy theories, politicians were scaring up the image not only of Soros, but also of hordes of people invading their countries from countries where people did not look like them.

The perfect other, Magyar told me, isn't Soros, or an urban liberal. The perfect other is someone who doesn't speak the language, or have the same skin color, or know the culture. The perfect other, for a politician looking to divide people so as to gain power, is a migrant.[71]

Soros, when seen as helping liberals, could be a worthy opponent whom politicians could attack without fear of giving a platform or legitimacy to the people actually running against them. And that was good.

But Soros, when seen as helping migrants, could be an existential threat. For the purposes of clinging to power, that was even better.

CHAPTER 9

Closed Society

Nothing—not being involved in the breaking of the Bank of England, not speculating on Asian currencies, not supporting Sarajevo during the war or civil society in Slovakia, not putting money toward defeating George W. Bush in the United States or election monitoring in Georgia in 2004, not even the financial crash of 2008—was as effective at cementing Soros's status as the bogeyman as was the migration crisis.

The conspiracy theory about Soros and migration—the one that says that Soros is trying to erode borders, pack Central Europe with refugees, flood the United States with caravans of asylum seekers—both wildly overstates Soros's activity in immigration and misses the crucial role he has actually had in supporting the rights of migrants.

Even so, it makes a certain sense that migration would, late in his life, be the thing tied to the idea of George Soros. His foundation is called Open Society. What is a better test of one society's openness than how it treats those fleeing another? Soros wanted to push the idea of a society based on the idea of civic participation rather than on ethnonationalism; migration, and the influx of more people from different ethnic and national backgrounds, tests the tolerance of a society—even one that tells itself bedtime stories about being a nation of immigrants and a melting pot of cultures— for that concept, that vision, that notion of what it means to belong.

ONE EVENING IN AUGUST 2019, I called up Muzaffar Chishti, director of the Migration Policy Institute at New York University School of Law (the institute, its spokesperson was quick to point out, is a recipient of Open Society funding). Before that, Chishti was director of the Immigration Project of the Union of Needletrades, Industrial and Textile Employees, and he is also on the boards of the New York Immigration Coalition and the Asian American Federation.

I called him because I wanted to speak to an immigration policy expert who could talk me through a brief history of U.S. immigration policy debates. I expected him to start maybe twenty years in the past. Instead, he started in 1882.

Eighteen eighty-two, Chishti explained, was the year that limits were put on legal immigration. They were qualitative, not quantitative: It wasn't about how many people were coming in, but what kind of people they were. Paupers, for example, were banned; new Chinese immigrants were banned, too.

Qualitative limits to legal immigration remained until 1921. In the interim, two things happened: There were waves of immigrants from Europe in the early twentieth century, and eugenics became popular and convinced American lawmakers that some Europeans were scientifically superior to others. Northern and western Europeans were desirable; southern and eastern Europeans were not. And so, in 1921, quantitative restrictions of legal immigration were imposed through the national origin quota system. The quota system was calibrated to give preference to northern and western Europeans.

The law was controversial—President Woodrow Wilson vetoed it. But so, too, was it popular enough that Congress overrode the veto, and the eugenics-inspired quota system became law until 1965.

Years later, when he was campaigning to be president, Senator John F. Kennedy promised that he would end the quota system, opening America up to the entire world (and stop the denigration of Italians, whose descendants' votes he wanted).

President Kennedy was assassinated without getting Congress to do much of anything about the law. But after his death, his successor, President Lyndon B. Johnson—who had voted to keep the quota system in place in the 1950s—asked Kennedy's advisors what Kennedy had promised that he, Johnson, now had to achieve. And they pointed to the quota laws.

Nine months later, the system was changed.[1] Family members and skilled workers were given priority in legal immigration lines. All Europeans were created equal. America was open to the whole world. Rights were wronged.

Except, of course, that new wrongs, or at least issues, were created. The law was designed with the idea that immigration would continue to be from Europe, when actually it was increasingly from Asia; in the first five years after the law passed, immigration from Asian countries more than quadrupled.[2] While the quota system was done away with, there were still caps on immigrants from each country, as well as on total immigration. Prior to the 1965 law, there had been no limits on *Western* Hemisphere immigration; suddenly, Mexico was put into the global pool from which immigrants could be chosen to come to America. This, coupled with the 1964 elimination of the bracero program through which Mexican workers came to America from 1948 to 1964, effectively led to the creation of unauthorized immigration from Mexico.

Under President Jimmy Carter, the immigration debate was not over what limits to put on legal immigration, but on how to deal with unauthorized immigration. Under President Ronald Reagan, amnesty was given to 3 million people, but sanctions were placed on those workplaces that hired unauthorized immigrants as workers (a right previously protected by arguably the most powerful law in America: capitalism). In the 1980s, the Immigration Reform and Control Act was enacted to stop unauthorized immigration by preventing the undocumented from getting jobs—a primary reason they were coming to the United States. And then, in 1994 in California, Proposition 187, which banned unauthorized immigrants from using nonemergency health care and public education, passed with almost 60 percent of the vote.

Then came 1996, the year Chishti described to me as the Before Christ/After Christ moment in U.S. immigration history.[3]

I MET FRANK SHARRY IN his office in late May 2019. He works in a coworking space in Washington, D.C., and I took advantage of the free coffee, over which Sharry told me his Soros story.

In 2008, Sharry founded America's Voice, an immigration reform group established, according to its online mission statement, "to harness the power of American voices and American values to enact policy change that guarantees full labor, civil and political rights for immigrants and their families." But before that, he worked for seventeen years for the National Immigration Forum, a coalition and policy group. It was there that he was brought into Soros's orbit.

"I remember the day that Aryeh Neier, Arthur Helton, and Gara LaMarche walked into my office at the National Immigration

Forum," he told me, referring to the men who were, respectively, head of Open Society, director of Open Society's Forced Migration Projects, and Open Society's U.S. programs director at the time. It was in 1996.

"I don't think I had heard of Open Society being involved in U.S. migration issues before that," he said. And he would have, had they been especially active in the space—he was, after all, in charge of fundraising for the forum.

"They walked in because George Soros—this was reported to me, I didn't hear this directly from him—the story goes that he read a front-page *New York Times* piece—I remember the piece, lower left-hand corner of the *New York Times*—that talked about how the welfare reform bill that had passed in 1996 was cutting off legal immigrants from food stamps. About a million legal immigrants were set to lose their food stamps." The same year that Clinton signed into law a bill that increased penalties on immigrants who broke U.S. law and made more people eligible for deportation.

"And about another 500,000 people were losing their SSI benefits," he added. SSI is not Social Security but a particular program for the disabled and elderly who aren't eligible for regular Social Security. The immigrants' benefits were being cut to pay for the welfare reform. That was the subject of the article Soros had read.

"He was really concerned about it and wanted to do something about it, so he asked his chief advisors to ask around." He wanted to "make a big splash" and "do something that would jump-start a whole new conversation," Sharry told me.

Helton told Sharry they'd just come off making a big investment in Bosnia, where they'd put in a significant amount of money through a few channels. And they wanted to replicate what they'd done in Bosnia again, but in the United States and to help legal immigrants who were losing their benefits. Could the National Immigration Forum be that conduit?

"It was clear that they were talking millions. A big number," Sharry said. Truthfully, it was too much money for the National Immigration Forum. "It would have blown up our organization."

"They ultimately hired Antonio Maciel . . . they basically said, Antonio, you're in charge. You're the main program officer. Here's fifty million dollars. And that was a huge amount of money."[4]

"Philanthropist Pledges to Help Immigrants," read the *New York Times* headline from October 1996.[5]

Maciel and company called it the Emma Lazarus Fund, named for the poet who wrote the lines "give me your tired, your poor, your huddled masses yearning to breathe free" inscribed on the Statue of Liberty. Originally, the fund was going to be used to replace the money that was being taken from immigrants. But once Maciel connected with immigrants' rights groups, "We said if you're just replacing people's food stamps, they're gonna be in the same boat," Cecilia Muñoz, then head of policy for National Council of La Raza, a Latinx advocacy group, now chair of Open Society's U.S. board, told me over the phone in August 2019. The immigrants' rights advocates (unsurprisingly) suggested Open Society invest in advocacy. And that is what it did.

"It really did transform our field, in a way," Sharry said. And Soros and company were very clear on what they wanted: the majority of the money was to go to directly help people. "I thought that was so interesting."

The majority of the money, Sharry said, went to help people become citizens. (The rest went to a combination of litigation and advocacy.) Why? Because the best way within the system as it exists for legal immigrants to protect their rights is to become citizens. "Because if they're citizens then they're no longer caught up in this netherworld of relying on SSI, a program designed for really disabled forty-year-olds that's being used by fifty- and sixty- and seventy-year-old legal immigrants because that was the only thing available to them."

Then–U.S. President Bill Clinton had said when he signed welfare reform into law that the issue of legal immigrants' benefits would have to be revisited. "It was a throwaway line," Sharry told me. He and others had met with Janet Murguía, head of UnidosUS (formerly National Council of La Raza), then a top legislative staffer for the Clinton administration. In an off-record meeting, Sharry said, she admitted that there was no energy around it—the energy had to be generated from the outside.

"Because of Open Society's funding, we were able to put on a local/national advocacy effort that was really one of the most successful things we've ever done as a movement," Sharry said. Restoring SSI benefits was the more expensive fight. "As I recall, we won an initial battle that wasn't that difficult to restore food stamps . . . the much bigger uphill battle was to restore benefits to legal immigrants."[6]

All the while, Soros, through Open Society, was funding local groups that were helping legal immigrants gain citizenship and funding and strengthening local coalitions—which were also involved in advocacy for benefits eligibility at the state level.

Muñoz, who largely led the effort, said that Soros, through Open Society, "seeded the field that worked all over the country to lift up the stories of the terribleness that was gonna happen, and to make sure that those stories were in the faces of folks and Congress. My memory of those years is of people thinking I was making stuff up because it sounded too extreme," she said.[7]

"I knew we were winning," Sharry said, "when Paul Ryan, a legislative director for Sam Brownback, senator from Kansas, both of whom we knew because they were the most pro-immigration guys around in the Republican Party at the time," called in Sharry and Angela Kelley (now a strategic advisor for immigration at Open Society) and opened a book of media materials about the harm that was being done to legal immigrants that the coalitions had sent out. "He opens the book and he says, 'How do we make this stop? It's killing us back home. What do we have to do?' We never would have had the capacity to build a local/national campaign to expose the horrors of these policies being implemented if it wasn't for the Soros advocacy money," Sharry said.[8]

"We worked like dogs over the course of that year, and we worked with the Clinton administration," Muñoz told me. Clinton had made a commitment. And they were going to hold him to it. "Once this law has passed, the notion that you were gonna undo part of it—people thought we were out of our minds," she added.

But they won.

Eventually, as part of the balanced budget deal, $12 billion for legal immigrants' benefits was restored. It had been cut because more money for legal immigrants was not a politically winning message; several months later, it was part of the deal, all while more people were becoming citizens through well-funded local groups.

The balm was retrospective, not preventative; that is, the benefits were only restored for immigrants who were already in the United States. Still, "The benefits thing was about undoing an enormous harm the Congress has done," Muñoz said, also noting, "The reason we were able to do it is because George Soros funded the campaign."

"Say what you will about George Soros," she added. "His focus has never been on protecting himself."

I asked her what she made of the argument that Soros, who made a lot of money and had a lot of influence, should perhaps not have outsized power in a field like immigration, where the subjects of the debates—that is, immigrants themselves—did not necessarily have money, power, or influence.

"He's giving money to organizing networks. He's not telling them what to do. There are lots of ways to use money to try to assert power," she said. "Supporting the center for community change and organizing immigrant leaders is not exactly a heavy-handed power grab."

And then she added something else: "Find me a pure source" of funding, she said. And of course, I couldn't do that. The Ford Foundation is tied to cars; Rockefeller, to oil. Everyone who got rich off society seems to have hurt that society in some way.[9]

I could have said that Soros contributed to the creation of the world in which some people had more money—a lot more money—than others. But I didn't, because the reality was that, in 1996, immigrants were in some cases literally considering taking their own lives because they were going to lose their benefits and didn't know what to do, and Soros gave money that helped stop the bleeding.

Still, one wonders about the health of a country in which it takes a billionaire-backed advocacy campaign to shame legislators into restoring legal immigrants' access to welfare. One wonders—I wonder, at least—about the health of a country that is comfortable having both billionaires and people who worry that it is impossible to both stay in America and stay alive.

TWO YEARS LATER, IN 1998, a Republican bill sought to make citizenship restrictions more stringent. In response, the advocacy coalition put together a campaign with the slogan "Citizenship delayed is democracy denied" and pushed Senator Ted Kennedy and Representative Dick Gephardt to put together a bill to, in Sharry's words, "restore citizenship to its rightful place" by speeding up the naturalization process. It, again, created the conditions for a budget deal to include more money for a path to citizenship.

"The Soros money came in, it resourced the advocacy that led to benefits being restored to a million legal immigrants on food stamps and a half a million on SSI benefits, it led to a huge citizenship drive that nearly overwhelmed the system, but because we had the local/national capacity to advocate in a new way, we ended up financing the citizenship system so that the backlogs could be reduced," Sharry said.

Soros then became a regular funder in the immigration space. But the focus was more on improving life for immigrants in America and on comprehensive immigration reform than it was on, say, migration from Central America and Mexico.

"Open Society became a big player," Sharry said. "But they weren't, like, a radical player. They weren't the leftiest of the foundations saying, 'We want open borders, we're only going to fund groups that are pushing the envelope.' Hardly!"[10]

"He's not an immigration radical at all," Muñoz said. "The groups that get the resources are groups that are trying to reform the immigration system going through Congress supported by 85 percent of the public."[11]

But Chishti, the expert at the Migration Policy Institute, asked me a question: Who did the people saying Soros wasn't a left-wing funder think *were* left-wing funders? Open Society, he said, is much more involved in supporting activism and advocacy than some others. "The foundation is a very important player in the immigration policy and advocacy world," he said. Soros's entrée into the immigration space may have been welfare reform, but "over time, it evolved into, how do you provide the advocacy, how do you support advocacy work on behalf of immigrants," Chishti said.[12]

THE YEARS FOLLOWING WERE NOT a steady set of steps toward more rights for immigrants. In 2000 and early 2001, Chishti said, people thought comprehensive immigration reform was a "fait accompli." George W. Bush had campaigned on closer and improved ties with Latin American countries, and Vicente Fox, who had been elected president of Mexico, was due to address Congress.

But after the attacks of September 11, 2001, Chishti said, immigration came to be seen through the lens of national security, and the apparatus that would later be used for mass deportations was established.[13]

In 2006, a bill for comprehensive immigration reform passed the Senate. Rather than push for compromise with the House, which passed its own tough-on-immigration bill that same year, immigration advocates decided to try again in 2007. But in 2007, "the bottom falls out," Muñoz told me. Anti-immigrant groups got better at pushing their message through Congress, and senators who had supported the 2006 bill were no longer there in 2007.

Muñoz, who went on to work in the Obama White House for eight years, said, "We can be faulted for not comprehending what we were seeing when the bottom started to fall out between 2006 and 2007."[14]

In President Barack Obama's first term, he deported so many undocumented immigrants that, in 2014, the aforementioned Janet Murguía, at what was still known as La Raza, nicknamed him the "deporter-in-chief"[15] (Obama's first-term chief of staff, Rahm Emanuel, had called on Clinton to be tough on immigration during his time as chief of staff in the Clinton administration after the 1996 reforms that Sharry et al. fought to reverse).[16] But so, too, did the Obama administration prioritize the deportation of serious criminals and recent arrivals,[17] and offer additional protection to DREAMers—children who entered the country without proper documentation as just that: children.[18]

In this context and among immigration advocacy funders, Open Society was notable for its pragmatism, Sharry said.[19] They funded comprehensive immigration reform and were part of that particular fight from the mid-2000s right up until President Donald Trump's election, when the terms of the fight changed.

THERE WAS NO SUCH SIMILAR exchange of views in Europe. There was a history of migration and movement of people, of course, but the national narrative about immigration—the story, however inaccurate, that people in the United States tell themselves about being a nation of immigrants—wasn't there.

"It is very different," Marta Pardavi, cochair of the Hungarian Helsinki Committee, told me when I interviewed her on that sweltering June day. Take Frank Sharry and his movement as an example. Sharry, she said, talks about building coalitions with people who agree on core principles but may disagree on particulars—for example, law-and-order Christian conservatives who want to work compassionately within the system can find allies in people who don't believe there should be borders but want to help asylum seekers given the system that exists. But that doesn't really work in Europe, she said. "When I look at the opposition in this country, it's easier for them to focus on the straightforward differences and the infighting and the past, present, and future injuries that they have caused and will cause to each other."

"It's a very American way of thinking that he has promoted to a European audience, where you have people from a variety of member states with a variety of all sorts of differences, where you can't really say, 'Well, our country was born out of immigration.' There's no such—the genesis is not about that. The traditional or classic narrative isn't really related to any value about migration, so you can't use that."[20]

It varied from country to country, Sharry said. Ireland was more pro-immigration; the United Kingdom, less so, especially after Prime Minister Tony Blair failed, in Sharry's view, to properly prepare for unprecedented economic migrants from Eastern Europe ("if you can't manage the issues of control," he told me, "you're fucked"). France, he said, "has always been a mess" regarding immigration.

And of Central and Eastern European countries, he said, "You could tell this was not a debate that these countries were ready for." Look at how they treated the Roma minority. Look at their language about Jews.[21]

There weren't the same narratives about migration in Europe. But migration itself was about to be turned into a very particular narrative.

ACCORDING TO THE INTERNATIONAL ORGANIZATION for Migration, over a million migrants traveled into Europe in 2015. They came by way of Turkey and Greece. And over half of the migrants and refugees crossing the Mediterranean came from Syria, fleeing the war that had already been ravaging that country for years.[22]

The dramatic influx of migrants and refugees shook the EU to its core. "We can do it," German Chancellor Angela Merkel said of taking in refugees, frustrating some in her own center-right party and other European countries.[23] An EU plan to spread asylum seekers across the EU member states was met with fury from Central European countries, with Hungary leading the charge. Some states inside the Schengen area—the part of Europe in which people are supposed to be able to move freely—put up border fences (Hungary, in the end, put up two).[24]

In September of that year, Soros wrote a column for a relatively little-read outlet in which many an august thinker has published: *Project Syndicate*. "The European Union needs to accept responsibility for the lack of a common asylum policy, which has transformed this year's growing influx of refugees from a manageable problem into yet another political crisis," it opened. It went on to outline five proposals for rebuilding the European asylum system: accept at least a million asylum seekers every year for the near future; provide adequate funding (by Soros's estimation, 8 to 10 billion euros) to Lebanon, Jordan, and Turkey to help support the millions of refugees living there; "immediately start building a single EU Asylum and Migration Agency and eventually a single EU Border Guard"; establish safe channels to get asylum seekers from Greece and Italy to their destination countries; and get NGOs, church groups, and businesses to act as sponsors to absorb and integrate those coming in.

The column concludes, "Hungarian Prime Minister Viktor Orbán has now also produced a six-point plan to address the crisis." But, he continued, the Orbán plan takes the inalienable human rights of those seeking asylum and subordinates them below border security. In doing so, Soros wrote, Orbán "threatens to divide and destroy the EU by renouncing the values on which it was built and violating the laws that are supposed to govern it."[25]

This piece was not the only thing Soros wrote about the crisis. In 2016, he also wrote in the better known *New York Review of Books* (apologies to *Project Syndicate*), calling on Europe to use its Triple A credit to provide adequate funding to frontline countries with the most refugees.[26] He also wrote for that prestigious publication on the war in Syria—the cause, he noted, of the migrant crisis—and bombing of Aleppo.[27]

But it was the *Project Syndicate* piece on which the Hungarian government seized (in our meeting, Zoltán Kovács, the Hungarian prime minister's spokesperson, referred to it as Soros's mouthpiece).[28] The column transformed, in Hungarian political discourse, into a plot, a white paper, a policy proposal. The Soros plan.

When, in 2015, a Sky News reporter came across a "travel guide" in Arabic with numbers for the Red Cross and U.N. Refugee Agency on a Greek beach, a YouTube video played the clip— with a voiceover saying the book had been paid for by Soros. As Elisabeth Zerofsky reported in the *New Yorker* in early 2019, the YouTube video was the beginning, not the end: *Magyar Idők*, a Hungarian outlet connected to Orbán's Fidesz Party, ran an article under the headline "George Soros Is Luring People with the Wealth of the White World."[29]

But propaganda with ties to the government was nothing compared to what the government itself could unleash against Soros and Open Society.

It wasn't only the 2017 law that made Hungarian nonprofits that accepted a certain amount of foreign money register as foreign agents. It wasn't only the 2018 law that criminalized aiding asylum seekers. It was that the Hungarian government turned the full force of its messaging against Soros and refugees. In 2017, a year before the "Stop Soros" bill that made it a crime to help those seeking asylum passed, the government began its "Stop Soros campaign." It sent out a survey asking Hungarians for their opinions on Soros, including language like "The goal of the Soros plan is to diminish the importance of the language and culture of European countries in order to make the integration of illegal immigrants happen sooner." The streets were plastered with billboards that shouted, "Stop Soros," some of which featured Soros's grinning face.[30]

The message was consistent and constant: immigration is a threat to Hungary, and Soros is the one responsible for the threat.

In reality, Soros was not working to flood Central Europe with migrants. To the extent that Open Society was putting money toward the issue of immigration, Marta Pardavi told me when we met on that café patio in June 2019, it was focused on legal protections—at first on funding refugee law clinics, training the next generation of lawyers to work on the issue, and then, after 2015, helping those organizations that were monitoring detention standards and working to provide and increase access to legal assistance. It was always, she said, focused on sustainable and systematic changes and improvements. They weren't advocating a radical political agenda. They were giving out grants.

Soros's point, Pardavi said, was that it was "an extremely dangerous time for Europe, and the EU should get its act together."

"In a way," she continued, "that's what Orbán says." But the two men took extremely different approaches. Soros's, she told me, was more comprehensive—of course there were needs beyond human rights, but human rights are important. Soros's vision, she argued, was more pragmatic. Orbán's plan hinged on keeping people out, but the people were already there.[31]

But "Soros's plan for immigrants is cautious, pragmatic, and focused on incremental and sustainable systematic reform" doesn't sound as threatening on a billboard, and doesn't sound like it warrants the cost of sending surveys out to Hungarian homes, and so that's not what the government told its citizens.

TO UNDERSTAND THE PARTICULAR ANTISEMITISM of saying that a Jew is trying to bring in immigrants to corrupt the Christian nation, one needs to understand that a core principle of antisemitism is that Jews are always the Other. In the Soviet Union, they were rootless cosmopolitans. In Hitler's Germany, they were not only not of the German people; they were not of the human species. These are extreme examples, but they are nevertheless part of history.

The idea of the Jew bringing in immigrants is, in a certain sense, the most perfect antisemitism. *Here is a person who is not tied, not really, to the country in which they claim to live, of which they claim to be, subverting and corrupting the true nation, the true people, the ones who really belong. Of course they want to subvert the values of the nation; they were never, could never, really be part of the nation in the first place. Of course they are helping the invaders; they are invaders themselves. Of course Jews are not helping refugees because they think it's right; their reason for helping them is the reason Jews do everything. Jews want only to corrupt.*

The beauty of this theory, if one is an antisemite, is that one does not even need to say the word "Jewish." The very image of a prominent Jewish person smuggling in people trying to destroy the soul of the nation is enough to make antisemites' synapses light up.

Here, someone normally offers that Benjamin Netanyahu, prime minister of Israel, was supportive of Orbán, meaning that he doesn't think that the attacks on Soros are antisemitic. But the two are perfectly compatible. Netanyahu did not mind these attacks on liberal Jews outside of Israel because he is the conservative leader of Israel. And plenty of people who want greater national purity are supportive of Israel; there, not here, is where Jews should be, the thinking goes.

"Orbán has managed to diffuse international condemnation on grounds of perceived anti-Semitism by forging a political marriage of convenience with Israeli Prime Minister Benjamin Netanyahu, an equally cynical, ruthless, and shrewd operator," the historian Paul Lendvai wrote. "Each side uses the other as a smokescreen to cover up ugly realities and offer pretexts to blunt liberal critics."[32]

Here, some others note that other rich people are criticized for spending money, and that attacks on them aren't dismissed as antisemitic. But the attacks on Soros are not antisemitic because they are a critique of money spent; they are antisemitic because they are a critique of money that has not and will never be spent. They are the invention and ascription of an agenda, a modern version of an old and hateful conspiracy.

Here, someone else might suggest that Soros is barely Jewish. This is correct if one thinks that the only way to be Jewish is to be both religious and tightly tied to Israel. Soros is neither of those things.

Zionism, he once said, didn't interest him because he was interested in the universal human condition.

But not being interested in Zionism is different from not being Jewish.

"Put yourself in my place," he told his interlocutor in that particular interview. "I was facing extermination at the age of 14 because I was Jewish. Wouldn't that make an impression on you?"[33]

FURY OVER SYRIAN REFUGEES DIDN'T stay in Hungary, or in Europe; the Syrian refugee crisis was the subject of heated debate in the United States, too. And the conviction that Soros was responsible for refugees didn't stay in Hungary, either.

President Donald Trump won the presidency after a campaign in which he called Mexican immigrants rapists and promised to ban Muslims from entering the country[34] (this, according to Chishti, was historic—a president had never won by campaigning on, or rather against, immigration before).[35] Trump, then, was not new to immigration conspiracy theories, nor was he new to antisemitic food for thought—during his campaign, he tweeted out an image of Democratic presidential candidate Hillary Clinton's face and the Star of David over piles of money[36] (Trump, of course, denied that there was anything antisemitic about this; elsewhere in the campaign, he told Republican Jews that they did not support him because he, Trump, couldn't be bought, and they, Republican Jews, liked to buy and control their candidates).[37]

But as the 2018 midterm elections approached, he combined xenophobia and antisemitism.

In late October 2018, Trump said he "wouldn't be surprised" if "someone" was paying for the migrant caravan that was making its way to the southern U.S. border. When one reporter helpfully shouted out, "George Soros?" Trump replied, "I don't know who, but I wouldn't be surprised. A lot of people say yes."[38]

I asked Muñoz if she was surprised to see immigration conspiracy theories and Soros conspiracy theories combined.

"It's all of a piece," she told me. "It's the same ugly crowd, and the same ugly set of arguments. It saddens me greatly, but it doesn't surprise me."[39]

In reality, what Soros and Open Society had done after Trump's election was to hire Angela Kelley—the woman with whom Frank Sharry went to see Paul Ryan—as a strategic advisor for immigration, and, through an antihate initiative, give "a lot of money to organizations at the local level, doing needed healing work," Kelley told me over the phone in August 2019.[40] Additionally, Open Society provides support to refugee and immigration advocacy groups. It's worked on the issues of family separation and supported groups that provide litigation and legal aid. Roughly five percent of OSF's budget in recent years has gone toward migration, refugee, and immigration issues. But that does not mean the caravan came from OSF.

"When I saw [Trump blame Soros for the caravan], I was just like—whoa, this is just Orbán's playbook that's come to America," said Sharry, the America's Voice founder. He remembered Soros becoming a bogeyman for the right wing back when he gave personal money to stop George W. Bush's reelection back in 2004, he told me—but he didn't remember it being so antisemitic.[41]

A few days before Trump wondered aloud whether Soros was funding the caravan, it should be noted, Chris Farrell, head of the conservative Judicial Watch, said the caravan was funded by the "Soros-occupied State Department."[42] That same day, a synagogue in Pittsburgh was attacked. Eleven people died. The massacre was thought to be the deadliest against Jewish people in U.S. history. The shooter was upset specifically over the Hebrew Immigrant Aid Society, a Jewish nonprofit that helps resettle refugees, which, he said, "likes to bring invaders that kill our people."[43]

THE ATTACK ON THE TREE of Life synagogue was a conflict between the language that Trump pushes and the ideals that Soros has funded. It was not the only one.

Then, in 2019, the Trump administration planned to change the census to track immigration status, which was quickly called out as a plan to scare undocumented immigrants and boost white voting power.

One day while I was in Budapest I checked my email, and a story in my daily Soros Google alerts caught my eye. It was sitting there amid the daily churn of conspiracy theories and diatribes. My friend and former *BuzzFeed News* colleague Nidhi Prakash had written it. The headline read, "Inside the Massive, Coordinated Push to Make Sure a Census Citizenship Question Does Not 'Distort Democracy.'"

The piece was about the fear from immigrants' rights groups that the threat of the question would deter immigrants, including green card holders, from participating in the census. So, too, was it about the coordinated advocacy work to make sure immigrants and their families were not left out—by offering helplines in multiple languages and doing community outreach—and the unprecedented support from philanthropic organizations, including Open Society.[44]

There is, again, an argument to be made that the very fact that those groups needed funding from a billionaire was already a distortion of democracy. But if the funding wasn't there, some of the most vulnerable people in the country would almost certainly be undercounted.

Shortly thereafter, the Supreme Court ruled that the citizenship question could not be added to the census. Activist groups doubled down to prevent an undercount of immigrants.[45]

THE STORY, OF COURSE, DOES not end there, with Soros beating Trump on the census and nothing else ever happening in the immigration space.

Weeks after the Supreme Court ruling, Trump told four freshmen members of Congress, all women of color, all U.S. citizens, three of whom were born in the United States and one of whom was a refugee, to go back from where they came.[46] He presided over a crowd that chanted of one of the women, Representative Ilhan Omar, "Send her back."[47] He made clear that he wanted to make the 2020 election about immigration, and xenophobia, and borders, and others. About the promise of a closed society, and an ethnonational conception of what it means to belong to it; the antithesis, in many ways, to Soros's life's work.

Democrats, too, are in a different place than they were in 2014, the year of "deporter-in-chief" and DREAMers. They are even in a different place than they were in 2016, when Secretary of State Hillary Clinton failed to win the presidency with her message of "Stronger Together." At one 2019 Democratic primary debate, Obama's former vice president, Joe Biden, asked Obama's former housing secretary, Julián Castro, whether he had objected to the mass deportations. "It seems one of us has learned the lessons of the past," Castro retorted, "and one of us hasn't."[48] Castro was running on decriminalizing illegal border crossings, something of a departure from Obama Chief of Staff Rahm Emanuel's tough-on-immigration line. I asked Soros whether he, too, supports de-criminalization; he did not provide an answer to this particular question. Republicans, Chishti told me, can't think of a single immigrant they like; Democrats can't think of a single enforcement measure they should support.[49]

"The number one difference is [that] it's become more partisan," Alex Nowrasteh, director of immigration at the Cato Institute, told me over the phone in August 2019 after I asked how the immigration debate and discourse has changed over the past several years.

"There were a large number of Republicans who thought liberalizing immigration was the right thing to do," he continued, citing the Gang of Eight—eight senators, four of whom were Republicans, who wrote a bill to modernize U.S. immigration (it passed the Senate and expired in the House under the leadership of Republican House Speaker John Boehner in 2013). Democrats were more likely to support liberalizing immigration, Nowrasteh allowed, "but it wasn't the massive imbalance you see today."

There is another difference, too, he said. "The rhetoric is more extreme."[50]

That doesn't mean the rhetoric is new, exactly. It's nothing that the people Soros funded back when he first got involved in migration policy hadn't heard before. "The anti-immigrant groups whose policy ideas are being implemented by the Trump administration have been around . . . for a really long time. I consider them the thing I've been fighting against my whole career," Muñoz told me[51]—although, as Kelley noted, Trump, when he came down the escalator to announce his candidacy in 2015 and called Mexicans rapists, was possibly unaware of the names of the restrictionist groups whose policies he would go on to implement. Still, "Every policy change that Trump comes out with is like the Christmas wish list of the restrictionist groups," Kelley said.[52]

"It's been there, but it [was] fringe. It's been a fringe until very recently," Muñoz told me. The same thing is true of Soros conspiracy theories, I noted. They've been around for decades. But now they're touted by people in the most powerful offices in their countries. In Trump's case, the most powerful office in the world.[53]

MULTIPLE STUDIES HAVE SHOWN THAT there are more people in America who think immigration is good than people who think immigration is an ill. But for people broadly supportive of immigration, according to Nowrasteh, the issue is probably not the main thing driving them to the polls. For nativists, he said, immigration, or opposition to it, is the number one concern. They don't know how many immigrants are in the country, they don't know how the complex U.S. immigration system works, or that no one person—even Soros—could control it. But the more ignorant the opinion, Nowrasteh said, the more likely the people holding it are to oppose immigration. They know that they don't want immigrants, and they will vote accordingly.[54] And Trump will encourage them to.

WILL THE PEOPLE WHO VOTE on that issue come out to vote? And if they do, will he win? And if he does, what does that mean, in the late years of Soros's life, for the legacy of a man who spent billions of dollars to counter this—Trump's—way of thinking about who gets to belong to and participate in a society?

I asked Charles Gati, the Johns Hopkins professor who knows Soros and was once quite friendly with Orbán, what he thought Soros's influence ultimately was.

It was still to be decided, he told me. It wouldn't be decided in Hungary—"Hungary for the time being is lost." It would be decided here, in the United States, in an election that it appears will be largely about whether this country wants to be an open society that allows different people from different backgrounds to have an equal shot at shaping the debate or a closed (and white) one.

"If Trump is defeated in 2020," he said, "then [Soros] will be seen as a major factor that stopped the growth of fascism in the world." That he decided, over fifteen years ago, to get involved in U.S. politics will be viewed as a "fine choice." He will be seen as one of the people who "began to turn the tide."

But if Trump is reelected—which, Gati said, seems likely—"then he will be seen as a good man who has failed. Which I regret very much," said Gati, "because he deserves better."

People say that it's better to have tried and failed, Gati said, adding, "But it's not a great saying."[55]

I asked Soros if he agreed with Gati. Did his legacy—does his legacy—hinge on whether Trump is reelected?

"No," he replied. "The open society is always endangered and each generation must fight for it to survive." There will always be people who would suppress others. In an open society wherein everyone is able to participate and express their opinion, those people have a right to express that opinion, too. But it is up to others who do not believe in ethnonationalism, ethnic cleansing, voter suppression, the stripping of the rights of citizens, border walls as substitute for other policy—it is up to those others to ensure that the participation of those who believe in a closed society does not come to mean the exclusion of all the people who disagree. It is up to the people who believe, still, even now, in the need for open societies.

CONCLUSION

On a very warm day in late June 2019, I got onto the tram near the Budapest train station. I found a seat between people holding bouquets, beaming. They were going, I knew, to the same place I was going. We were all going to the Palace of Arts for Central European University's last graduation in Budapest.

I made my way into the lobby where graduates and their presumably proud parents sipped glasses of water and flutes of champagne. Pink and gold saris peeked out from under graduation robes; some of the young women had head scarves under their caps. Maybe I noticed these things—these markers, at least to me, a white American traveling in Central Europe, of multiculturalism and diversity—because I hadn't seen them elsewhere in Budapest; maybe it was because I was looking for them.

I found a CEU staffer, who brought me upstairs to another CEU staffer, who asked me to wait before they brought me to my seat. I scrolled through Twitter on my phone while I waited. I noticed that Laura Silber, Open Society's top communications official, had tweeted out a *New York Times* article. It was about an open letter published on the website Medium in which a collective of very rich individuals called for "a moderate wealth tax on the fortunes of the richest one-tenth of the richest 1 percent of Americans—on us." Signatories included Abigail Disney, Facebook cofounder Chris Hughes, and George Soros, whose photo the *Times* had selected to adorn the virtual page. "A Message from the Billionaire's Club: Tax Us," the headline read.[1] Alexander Soros, the son who Soros has signaled is interested in carrying on his work, had signed on, too.

I was finally allowed in, and was surprised that I was seated not at the very back of the room, but in a box to the side. I was next to Ildikó Nagy Moran, external advisor to Michael Ignatieff, CEU's president and rector. We were seated by the ambassadors from Canada, Norway, Argentina, and Ireland. I noted to Moran that it was a very international audience. "Of course it is," she told me. She repeated it twice more.

The ceremony began with an academic procession. There were opening remarks in Hungarian. Then the master of ceremonies—Liviu Matei, the university's provost—introduced a musical performance. There would be pieces by Béla Bartók, the last of which was called "Far Behind I Left My Country." "Which is perhaps something to be reflected on," the provost quipped.

"Far behind I left my country, my esteemed little Hungary," the song goes, according to the translation in my program. "Halfway gone, I looked back, My eyes were brimmed with tears."

"Now all the Hungarians are crying," Moran whispered to me, adding, "and I am, too."

The graduation, Ignatieff said, was "obviously a bittersweet moment." They were saying goodbye to this place—there would still be the CEU building, and the archives, and some programming. But the U.S.-accredited institution of higher education was

Conclusion

moving to Vienna, and this seemed likely to be the last graduation in Budapest.

"That's the bitter part," he said, and then, to the students, added, "The sweet part is you."

The whole thing was like that. It was a celebration for the students and a funeral for the university as it was.

"You know how hard we fought to stay," Ignatieff said in his speech. "Our efforts have been in vain," though he vowed, "This city will remain our spiritual home."

Alexander Soros, who is on CEU's board of trustees, made an appearance not marked on the program ("That's Alex!" Moran told me excitedly while he was introduced). "It is a disgrace," he said of CEU's removal from Hungary. It was, he said, the first time in the history of the European Union that an EU member state had banned a university. He announced that Open Society was committed to the recapitalization of the endowment, and that "we will never give up on Hungary or the Hungarian people." And then he left.

Leon Botstein, chairman of the board, spoke, promising that CEU will never leave Budapest, and added, "This is not about Hungary. This is about a particular political movement."

I wondered, listening to the speeches, if the students were sad, or mad, or just wanted everyone to hurry up so that they could go enjoy a late lunch with their families.

It wasn't until the degrees were awarded and the students lined up department by department, program by program, degree by degree, one by one, that I got it. Sitting in Budapest, I watched a young woman from Mexico walk across the stage to collect a degree in medieval studies. The political science program alone had students from Argentina, Russia, Nigeria, the Netherlands, Slovakia, the United States, Ukraine, Pakistan, Turkey, Georgia, India, Hungary, North Macedonia, Serbia, China, Romania, the Czech Republic, and Germany.

I wondered who, thirty years ago, could have imagined that all of those people from all of those places would graduate with political science degrees in Budapest. And then I realized that, of course, there was one person who could have, and did.

The last thing before we dispersed was the awarding of the 2019 Open Society Prize. It went to Joseph Stiglitz, renowned economist of Columbia University, formerly of the World Bank. "I've always viewed my academic work as not just an end in itself, but as a means to an end—creating a more just society, a more open society, a society with more respect for human rights," Stiglitz said. "Nothing is more symbolic of the meaning of an open society than a free press and academic freedom."

He was praised for his commitment to progressive capitalism, for the success with which the World Bank helped countries transition from Communism to market economies. That the current result of this transition was Viktor Orbán and the exile of CEU seemed not to occur to anyone; or, if it did, they didn't seem to dwell on it.

IT WAS THE NEXT DAY that I went to see István Rév, who had been with CEU since the beginning and is now its archival director. We talked about how CEU got started, and how Orbán had rewritten Hungarian history, and what the university was in Budapest and why it wouldn't be the same in Vienna.

Toward the end of our interview, I asked him the same thing that I'd asked Charles Gati, the Johns Hopkins professor. What was Soros's legacy, his influence? Could you, looking around the world—at his country, at mine—say that it was moot?

You couldn't, he told me. Or he wouldn't, anyway. Soros tried to build something. It may look, now, like what he'd spent his life building was destroyed. But that doesn't mean he never should have tried.

Conclusion

"You have to start from scratch all the time," he told me. "Something horrible always happens. Then you, or somebody, should start once more."

He asked me what he should say. That there's Orbán, there's Trump, there's whoever else, we're doomed?

"Yes, we are doomed," he said. "But we are alive." And so long as you are alive, you have to try to make things a little less doomed. "You don't have any other choice."

Would it have been better, he asked me, if Soros had spent his money on paintings?[2]

I DID NOT ANSWER ISTVÁN Rév, because I did not have my answer then. I am not sure I have it now. But I think that it would not have been better if Soros had spent his money on paintings. And it is remarkable that he did not. It is remarkable that what mattered to him was creating conditions for more people to be more able to live with decency and dignity, and to share their voices, and to contribute their own fallacies and fallibility in the hope that all of us together might reach clearer understanding. Soros grew up in a world where people are free to become billionaires. It is my opinion that the fact that he used his billions to try to open society is to his credit, and that the reality is that he was able to do as much as he did because he made money before trying to live his values.

But it is also my opinion that he should not have had the billions to begin with, because a society in which one person can amass so much personal wealth, power, and influence while some don't have any can never be open.

The people to whom I spoke, from Bosnia to Baltimore, were grateful that Soros gave them his money, and each one said that he gave it without trying to exert undue influence.

But he had the kind of money that could change things and the people I spoke with didn't. This is, to a certain extent, the paradox of and the problem with billionaire philanthropists: at the end of the day, they're still the ones with the money, and the power to decide what to do with it. But it's a tension one sees more clearly when the philanthropist in question is working from the central idea that everyone should have an equal chance at participating fully in society (and throwing his personal financial backing behind particular politicians in the process), as opposed to providing mosquito nets.

That the global financial system as it exists is incompatible with an open society is something Soros himself has admitted repeatedly. "My defense is that I operate within the rules," Soros said in 1995. "If there is a breakdown in the rules, that is not my fault as a lawful participant but the fault of those who set the rules. I think that is a very sound and justified position, and I have absolutely no moral qualms in being branded a speculator . . . I think that it behooves the authorities to design a system that does not reward speculators. When speculators profit, the authorities have failed in some way or another."[3]

And it wasn't only unchecked speculation that he criticized.

"I believe we must strive for certain fundamental values, such as social justice, which cannot be attained by unrestrained competition," he said that same year. "It is exactly because I have been successful in the marketplace that I can afford to advocate those values. I am the classic limousine liberal. I believe that it behooves those who have benefited from the system that they should exert themselves to make the system better."[4]

He also noted that he himself didn't start giving his money away and living a life around his core values until he had made millions. It wasn't just that money brought him influence and power; it was that he wouldn't have necessarily been actively committed to the cause without it.

Conclusion

"The main enemy of the open society, I believe, is no longer the communist but the capitalist threat," he said in 1997. "The laissez-faire idea that markets should be left to their own devices remains very influential. I consider it a very dangerous idea."[5]

"Systemic reforms need broad public participation and support," Soros wrote in 2011. "That is what makes them irreversible."[6]

A wealth tax "would make America healthier. It is a fair way of creating opportunity. And it strengthens American freedom and democracy," the letter that he and his son signed on to in 2019 read. "It is not in our interest to advocate for this tax, if our interests are quite narrowly understood. But the wealth tax is in our interest as Americans."[7]

One could argue that this is hypocritical—that it's easy to criticize a system that allows people to amass great sums of money through speculation after one has done exactly that. That regret at a financial system is easy to express after one has used it to become rich, live in luxury, and exert great influence.

But one could also argue that it is also the natural conclusion of a life's work spent trying to create a more equitable world. Soros's life was, in some ways, defined by this dissonance, this tension. That tension has to give.

I do not think it would have been better for the world if Soros had spent his money on paintings. I do think that if there is to be an open society, and if the roots of inequality within and between countries are to be addressed, more people need to be less dependent on eccentric and impassioned billionaires.

"That is a real conversation that has really erupted in a mainstream way . . . the question is, how do you give in ways that reduce the power of rich people? Which is a very paradoxical form of giving," said Anand Giridharadas, who has spent much of the time after the publication of his book on the problem of philanthropy trying to bring the discussion further into public view. "I do think he really has an opportunity here. There is a conversation happening right now at the highest levels of philanthropy . . . I think he could really be a leader in the conversation in the coming years."[8]

I thought of how Soros, for all his faults, had been ahead of his time in seeing the threat of nationalism in Central and Eastern Europe after the dissolution of the Eastern Bloc; in recognizing that treating drug addiction like a criminal problem was wrong; in understanding the threat that propagandistic right-wing news posed to this country. I wondered if, toward the end of his life, he could be ahead of his time in this, too.

NOT LONG AFTER I LEFT the CEU graduation, I learned that there previously had been a poster campaign in the university's main building. On one half, there was a picture of Lenin speaking to a crowd, photoshopped so that Lenin was promising a mass of people—meant to represent CEU students—town halls and integrated feedback about the future of the university. On the other half, there was a tumbleweed blowing through a desert. At the top, it read DEMOCRACY AT CEU. At the bottom, a line from the university's rules and academic regulations that said students could publicize their opinion by print. The removal of the poster would be taken as a violation of student rights, the poster's writer concluded.

It was perfect. The students had been taught to think freely, and now they were doing so. If the university's administrators didn't like their conclusions, it only meant that they'd done their jobs well.

I wondered what the students would do now, after graduation, unleashed onto the world. Some of them, I thought, had to be true believers in CEU's mission. Some of them, I thought, or maybe just hoped, were surely set to go back to their home countries—or stay in Hungary, if that is their home country—and try to empower themselves and others to make society freer and more equitable. And try to create a world where people are less reliant on others for that empowerment.

I have come to believe that I disagree with Gati. I don't think Soros's legacy hinges on Trump. I think it is in every person in Sarajevo. I think it was there in Slovakia when they elected their first woman president, a woman who ran and won on an anticorruption platform. I think it is walking around in everyone who managed to graduate from CEU the year it was being pushed out of Budapest and to protest both the Hungarian government and their own university. I think it is in the people who work for asylum seekers in Hungary even when they risk being considered criminals for it. I think it is in people who push for greater voter enfranchisement in the United States. And when those same people turn around and ask why there are billionaires and why they are not able to enfranchise and empower themselves—I think it is in them, too.

There will never be another George Soros. The conditions that created him were unique, and he is, too. And if society is to be open, I don't think there *should* ever be another.

But perhaps conditions can be created such that there are many more like him: empowered, enfranchised, and invested in the preservation, protection, and promotion of open societies.

ACKNOWLEDGMENTS

This book was reported in Bosnia, the Czech Republic, Hungary, Romania, Slovakia, and the United States, and includes interviews with people based in Georgia, New Zealand, Poland, Serbia, and the United Kingdom. I want to first say that I do not have the words to express how grateful I am to everyone in each of those places who took a moment out of their lives to discuss Soros and his influence on their societies and themselves with me. Thank you all, and thank you to anyone who put me in touch with anyone. Thank you especially to Szabolcs Panyi, a journalist's journalist and a moral compass in Budapest. I think we first became friends when you tweeted at me after I mispronounced Soros's name on a podcast; I am so glad you did. And to Johana Sedláčková Vamberská for her hospitality in Prague, guidance in all things Central and Eastern Europe, and friendship—thank you.

Laura Silber at Open Society was one of the very first people I told I was thinking of doing this, and I am indebted to her, as well as the Soros Fund's Michael Vachon, for their help, advice, and

Acknowledgments

openness. Thank you also, of course, to George Soros for taking the time to answer my questions (even if it was over email), and also—how do I put this?—for having a life worth writing about.

This book would not exist if Noah Ballard at Curtis Brown had not reached out one day to ask if I wanted to write a book on George Soros (I did, as it turns out), so high-up thanks go to him, too. Thank you for everything, Noah.

Thank you to Stephanie Hitchcock (formerly of Harper, now of Atria) for taking a chance on this project and on me. Thank you to Rebecca Raskin (still of Harper, thank God!) for getting what I was trying to do before I did, for email pep talks, for patient and gracious edits, and for generally being the best. Actually, thank you to everyone at Harper—I still can't believe you let me do this, but I'm very glad you did.

Martin de Bourmont, thank you for checking my facts and for being my friend.

I would be remiss if I did not also thank Sharon Weinberger and Mark Seibel, editors who made me better and also made me write long articles on Soros. I can honestly say this book would never have happened if they hadn't. Thank you also to Keith Johnson for telling me to write it tight, to Lara Jakes for making me a journalist, and to Fuzz Hogan for so much. I have many hopes for this book, but one of them is that I make the five of you, my forever editors, proud.

To Professor Popkin (aka Cathy) of Columbia University—I still think about that undergrad Chekhov class all the time.

To friends who offered to read a chapter for free—Rachel Barclay (and her husband, Paul Jones, who took my author photo) and Brandon Tensley—thank you. I'll never forget it. Thank you to Katie David and Hannah Miranda Miller for talking through different parts of this book with me. And thank you to David Hinds for working with me (for no money!) the first time I tried to sell a book proposal. It didn't work out, but also, in the end, it did.

Acknowledgments

Thank you also to Akbar Shahid Ahmed, Vera Bergengruen, Jacob Brogan, Boer Deng, Lauren Fish, Chris Geidner, Steve Lucas, and Veronica Mooney for your support; to my FP crew for being like colleagues long after we stopped working together; to the women of BuzzFeed World for always helping to find the humor in the situation; to Sid Mahanta for everything; to Ruby Mellen for the Gchats; to college girlses (not a typo) Devin Briski, Amanda Cormier, Paula Gergen, Christine Jordan, and Sarah Quereshi for the texts and WhatsApps; to my grad school clique—Jake Brockman, Paul Sander, and others whose names I will leave out of a book on Soros for professional reasons—for the Facebook Messenger missives; and to Matt Deinhardt because you wouldn't let me hear the end of it if I didn't thank you.

My fiancé told me he would do anything if, in these acknowledgments, I admitted that noted British television series *Midsomer Murders* was with me from the time I started working on the proposal and through the writing of this book, so—*Midsomer Murders*, thank you.

My siblings, Elizabeth and Nicholas Tamkin, kept me humble. My father, Dan Tamkin, challenged my way of looking at the world (and worried while I traveled to report out the book). My mother, Cindy Cardinal, is my first and best reader, and looked at and edited every chapter, sometimes more than once, before I showed it to anyone else. She gave me so much of her time and energy, and I will always think of this as our book. Also, I once texted her that I was worried this book would be bad, and she responded, "So make it good." And so, to my family: Thank you for all that, and for everything else, too.

And finally, to Neil Bhatiya (and our dog, Shiloh, a good girl): This little line isn't enough to thank you for your being there for and with me throughout this whole thing—or for telling me that someone would buy my proposal, for assuring me I would meet my deadlines, for reading a draft of almost every chapter, for telling

Acknowledgments

me my interview requests would be answered if I was just patient and persistent, for waiting while I went out and reported, for letting me turn our coffee table and couch into my office, for not complaining while I worked on this book on vacation, for ironing the dress in my author photo, and especially for never once telling me to stop talking about Soros, even as you asked if he was becoming the third person in our relationship—but thank you, all the same. You are the great joy of my life. I love you.

NOTES

Introduction

1. Ali Kucukgocmen and Gulsen Solaker, "Soros Foundation to Close in Turkey After Attack by Erdogan," Reuters, November 26, 2018.

2. Nati Tucker, "Netanyahu Shared Fake News About George Soros. Now He and Facebook Have to Answer to the Court," *Haaretz*, September 12, 2018.

3. Palko Karasz, "Protests Rock Romania After Government Weakens Corruption Law," *New York Times*, February 2, 2017.

4. Petru Clej, "George Soros Tried to Kill Me, Romanian Leader Liviu Dragnea Hints," *Jewish Chronicle*, August 22, 2018.

5. Radoslav Tomek, "Ousted by Mass Protests, Ex-Premier's Comeback Plan Stirs Anger," Bloomberg, February 3, 2019.

6. Jane Coaston, "Trump Repeats a George Soros Conspiracy Theory Right Before Kavanaugh Vote," *Vox*, October 5, 2018.

7. Patrick Lovett, "'Anti-Soros': Orban's Reelection Campaign's Centerpiece to Become Law," France24, June 1, 2018.

8. Emily Tamkin, "Hungary's Decision to Close a Soros-Linked University Shows the Limits of Trump's Influence," *BuzzFeed News*, December 3, 2018.

9. Cristina Cabrera, "Tucker Carlson Claims George Soros Is 'Remaking This Country,'" *Talking Points Memo*, June 11, 2019.

10. Michelle Malkin, "Beware Soros-Funded Hijacking of US Census," *Daily Signal*, April 24, 2019.

11. Sheera Frankel et al., "Delay, Deny, and Deflect: How Facebook's Leaders Fought Through Crisis," *New York Times*, November 4, 2018.

12. Japhy Wilson, "Counting on Billionaires," *Jacobin*, March 3, 2015.

13. Karl Popper, *The Open Society and Its Enemies* (Princeton and Oxford: Princeton University Press, 1994).

14. https://www.opensocietyfoundations.org/newsroom/open-society-foundations-and-george-soros.

15. https://www.opensocietyfoundations.org/who-we-are.

16. Maggie Severns, "Soros Launches Super PAC for 2020," *Politico*, August 6, 2019.

Chapter 1: Birth of a Myth

1. Laura King, "How Billionaire-Philanthropist George Soros Became a Favorite Far-Right Target, Especially in His Native Hungary," *Los Angeles Times*, August 10, 2018.

2. Michael T. Kaufman, *Soros: The Life and Times of a Messianic Billionaire* (New York: Knopf, 2002), 23.

3. Paul Lendvai, *The Hungarians: A Thousand Years of History in Defeat* (Princeton: Princeton University Press, 2003), 329.

4. Ibid., 332.

5. Kati Marton, *The Great Escape: Nine Jews Who Fled Hitler and Changed the World* (New York: Simon & Schuster, 2006), 18.

6. Ibid., 337.

7. Kaufman, 8.

8. George Soros, *Soros on Soros: Staying Ahead of the Curve* (New York: Wiley, 1995), 27.

Notes

9. Lendvai, *The Hungarians*, 365–370.

10. Ibid, 379.

11. Ibid., 369–372.

12. Ibid., 373–375.

13. Ibid., 377–378.

14. Ibid., 384.

15. Ibid., 334.

16. Kaufman, 23.

17. Ibid., 24.

18. Tivadar Soros, *Masquerade: The Incredible True Story of How George Soros' Father Outsmarted the Gestapo* (New York: Arcade Publishing, 2011), 2.

19. Júlia Tar, "Former PM Pál Teleki's Second Suicide Note Found," *Hungary Today*, April 3, 2019.

20. Tivadar Soros, 2.

21. Kaufman, 28.

22. Tivadar Soros, 3–4.

23. Ibid., 16–18.

24. Kaufman, 32.

25. Tivadar Soros, 21.

26. Ibid., 23.

27. Ibid., 53–58.

28. Kaufman, 34–38.

29. Jane Coaston, "George Soros Is Not a Nazi, Explained," *Vox*, June 11, 2018.

30. TOI Staff and JTA, "Roseanne Barr Apologizes for George Soros Was a Nazi Tweet," *Times of Israel*, June 12, 2018.

31. "Timeline of Events: Deportation of Hungarian Jews," United States Holocaust Memorial Museum, https://www.ushmm.org/learn/timeline-of-events/1942-1945/deportation-of-hungarian-jews.

32. George Soros, *Soros on Soros*, 28.

33. Tivadar Soros, 165.

34. Ibid., 97–103.

35. Ibid., 96.

36. Ibid., 203.

37. Soros, *Soros on Soros*, 28. (From here on "Soros" alone as author will refer to George Soros.)

38. István Rév, personal interview, Budapest, June 2019.

39. Kaufman, 52.

40. Soros, *Soros on Soros*, 31.

41. Kaufman, 56.

42. Ibid., 60.

43. Soros, *Soros on Soros*, 33.

44. George Soros, *The Soros Lectures at the Central European University* (New York: PublicAffairs, 2010), 55.

45. Kaufman, 67–68.

46. George Soros, *Underwriting Democracy: Encouraging Free Enterprise and Democratic Reform Among the Soviets and in Eastern Europe* (New York: PublicAffairs, 1991), 4–5.

47. Soros, *Soros on Soros*, 35–36.

48. Ibid.

49. Andrew Morrison, personal interview, Washington, D.C., May 2019.

50. Kaufman, 83–86.

51. Taylor Nicole Rogers, "What George Soros' Life Is Really Like," *Business Insider*, June 28, 2019.

52. Kaufman, 101.

53. Soros, *Soros on Soros*, 33.

54. Kaufman, 117–118.

55. Ibid., 119.

56. Soros, *Soros on Soros*, 43–46.

57. Kaufman, 134.

58. Sebastian Mallaby, *More Money Than God: Hedge Funds and the Making of a New Elite* (New York: Penguin Press, 2010), 86.

Notes

59. Kaufman, 145.

60. Ibid., 120.

61. Mallaby, 87.

62. Ibid., 86.

63. Morrison, personal interview.

64. Ibid.

65. Soros, *Soros on Soros*, 54.

66. Kaufman, 149–151.

67. Jennifer Ablan, "Soros to Marry for Third Time with Three-Day New York Celebration," Reuters, September 20, 2013.

68. Mallaby, 90–93.

69. Ibid., 94–95.

70. Ibid., 95.

71. Jonathan Soble, "Japan Kept Its Cool in the 1987 Crisis," *Financial Times*, October 18, 2007.

72. Mallaby, 96–98.

73. Ibid., 98.

74. Ibid., 100–101.

75. Ibid., 101–102.

76. George Soros, "My Philanthropy," in Chuck Sudetic, *The Philanthropy of George Soros: Building Open Societies* (New York: Public Affairs, 2011), 11.

77. Kaufman, 147–148.

78. Ibid.

Chapter 2: 1984

1. Ibid., 170–171.

2. Soros, *Underwriting Democracy*, 4.

3. Ibid.

Notes

4. Soros, "My Philanthropy," in Sudetic, *The Philanthropy of George Soros*, 12–13. (Hereafter: Soros, in Sudetic, 00.)

5. Soros, *Soros on Soros*, 114–115.

6. Kaufman, 171.

7. Soros, *Soros on Soros*, 114–115.

8. Open Society Foundations, "The Open Society Foundations in South Africa," https://www.opensocietyfoundations.org/newsroom /open-society-foundations-south-africa.

9. Soros, in Sudetic, 13–14.

10. Soros, *Soros on Soros*, 116–117.

11. Ibid.

12. Kaufman, 211.

13. Lendvai, *The Hungarians*, 499.

14. Ibid., 194–195.

15. "Imre Nagy Executed Illegally After Show Trial, Hungary Regime Says," *Los Angeles Times*, May 30, 1989.

16. Soros, *Soros on Soros*, 118.

17. Soros, *Underwriting Democracy*, 4–5.

18. Ibid., 8–9.

19. Kaufman, 198–199.

20. András Bozóki, personal interview, Budapest, June 2019.

21. Soros, *Soros on Soros*, 121.

22. Szabolcs Panyi, personal interview, Budapest, June 2019.

23. Bálint Magyar, personal interview, Budapest, June 2019.

24. Gábor Horn, personal interview, Budapest, June 2019.

25. Soros, *Soros on Soros*, 122.

26. Timothy Garton Ash, personal interview, Washington, D.C., June 2019.

27. Paul Lendvai, *Orbán: Europe's New Strongman* (Oxford: Oxford University Press, 2017), 17–18.

28. Ibid., 23.

Notes

29. Soros, *Underwriting Democracy*, 10.

30. Magyar, personal interview.

31. Kaufman, 215–216.

32. Ibid., 217.

33. Ibid., 218.

34. Ibid.

35. Ibid., 219.

36. Soros, *Underwriting Democracy*, 13.

37. Soros, *Soros on Soros*, 127.

38. Ibid.

39. Kaufman, 230–231.

40. Aleksander Smolar, personal interview, Washington, D.C., May 2019.

41. Garton Ash, personal interview.

42. Ibid.

43. Smolar, personal interview.

44. Kaufman, 222–223.

45. Anna Porter, *Buying a Better World: George Soros and Billionaire Philanthropy* (Toronto: TAP Books, 2015), 108.

46. Soros, *Soros on Soros*, 128–130.

47. Ibid.

48. Ibid.

49. Ibid., 130.

50. Ibid., 123–124.

51. Paul Stubbs, personal interview, Washington, D.C., October 2017.

52. Soros, *Soros on Soros*, 178.

53. Soros, in Sudetic, 21.

54. István Rév, personal interview, Budapest, June 2019.

55. Bozóki, personal interview.

56. Porter, 88.

57. Soros, *Soros on Soros*, 133–135.

58. Rév, personal interview.

59. Soros, *Soros on Soros*, 136–137.

60. Attila Bátorfy and Mark Tremmel, "Data Visualization: The Definitive Timeline of Anti-Soros Conspiracy Theories," *Átlátszó*, February 10, 2019, https://english.atlatszo.hu/2019/02/10/data-visualization-the-definitive-timeline-of-anti-soros-conspiracy-theories/.

61. Rév, personal interview.

62. Zselyke Csaky, personal interview, Budapest, June 2019.

63. Rév, personal interview.

64. Soros, *Soros on Soros*, 175.

65. Ibid., 123.

66. Kaufman, 211.

67. Ibid., 211–212.

68. Soros, in Sudetic, 23.

69. Kenneth Roth, personal interview, Washington, D.C., July 2019.

70. Garton Ash, personal interview.

71. Michael Lewis, "The Speculator," *New Republic*, January 10, 1994.

Chapter 3: Breaking the Banks

1. George Soros, *The Soros Lectures at the Central European University* (New York: PublicAffairs, 2010), 40.

2. Stanley Druckenmiller, personal interview, Washington, D.C., 2019.

3. http://www.europarl.europa.eu/RegData/etudes/BRIE/2015/551325/EPRS_BRI(2015)551325_EN.pdf.

4. https://www.bbc.com/news/av/uk-politics-27053535/euro-moments-uk-joins-exchange-rate-mechanism.

5. Mallaby, 152–153.

6. Druckenmiller, personal interview.

7. Mallaby, 153.

8. Ibid., 154–156.

Notes

9. Rob Johnson, personal interview, Washington, D.C., September 2019.

10. Mallaby, 157.

11. Paul La Monica, "Bill Ackman's Herbalife Disaster Is Finally Over," CNN *Business*, March 1, 2018.

12. Johnson, personal interview.

13. Mallaby, 158–159.

14. Ibid., 160–161.

15. Druckenmiller, personal interview.

16. Johnson, personal interview.

17. Mallaby, 163.

18. Phillip Inman, "Black Wednesday 20 Years On: How the Day Unfolded," *The Guardian*, September 13, 2012.

19. Mallaby, 166.

20. Ibid., 167.

21. Connie Bruck, "The World According to George Soros," *New Yorker*, January 23, 1995.

22. Martin Vander Weyer, "Black Wednesday: The Moment Power Shifted to the Markets," *The Telegraph*, September 13, 2012.

23. Mallaby, personal interview.

24. Druckenmiller, personal interview.

25. Soros, in Sudetic, 26.

26. Soros, *Soros on Soros*, 83.

27. David Kowitz, personal interview, Washington, D.C., September 2019.

28. Rodney Jones, personal interview, Washington, D.C., September 2019.

29. Mallaby, 197.

30. Sudetic, 176–177.

31. Kowitz, personal interview.

32. Mallaby, 199–200.

33. Kowitz, personal interview.

34. Mallaby, 200–201.

35. Jones, personal interview.

Notes

36. Mallaby, 206–207.

37. Seth Mydans, "Malaysian Premier Sees Jews Behind Nation's Money Crisis," *New York Times*, October 15, 1997.

38. Yaron Steinbuch, "Malaysian Prime Minister: My Jewish Friends Are 'Not Like Other Jews,'" *New York Post*, June 18, 2019.

39. Kowitz, personal interview.

40. Mallaby, 207.

41. Jones, personal interview.

42. Johnson, personal interview.

43. Soros, *Soros on Soros*, 142–144.

44. Mallaby, 212–219.

45. Mallaby, personal interview.

46. Druckenmiller, personal interview.

47. Anand Giridharadas, personal interview, Washington, D.C., September 2019.

48. Soros, *Soros on Soros*, 237–239.

Chapter 4: The Humanitarian Exception

1. Dženeta Karabegović, personal interview, Sarajevo, June 2019.

2. Ibid.

3. Mark Mazower, *The Balkans: A Short History* (New York: Modern Library, 2002), 140.

4. Ibid.

5. Misha Glenny, *The Balkans: Nationalism, War, and the Great Powers, 1804–2011* (New York: Penguin Books, 2012), 634–635.

6. Ibid., 637.

7. Ibid., 637–638.

8. Ibid., 642.

9. Dušan Stojanović, "Bosnian Independence Referendum Begins," Associated Press, February 29, 1992.

Notes

10. Glenny, 644.

11. Ibid., 646–647.

12. Ibid., 649–650.

13. United States Holocaust Memorial Museum, "Bosnia-Herzegovina," https://www.ushmm.org/confront-genocide/cases/bosnia-herzegovina.

14. Sue Turton, "Bosnian War Rape Survivors Speak of Their Suffering 25 Years On," *The Independent*, July 21, 2017.

15. Mark Malloch-Brown, personal interview, Washington, D.C., May 2019.

16. Ibid.

17. Open Society Foundations, "Saving Bosnia: Looking Back at George Soros's $50 Million Intervention After 25 Years," https://www.opensocietyfoundations.org/events/saving-bosnia-looking-back-george-soros-s-50-million-intervention-after-25-years.

18. Malloch-Brown, personal interview.

19. Soros, *Soros on Soros*, 179.

20. Malloch-Brown, personal interview.

21. Ibid.

22. Jakob Finci, personal interview, Sarajevo, June 2019.

23. Soros, in Sudetic, 27.

24. Open Society Foundations, "Saving Bosnia: Looking Back at George Soros's $50 Million Intervention After 25 Years," https://www.opensocietyfoundations.org/events/saving-bosnia-looking-back-george-soros-s-50-million-intervention-after-25-years.

25. Soros, in Sudetic, 27.

26. Open Society Foundations.

27. Owen Bowcott, "Bosnian Croat War Criminal Dies After Taking Poison in UN Courtroom," *The Guardian*, November 29, 2017.

28. United Nations, International Criminal Tribunal for the Former Yugoslavia, "International Criminal Tribunal for the Former Yugoslavia," http://www.icty.org.

29. Open Society Foundations.

Notes

30. Owen Bowcott and Julian Borger, "Ratko Mladić Convicted of War Crimes and Genocide at UN Tribunal," *The Guardian*, November 22, 2017.

31. United Nations, International Criminal Tribunal for the Former Yugoslavia, "Slobodan Milosevic Transferred into Custody of the International Criminal Tribunal for the Former Yugoslavia," http://www.icty.org/en/press/slobodan-milosevic-transferred-custody-international-criminal-tribunal-former-yugoslavia.

32. Sylvia Poggioli, "Radovan Karadzic Gets Life as Hague Court Upholds Genocide Conviction," NPR, March 20, 2019.

33. Emily Tamkin, "John Bolton Took Aim at the International Criminal Court, Declaring It 'Dead to Us,'" *BuzzFeed News*, September 10, 2018.

34. Malloch-Brown, personal interview.

35. Sonja Licht, personal interview, Prague, May 2019.

36. Ibid.

37. Suzanne Arbanas, ed., *10 Years Open Society Fund Bosnia & Herzegovina Report 2002* (Sarajevo: Open Society Fund Bosnia & Herzegovina, 2003), 5.

38. Finci, personal interview.

39. Dobrila Godevarica, personal interview, Sarajevo, June 2019.

40. Dženana Trbić, personal interview, Sarajevo, June 2019.

41. Hrvoje Batinić, personal interview, Sarajevo, June 2019.

42. Godevarica, personal interview.

43. Batinić, personal interview.

44. Jasmin Mujanović, personal interview, Washington, D.C., May 2019.

45. Licht, personal interview.

46. Finci, personal interview.

47. Trbić, personal interview.

48. Paul Stubbs, personal interview, Washington, D.C., September 2017.

49. Connie Bruck, "The World According to George Soros," *New Yorker*, January 23, 1995.

50. Paul Stubbs, "Flex Actors and Philanthropy in (Post-)Conflict Arenas: Soros' Open Society Foundations in the Post-Yugoslav Space," *Politička Misao* L/2013, 5 (2013): 114–138.

Notes

51. Finci, personal interview.

52. Mazower, 147.

53. Michael Kaufman, "The Dangers of Letting a President Read," *New York Times*, May 22, 1999.

54. Soros, *Soros on Soros*, 179.

55. Slavenka Drakulić, *Café Europa: Life After Communism* (New York: Penguin Books, 1999), 211.

56. Glenny, 640–641.

57. Ibid., 647.

58. Ibid., 649.

59. Ibid., 650–651.

60. https://hudoc.echr.coe.int/eng?i=001-96491.

61. Emily Tamkin, "Bosnia Is Teetering on the Precipice of a Political Crisis," *Foreign Policy*, March 21, 2018.

62. Mitch Prothero, "A Serbian Politician Has Become a Flashpoint in Bosnia's Election Campaign," *BuzzFeed News*, October 6, 2018.

63. Batinić, personal interview.

Chapter 5: Rocking the Vote

1. Emily Tamkin, "In Charter 77, Czech Dissidents Charted New Territory," *Foreign Policy*, February 3, 2017.

2. Michael Žantovský, *Havel: A Life* (New York: Grove Press, 2014), 252–253.

3. Soros, *Soros on Soros*, 132–133.

4. Žantovský, 401.

5. Dominik Jún, "Czechs and Slovaks—More Than Just Neighbors," Radio Prague International, October 28, 2016.

6. Žantovský, 403–425.

7. Martin Bútora, "OK '98: A Campaign of Slovak NGOs for Free and Fair Elections," in *Reclaiming Democracy: Civil Society and Electoral Change in Central and Eastern Europe* (2007): 21–52.

8. Stephen Kinzer, "West Says Slovakia Falls Short of Democracy," *New York Times*, December 26, 1995.

9. Soros, *Soros on Soros*, 173.

10. Pavol Demeš, *A Collective Portrait: The U.S. Contribution to the Development of Civil Society in Slovakia* (German Marshall Fund, 2012), 15.

11. Jan Orlovsky, personal interview, Bratislava, September 2017.

12. Bútora, 25.

13. Demeš, *A Collective Portrait*, 23.

14. Orlovsky, personal interview.

15. Bútora, 26.

16. Marek Kapusta, personal interview, Washington, D.C., April 2019.

17. Ibid.

18. Demeš, personal interview, Washington, D.C., April 2019.

19. Bútora, 30.

20. Ibid., 39.

21. Rasťo Kužel, personal interview, Washington, D.C., April 2019.

22. Kapusta, personal interview.

23. Orlovsky, personal interview.

24. "Slovakia Slips Backwards," *New York Times*, August 14, 1995.

25. Kužel, personal interview.

26. Kapusta, personal interview.

27. Soros, *Underwriting Democracy*.

28. Demeš, personal interview.

29. Orlovsky, personal interview.

30. Daniel Milo, personal interview, Washington, D.C., April 2019.

31. https://spectator.sme.sk/c/22035444/slovaks-do-not-consider-anti-semitism-a-problem.html.

32. Shaun Walker, "How a Slovakian Neo-Nazi Got Elected," *The Guardian*, February 14, 2019.

33. Kapusta, personal interview.

Notes

34. Pavol Demeš and Joerg Forbrig, "Introduction," in *Reclaiming Democracy: Civil Society and Electoral Change in Central and Eastern Europe* (German Marshall Fund, 2007), 9.

35. Bútora, 51.

Chapter 6: To Baltimore

1. Soros, in Sudetic, 28–29.

2. http://www.drugpolicy.org/issues/brief-history-drug-war.

3. Heidi Gillstrom, "Clinton's 'Superpredators' Comment Most Damaging by Either Candidate," *The Hill*, September 20, 2016.

4. German Lopez, "Joe Biden's Long Record Supporting the War on Drugs and Mass Incarceration, Explained," *Vox*, July 31, 2019.

5. Lopez, "Joe Biden's Criminal Justice Reform Plan, Explained," *Vox*, July 23, 2019.

6. http://www.drugpolicy.org/issues/brief-history-drug-war.

7. Michael Kaufman, *Soros: The Life and Times of a Messianic Billionaire* (New York: Knopf, 2002), 304–305.

8. Sudetic, 273.

9. Kurt Schmoke, personal interview, Washington, D.C., August 2019.

10. Nicole Porter, personal interview, Washington, D.C., August 2019.

11. Sudetic, 275–276.

12. Peter Beilenson, personal interview, Washington, D.C., August 2019.

13. Schmoke, personal interview.

14. Sudetic, 276.

15. Ibid., 280–281.

16. Christopher Welsh, personal interview, Washington, D.C., August 2019.

17. Schmoke, personal interview.

18. Welsh, personal interview.

19. Sudetic, 285–286.

20. Ibid., 291.

21. Lauren Abramson, personal interview, Washington, D.C., August 2019.

22. Beilenson, personal interview.

23. Schmoke, personal interview.

24. Porter, personal interview.

25. Kaufman, 308–313.

26. Beilenson, personal interview.

27. Kaufman, 314.

28. Schmoke, personal interview.

29. German Lopez, "Congress's Prison Reform Bill, Explained," *Vox*, May 22, 2018.

30. Jonathan Blanks, personal interview, Washington, D.C., August 2019.

31. Abramson, personal interview.

32. Christine Zhang, "Maryland's Prison Population Drops to 1980s Levels, Continuing a Multiyear Decline," *Baltimore Sun*, April 24, 2019.

33. Schmoke, personal interview.

34. Amina Khan, "Getting Killed by Police Is a Leading Cause of Death for Young Black Men in America," *Baltimore Sun*, August 16, 2019.

35. https://twitter.com/realdonaldtrump/status/1155073965880172544?lang=en.

36. Porter, personal interview.

37. Scott Bland, "George Soros's Quiet Overhaul of the US Criminal Justice System," *Politico*, August 30, 2016.

38. https://www.laadda.com/the-ongoing-attempt-to-buy-the-criminal-justice-system/.

Chapter 7: The Elections of 2004

1. George Soros, interview by Brian Lamb, "The Bubble of American Supremacy: Correcting the Misuse of American Power," C-SPAN, February 29, 2004.

Notes

2. Julian Borger and Ewen MacAskill, "Iran Was Illegal and Breached UN Charter, Says Annan," *The Guardian*, September 15, 2004.

3. "Transcript of President Bush's Address," CNN, September 21, 2001, http://edition.cnn.com/2001/US/09/20/gen.bush.transcript/.

4. Julian Borger, "Financier Soros Puts Millions into Ousting Bush," *The Guardian*, November 12, 2003.

5. Jane Mayer, "The Money Man," *New Yorker*, October 10, 2004.

6. Tom Novick, personal interview, Washington, D.C., May 2019.

7. Ibid.

8. Ibid.

9. Mayer.

10. Novick, personal interview.

11. Mark Steitz, personal interview, Washington, D.C., May 2019.

12. Ibid.

13. Joe Garofoli, "MoveOn, a Political Force Online, Receives $5 Million Matching Gift / Soros' Pledge Moves Right Wing to Slam the Progressive Group," *SFGate*, November 23, 2003.

14. Mayer.

15. Borger.

16. Ibid.

17. Ivan Levingston, "George Soros Returns to Politics with $25 Million Splash: Report," CNBC, July 27, 2016.

18. Mayer.

19. Ibid.

20. "2004 Presidential Race," OpenSecrets.org, https://www.opensecrets.org/pres04/.

21. Ken Vogel, "Kerry, Swift Boat Backer Meet," *Politico*, March 2, 2010.

22. Kate Zernike, "T. Boone Pickens Says No Deal on Swift Boat Bounty," *New York Times*, June 25, 2008.

23. Matthew Dowd, personal interview, Washington, D.C., 2019.

24. Ibid.

25. Ibid.

26. Mayer.

27. Novick, personal interview.

28. Anand Giridharadas, personal interview, Washington, D.C., September 2019.

29. Nahum Barnea, "Why They Hate George Soros," *Ynetnews*, April 25, 2018.

30. George Soros, *The Bubble of American Supremacy: The Costs of Bush's War in Iraq* (London: Weidenfeld & Nicolson, 2004), 4–7.

31. Ibid., 9.

32. Ibid., 10.

33. Ibid., 14–15.

34. Ibid., 10.

35. Ibid., 11.

36. Ibid., 12–13.

37. Ibid., 19–20.

38. Ibid., 176.

39. Dowd, personal interview.

40. Steitz, personal interview.

41. Mayer.

42. Steitz, personal interview.

43. Mayer.

44. Matthew Garrahan and Kara Scannell, "Bill O'Reilly Out at Fox News After Harassment Allegations," *Financial Times*, April 19, 2017.

45. Jack Shafer, "Dennis Hastert on Dope," *Slate*, September 1, 2004.

46. Jack Shafer, "Dennis Hastert, Liar or Fool?" *Slate*, September 2, 2004.

47. Aamer Madhani, "Ex-Speaker Dennis Hastert Released from Federal Prison," *USA Today*, July 18, 2017.

48. Rob Johnson, personal interview, Washington, D.C., September 2019.

49. Novick, personal interview.

50. Dowd, personal interview.

51. Soros, *The Bubble of American Supremacy*, 189.

Notes

52. Novick, personal interview.

53. Stephen Jones, *Georgia: A Political History Since Independence* (London: I. B. Tauris, 2013), 118.

54. Soros, in Sudetic, 32–35.

55. Darko Janjevic, "Saakashvili: Georgian Reformist Battles Ukraine's President," *DW*, February 13, 2008.

56. Robert Coalson and Eka Kevanishvili, "Out of Power, Georgia's United National Movement Seeks New Role," *RFERL*, November 12, 2013.

57. Soros, in Sudetic, 32–35.

58. Ibid.

59. Paul Stubbs, personal interview, Washington, D.C., September 2017.

60. Marlene Spoerri, *Engineering Revolution: The Paradox of Democracy Promotion in Serbia* (Philadelphia: University of Pennsylvania Press, 2014), 85–86.

61. Robyn E. Angley, "Escaping the Kmara Box: Reframing the Role of Civil Society in Georgia's Rose Revolution," *Studies of Transition States and Societies* 5, no. 1 (2013).

62. Lincoln Mitchell, "Georgia's Rose Revolution," *Current History* 103, no. 675 (2004): 346.

63. Peter Baker, "Tbilisi's 'Revolution of Roses' Mentored by Serbian Activists," *Washington Post*, November 25, 2003.

64. Soros, in Sudetic, 32–35.

65. Tamkin, "Who's Afraid of George Soros?"

66. Soros, in Sudetic, 33–34.

67. Misha Dzhindzhikhashvili, "Soros Downplays Role in Georgia Revolution," Associated Press, May 31, 2005.

68. Tamkin, "Who's Afraid of George Soros?"

69. Max Seddon, "The Rise and Fall of Mikheil Saakashvili," *BuzzFeed News*, October 28, 2013.

70. Emily Tamkin, "The Man Without a State," *Foreign Policy*, August 22, 2017.

71. Marc Behrendt, personal interview, Washington, D.C., August 2017.

72. Ibid.

73. Soros, in Sudetic, 32–35.

74. Ibid.

75. Ian Traynor, "US Campaign Behind the Turmoil in Kiev," *The Guardian*, November 26, 2004.

76. Soros, *Soros on Soros*, 131.

77. "Remarks by President Trump and President Putin of the Russian Federation in Joint Press Conference," whitehouse.gov, July 16, 2018, https://www.whitehouse.gov/briefings-statements/remarks-president -trump-president-putin-russian-federation-joint-press-conference/.

78. Tamkin, "The Man Without a State."

79. Soros, in Sudetic, 32–35.

80. Soros, *The Bubble of American Supremacy*, 94.

81. https://www.icij.org/investigations/paradise-papers/paradise-papers -exposes-donald-trump-russia-links-and-piggy-banks-of-the-wealthiest -1-percent/.

82. Steitz, personal interview.

83. Tea Khorguashvili and Natia Khorguashvili, "The Current Trends of Globalization in Georgia," *European Journal of Sustainable Development 5*, no. 3 (2016).

84. https://europa.eu/european-union/about-eu/history/2000-2009_en.

Chapter 8: United We Fall

1. Goran Buldioski, personal interview, Eagle Rock, Virginia, July 2019.

2. Tamkin, "Who's Afraid of George Soros?"

3. Open Society Foundations, "Our History," https://www.opensociety foundations.org/who-we-are/our-history.

4. Kenneth Roth, personal interview, Washington, D.C., July 2019.

5. Aleksander Smolar, personal interview, Washington, D.C., May 2019.

6. Marta Pardavi, personal interview, Budapest, June 2019.

7. András Bozóki, personal interview, Budapest, June 2019.

Notes

8. Emily Smith and Julia Marsh, "George Soros' Ex Goes Berserk in Court, Has $50M Suit Tossed," *New York Post*, February 6, 2015.

9. Emily Smith, "Soros' Jilted Ex on Their 5-Year Affair and His Sudden Change of Heart," *New York Post*, August 13, 2011.

10. Jennifer Ablan, "Billionaire Soros Weds Consultant in Third Marriage," Reuters, September 21, 2013.

11. Soros, *The Bubble of American Supremacy*, 90–91.

12. Rob Johnson, personal interview, Washington, D.C., September 2019.

13. https://www.influencewatch.org/non-profitinstitute-for-new
-economic-thinking/.

14. Stefan Wagstyl, "George Soros Gives $100M Gift to Europe," *Financial Times*, June 18, 2009.

15. https://ec.europa.eu/environment/enveco/memberstate_policy/pdf
/Differences%20in%20costs.pdf.

16. https://www.oxfordscholarship.com/view/10.1093/acprof:oso
/9780199602315.001.0001/acprof-9780199602315-chapter-1.

17. Soros, *The Soros Lectures at the Central European University*, 40.

18. http://hungarianspectrum.org/2014/06/10/maria-schmidts-revisionist
-history-of-world-war-ii-and-the-holocaust-part-ii/.

19. Krisztina Than and Gergely Szakacs, "Fidesz Wins Hungary Election with Strong Mandate," Reuters, April 11, 2010.

20. Péter Balázs, personal interview, Prague, May 2019.

21. Drew Hinshaw and Anita Komuves, "In a Reversal, U.S. to Host Hungarian Prime Minister," *Wall Street Journal*, May 12, 2019.

22. Charles Gati, personal interview, Washington, D.C., July 2019.

23. Bálint Magyar, personal interview, Budapest, June 2019.

24. Conrad Duncan, "Hungary's Viktor Orban Faces Scrutiny over Government Corruption as Showdown with EU Looms," *The Independent*, March 17, 2019.

25. Gati, personal interview.

26. Lili Bayer and Larry Cohler-Esses, "Evil Soros: Dog Whistling Anti-Semitism in Viktor Orban's Hungary," *The Forward*, May 30, 2017.

27. Hannes Grasseger, "The Plot Against George Soros," *BuzzFeed News*, January 20, 2019.

28. István Rév, personal interview, Budapest, June 2019.

29. Eleni Kounalakis, *Madam Ambassador: Three Years of Diplomacy, Dinner Parties, and Democracy in Budapest* (New York: New Press, 2015).

30. Balázs, personal interview.

31. Tamkin, "Who's Afraid of George Soros?"

32. Emily Tamkin, "They Spent Months Protesting Corruption. Now What?" *Foreign Policy*, September 29, 2017.

33. Peter Laca and Radoslav Tomek, "Slovak Premier Sees Soros Behind Plan to Topple His Government," Bloomberg, March 6, 2018.

34. "Erdoğan Slams 'Hungarian Jew Soros' While Warning Europe over 'Terror Support,'" *Hürriyet Daily News*, November 21, 2018.

35. Tucker, "Netanyahu Shared Fake News About Soros."

36. Allison Kaplan Sommer, "Why Netanyahu Hates George Soros So Much," *Haaretz*, September 10, 2017.

37. White House, "Remarks by President Trump and President Putin of the Russian Federation in Joint Press Conference," July 16, 2018.

38. Tamkin, "Who's Afraid of George Soros?"

39. Josh Lederman, "How a Conspiracy Theory about George Soros Is Fueling Allegations of Ukraine Collusion," NBC News, December 5, 2019.

40. https://twitter.com/realdonaldtrump/status/1048196883464818688?lang=en.

41. John Fund, "Look Who Was Behind the Jeff Flake Elevator Setup," *New York Post*, October 1, 2018.

42. Shaun Walker, "Hungarian Leader Says Europe Is Now 'Under Invasion' by Migrants," *The Guardian*, March 15, 2018.

43. Larry Cohler-Esses, "George Soros Denounced by Hungary as 'Satan' Seeking to Destroy 'Christian Europe,'" *The Forward*, October 11, 2017.

44. Jennifer Ablan, "Russia Bans George Soros Foundation as State Security 'Threat,'" Reuters, November 30, 2015.

45. Yasmeen Serhan, "Hungary's Anti-Foreign NGO Law," *The Atlantic*, June 13, 2017.

46. Csaba Csontos, personal interview, Washington, D.C., June 2019.

47. Marton Dunai, "Hungary Approves 'STOP Soros' Law, Defying EU, Rights Groups," *Reuters*, June 20, 2018.

48. Gabriel Petrescu, personal interview, Bucharest, September 2017.

49. Tamkin, "Who's Afraid of George Soros?"

50. Pardavi, personal interview.

51. "Hungary Orban: Europe's Centre-Right EPP Suspends Fidesz," BBC, March 20, 2019.

52. Gati, personal interview.

53. Rév, personal interview.

54. Balázs, personal interview.

55. Emily Tamkin, "Hungary Passes Law Targeting Soros-Founded University," *Foreign Policy*, April 4, 2017.

56. Tamkin, "Hungary's Decision to Close a Soros-Linked University Shows the Limits of Trump's Influence."

57. CEU, "CEU Suspends Education Programs for Registered Refugees and Asylum Seekers," August 28, 2018, https://www.ceu.edu/article/2018-08-28/ceu-suspends-education-programs-registered-refugees-and-asylum-seekers.

58. Elizabeth Redden, "Hungary Officially Ends Gender Studies Programs," *Inside Higher Ed*, October 17, 2018.

59. https://www.ceu.edu/article/2017-10-03/ceu-signs-mou-bard-college-retains-aim-stay-budapest.

60. Sandor Peto, "Thousands Rally to Keep Soros-Founded University in Hungary," *Reuters*, October 26, 2018.

61. Bozóki, personal interview.

62. Rév, personal interview.

63. Kati Marton, personal interview, Washington, D.C., August 2019.

64. Valerie Hopkins and Amie Williams, "Trump Praises Hungary's Orban in White House Visit," *Financial Times*, May 13, 2019.

65. Zoltán Kovács, personal interview, Budapest, June 2019.

66. Paul Hanebrink, *A Specter Haunting Europe* (Cambridge, MA: Belknap Press of Harvard University Press, 2018), 8.

67. Allison Kaplan Sommer, "How Did the Term 'Globalist' Become an Anti-Semitic Slur? Blame Bannon," *Haaretz*, March 13, 2018.

68. Kovács, personal interview.

69. George Soros, *On Globalization* (New York: Public Affairs, 2002), 12.

70. Kovács, personal interview.

71. Magyar, personal interview.

Chapter 9: Closed Society

1. Muzaffar Chishti, personal interview, Washington, D.C., August 2019.

2. https://www.history.com/topics/immigration/us-immigration-since-1965.

3. Chishti, personal interview.

4. Frank Sharry, personal interview, Washington, D.C., May 2019.

5. Eric Schmitt, "Philanthropist Pledges to Help Immigrants," *New York Times*, October 1, 1996.

6. Sharry, personal interview.

7. Cecilia Muñoz, personal interview, Washington, D.C., August 2019.

8. Sharry, personal interview.

9. Muñoz, personal interview.

10. Sharry, personal interview.

11. Muñoz, personal interview.

12. Chishti, personal interview.

13. Ibid.

14. Ibid.

15. Reid Epstein, "NCLR Head: Obama 'Deporter-in-Chief,'" *Politico*, March 4, 2014.

16. Eric Carlson, "White House Memos Reveal Emanuel's Agenda on Immigration, Crime," NBC Chicago, June 20, 2014.

17. Chishti, personal interview.

18. Eyder Peralta, "Obama Goes It Alone, Shielding Up to 5 Million Immigrants from Deportation," NPR, November 20, 2014.

19. Sharry, personal interview.

20. Marta Pardavi, personal interview, Budapest, June 2019.

21. Sharry, personal interview.

22. "Migrant Crisis: One Million Enter Europe in 2015," BBC, December 22, 2015.

23. Janosch Delcker, "The Phrase That Haunts Angela Merkel," *Politico Europe*, August 19, 2016.

24. Saim Saeed, "Hungary's Second Border Fence Is Finished, Says Orban," *Politico Europe*, April 28, 2017.

25. George Soros, "Rebuilding the Asylum System," *Project Syndicate*, September 26, 2015.

26. George Soros, "Europe: A Better Plan for Refugees," *New York Review of Books*, April 9, 2016.

27. George Soros, "On the Bombing of Aleppo," *New York Review of Books*, November 10, 2016.

28. Zoltán Kovács, personal interview, Budapest, June 2019.

29. Elisabeth Zerofsky, "Viktor Orbán's Far-Right Vision for Europe," *New Yorker*, January 7, 2019.

30. Ibid.

31. Pardavi, personal interview.

32. Lendvai, *Orbán: Europe's New Strongman*, 230.

33. Soros, *Soros on Soros*, 240.

34. German Lopez, "Donald Trump's Long History of Racism, from the 1970s to 2019," *Vox*, July 15, 2019.

35. Chishti, personal interview.

36. Jeremy Diamond, "Donald Trump's 'Star of David' Tweet Controversy, Explained," CNN, July 5, 2016.

37. Tim Hains, "Trump to Jewish Republicans: 'You're Not Going to Support Me Because I Don't Want Your Money,'" *Real Clear Politics*, December 3, 2015.

38. Bess Levin, "Trump: 'A Lot of People Say' George Soros Is Funding the Migrant Caravan," *Vanity Fair*, October 31, 2018.

39. Muñoz, personal interview.

40. Angela Kelley, personal interview, August 2019.

41. Sharry, personal interview.

42. https://twitter.com/joshtpm/status/1056324117329297409?lang=en.

43. Alejandro de la Garza, "Pittsburgh's Synagogue Shooter May Have

Targeted HIAS on Social Media. Here's What to Know About the Organization," *Time*, October 29, 2018.

44. Nidhi Prakash, "Inside the Massive, Coordinated Push to Make Sure a Census Question Does Not 'Distort Democracy,'" *BuzzFeed News*, June 24, 2019.

45. Sarah Parvini, "With Citizenship Question off the Census, California Groups Push for Participation," *Los Angeles Times*, August 9, 2019.

46. Martin Pengelly, "'Go Back Home': Trump Aims Racist Attack at Ocasio-Cortez and Other Congresswomen," *The Guardian*, July 15, 2019.

47. Tom McCarthy, "Trump Rally Crowd Chants 'Send Her Back' After President Attacks Ilhan Omar," *The Guardian*, July 18, 2019.

48. Jonathan Easley, "Castro to Biden: 'One of Us Has Learned the Lessons of the Past and One of Us Hasn't,'" *The Hill*, July 31, 2019.

49. Chishti, personal interview.

50. Alexander Nowrasteh, personal interview, Washington, D.C., August 2019.

51. Muñoz, personal interview.

52. Kelley, personal interview.

53. Muñoz, personal interview.

54. Nowrasteh, personal interview.

55. Charles Gati, personal interview, Washington, D.C., July 2019.

Conclusion

1. Patricia Cohen, "A Message from the Billionaire's Club: Tax Us," *New York Times*, June 24, 2019.

2. Rév, personal interview.

3. Soros, *Soros on Soros*, 83.

4. Ibid., 196.

5. Mallaby, *More Money Than God*, 207.

6. Soros, in Sudetic, 35.

7. Cohen.

8. Giridharadas, personal interview.

INDEX

Index

Index

Index

Index

Index

Index

Index

Index

Index

Index

Index

Index

Index

Romanian Open Society, 205
Rose Revolution, Georgia, 172–75, 176, 178
Rosenblatt, Lionel, 98
Roth, Kenneth, 185
Rothman, David, 142
Rove, Karl, 160
Rumsfeld, Donald, 164
rural farmers association, Hungary, 44
Russia
    and Bosnian War, 119
    Mečiar attempting to align Slovakia with, 129
    Putin, 172, 175–79, 200, 202
    robber capitalist episode, 54, 83–84
    and Soros, 82–84, 200
    See also Soviet Russia
Ryan, Alan, 142
Ryan, Paul, 225–26

Saakashvili, Mikheil
    anticorruption program of, 172
    policies contradict his stated plans, 175–76
    post-Georgian presidency, 179
    and Putin, 177–78
    running against Shevarnadze, 172–73
    and Russo-Georgian War, 175
    on Soros playing politics, 179
    Soros's support for, then criticism of, 173, 176
Sakharov, Andrei, 38, 52–53
Sarajevo, Yugoslavia
    Bosnian Serbs attack, 93
    foreign journalists in, 99–100
    humanitarian relief for, 89–90
    Mostar Bridge blown up, 101
    NATO says Bosnian Serbs must withdraw from, 93

praise for Soros's role in, 100
Russia sending troops to Sarajevo, 94
water purification plant built in, 100–101
See also humanitarian relief for Yugoslavia
Sarajevo Open Society Foundation, 99–100, 106–13
Scanlon, T. M., 142
Schlesinger, Helmut, 69, 72–73, 76
Schmidt, Helmut, 67
Schmidt, Maria, 191–92
Schmoke, Kurt, 146–49, 151, 152, 154
Schwartz, György, 7. See also Soros, George
Schwartz, Tivadar, 7, 8–9. See also Soros, Tivadar (father)
Senate Banking Committee, 69–70
September 11, 2001, terrorist attacks, 158–59, 229
Serbian Republic (Republika Srpska), 92, 119, 122
Sharry, Frank, 222–26, 227–28, 229–31
Shatalin plan for Soviet Russia, 53, 70
Shevardnadze, Eduard, 172–73, 174, 175–76, 177, 178
Shirley, Craig, 197
shorting currencies
    overview, 71
    the British pound, 3–4, 27–28, 68–69, 71–77, 136
    the Thai baht, 77, 78–79
    the U.S. dollar, 31
Silber, Laura, 184–85, 243–44
Singer & Friedlander, London, 23
60 Minutes (TV program), 16
Skopje, Macedonia, Open Society Foundation, 115

Index

Index

Index

Index

Tudjman, Franjo, 92, 94, 120, 134
Tunisia office of Open Society, 185

U.N. High Commission for
    Refugees (UNHCR), 97–98
U.N. Protection Force troops in
    Sarajevo, 94
U.N. Tribunal in the Hague, 102–4
Underwriting Democracy (Soros),
    46
    on the foundation in China,
        48–49
United Kingdom joins European
    Exchange Rate Mechanism, 67
United States
    Ehrlichman on making hippies
        and blacks public enemies,
        143
    Iraq War, 163–64
    "lift and strike" strategy in
        Bosnian War, 118, 119
    migrant caravan heading to
        southern border, 2, 237–38
    migrant crises in Europe and, 2,
        200–201, 216–17
    political history of illegal drugs
        and drug users in, 142–45
    post-9/11 morph from victim into
        perpetrator, 166
    and Slovakia's developing
        authoritarianism, 128
    Soros conspiracy theories, 202–4
    Syrian refugee crisis, 236
    Tamkin wondering about the
        health of, 227
    violent and unforgiving criminal
        justice system for black
        Americans, 154–55
United States election of 2004
    overview, 157–58, 182
    Republican response to Soros's
        attempt to defeat Bush in
        2004, 167–71

Soros becomes involved in
    partisan politics, 158–61
total contributions of $880.5
    million, 161
University of Cape Town, South
    Africa, 37

Vander Weyer, Martin, 75
Vásárhelyi, Miklós, 39, 193
Velvet Divorce, Czech Republic and
    Slovakia, 126–27
Vilakazi, Herbert, 36
voter mobilization, 160, 161
Vuco, Beka, 101

Wall Street Journal, 168
Wallace, Chris, 169
War Childhood Museum, Sarajevo,
    92
war on drugs, 142–43, 146–47, 154
Ward, Marty, 146
water purification plant in Sarajevo,
    100–101
wealth tax, 243–44, 249
Weber, Susan, 29, 39, 187, 193
welfare reform bill's effect on legal
    immigrants, 223–28
Welsh, Christopher, 148–49
Wertheim & Co., New York City,
    24
Williams, Bernard, 142
Wilson, Woodrow, 221
Winners Take All (Giridharadas),
    86
Witschak, Annaliese, 24
Wolff, Jonathan, 25
Wolfowitz, Paul, 99, 164
World Bank, 80
World War I, 8, 9, 10–12
World War II, 7, 13–20

Yeltsin, Boris, 53
Yovanovitch, Marie, 202–3

Index

ABOUT THE AUTHOR

EMILY TAMKIN is the U.S. editor of the *New Statesman*. Her work has appeared in the *Columbia Journalism Review*, the *Economist*, the *New Republic*, *Politico*, *Slate*, and the *Washington Post*, among other publications. She previously covered foreign affairs on staff at *Foreign Policy* and *BuzzFeed News*. She studied Russian literature and culture at Columbia University and Russian and East European studies at the University of Oxford. She has conducted research on Soviet dissidence on a Fulbright Fellowship in Germany. She was also a Council on Foreign Relations International Affairs Fellow in New Delhi, India. She lives in Washington, D.C.